ENGINE BLUEPRINTING
BY RICK VOEGELIN

ENGINE BLUEPRINTING

EDITED BY LARRY SCHREIB
PRODUCTION BY LARRY ATHERTON

COVER PHOTOGRAPH BY RICK VOEGELIN
DRAWINGS BY JIM DENNEWILL

CONTENTS

INTRODUCTION

WHAT IS BLUEPRINTING?

"Blueprinting" is without question the most used—and most abused—term in engine building. Ask any enthusiast about his motor, and chances are he'll proudly describe it as having been blueprinted all the way from the air cleaner to the oil pan plug. Press him for further details and you may discover that this entire procedure consisted of rebuilding the carburetor, installing a distributor curve kit, and changing the oil filter. And, yes, a friend of his uncle once adjusted the valves. That may be what "blueprinting" means to some people—but not to the beginning engine builders who have read this book.

In a very strict sense, *every* engine is blueprinted. By that we simply mean that before an automaker introduces a new powerplant, the design engineers must first transfer their ideas into elaborate drawings that will guide the pattern makers and tooling specialists. But this is an imperfect world, and not every component that falls off the end of the assembly line meets the engineers' exact specifications. Drill bits and machine tools become dull. Grinding stones wear out. Gauges don't always read properly. Lathes run untrue, and mills flex. In any piece of machinery as complex and complicated as an internal combustion engine, all these inaccuracies add up. Sometimes the mistakes cancel each other out, and the finished part is just what the original blueprints called for. More often, though, they combine to produce a component that is often somewhat less than ideal.

An assembly line is no place for a perfectionist. If engines were built to exact dimensions, even Arab sheiks couldn't afford Chevettes. The car manufacturers are willing to accept parts that are "almost right" or "pretty close"—so long as their deviations aren't so great that they will cause the engine to disassemble itself the instant its new owner takes delivery. Of course, there has to be a reliable means of determining whether a part is "close enough." And that's what a *tolerance* figure does.

Which brings us back to the blueprints. All of the critical dimensions are assigned a tolerance. For example, a hole that is required to be 0.50-inch in diameter may have a range of +/- 0.005-inch. This "plus or minus" figure gives the range of acceptable or "tolerable" variation from the stated dimension. Thus the actual hole could measure between 0.245- and 0.255- inch and still be considered within tolerance. In theory, a hole that is larger or smaller than this range would be reason to scrap the part—or at least set it aside for repair.

Some tolerances are more critical than others. A hole that simply functions as an oil drain might be one-tenth of an inch (0.10) larger or smaller than the blueprints called for, and yet it could still perform its function perfectly. The hole in the small end of a connecting rod, though, has to be within *one ten-thousandth of an inch* (0.0001) of the specified diameter if it is to do the job properly. In short, boring the hole in the small end of a connecting rod calls for a thousand times more accuracy than drilling an oil drain hole.

Machine tools and their operators occasionally have bad days. When this happens, the problem of "tolerance stack-up" sometimes arises. It's possible for all of the *individual* machine operations to be within tolerance, yet the final part may be far out of spec. For example, if a series of holes are all drilled on the "high side" (larger) of the specified tolerance, and the size of these holes is later used as a reference point for a series of machining operations, that may also happen to favor the high side of the specifications, the final result could be a component of very bad quality. And a component that is the victim of this tolerance stack-up can be difficult to spot, since it can meet the blueprint specs at each point during the manufacturing process. So an engine piece like this is a mechanical time bomb that's almost certain to cause trouble at some time in the future.

Thus, in a sense, even the engine in your grandmother's Malibu is blueprinted—that is, its components fall within the manufacturer's design specifications (assuming they were at least inspected sometime during their

In circle-track and road-racing competition, engine durability is vital. A motor assembled with the correct clearances will outlast the competition.

As interest in restoring Sixties-style supercars continues to grow, more enthusiasts are discovering that a blueprinted engine offers improved performance even with today's low-octane pump gasoline.

Drag racing demands a powerplant that can produce horsepower at extremely hgh rpm levels. Careful blueprinting will help an engine survive quarter-mile sprints at 10,000 rpm.

creation). But that's little comfort for racers and performance enthusiasts. In many instances, the acceptable tolerances cover such a wide range, it's a wonder that any production engine is able to live a long and productive life—and yet millions do. The range of permissible main bearing clearances for a Chevrolet V-8, for example, runs from 0.0007- to 0.0035-inch—a spread of almost 0.003-inch. Such a wide variation may be all right for a commuter motor that never sees the far side of 4000rpm, but it's hardly suitable for a 600-horsepower big-block!

Engines have an amazing tolerance for abuse. On a fast-moving assembly line, banks of pistons are slammed into cylinder blocks with hydraulic rams. Pneumatic gang wrenches torque down cylinder heads in a matter of seconds. For a conscientious engine builder who devotes an entire weekend assembling a short block, such quick-and-dirty techniques may be shocking. But economics are on the side of the assembly line.

The most basic form of blueprinting, then, is simply making sure that all of the tolerances fall within factory specifications. High-volume engine rebuilders generally adopt this approach, which can be characterized by the statement, "if the crank turns, it's good enough." During a straightforward rebuild, as on the factory production line, there is no attempt to *optimize* clearances between components. At this level, the performance of the engine is simply a matter of luck—the result of the random selection of parts from a bin. Although you might be technically correct in describing a low-buck rebuilt engine as "blueprinted," it is no more deserving of the title than a lawnmower motor.

In the eyes of most knowledgeable enthusiasts, blueprinting an engine means not only *checking* clearances but *correcting* them as well. Careful blueprinting demands that the engine builder pay attention to how the hundreds of parts in an engine all work together. The engine builder must then recognize that changing one component has an effect on many other pieces. In many instances, shop manuals offer no guidelines; the factories never anticipated the high-lift camshafts, high-compression pistons, and high-tech cylinder heads that have become a part of the high-performance scene. Today's performance engine builder must be a part-time automotive engineer, since he has to make sure that the components he has selected will work

A blueprinted small-block outfitted with a single four-barrel carburetor and a selection of carefully coordinated components is an ideal engine for both weekday commuting and weekend cruising.

together. Moreover, the term "blueprinting" embraces a tremendous range of engine building skills. Even the most experienced professional engine builder continually discovers new tricks and techniques that will make his motors more powerful, more reliable, or more affordable.

Blueprinting is a constantly evolving science. Any sharp automotive machinist will agree that before a motor has earned the distinction of being blueprinted, the block must first be square and true, the crankshaft straight, its clearances correct, and the cylinder heads completely reconditioned. These are the basics of engine blueprinting, and they'll be covered in detail on the following pages. But there's much more to precision engine building than just covering the basics. The details make the difference—the alignment of the intake manifold with the cylinder head ports, the carefully matched rockerarm ratios, the end play of the distributor shaft. You probably couldn't pay a professional builder enough money to double-check every possible detail in an engine—but in many instances, you can do the work yourself for free. And while you'll undoubtedly have to send out some pieces for major machine operations (like boring and surfacing), most of the critical "massaging" of small parts can be done on a garage workbench with simple hand tools. By the time you have trial assembled an

It's sometimes difficult to tell the difference between today's high-tech street machines and all-out race cars. With blowers, turbochargers, and nitrous-oxide injection now commonplace on street engines, blueprinting has become essential for maximum performance and reliability.

When you are investing thousands of dollars in a purebred racing engine, it pays to take the time to double-check every component.

engine several times—checking and rechecking each component at every step in the process—you will have developed a unique understanding of the mechanics of motor building.

The cardinal rule of engine blueprinting is really simple: NEVER ASSUME ANYTHING. Copy this quotation on the biggest piece of cardboard you can find and tape it over your tool box. Whenever the words "I'm sure it's okay" pass your lips, remember this rule! When it's late on Saturday night and you are putting away the tools, even though you *know* you should have checked the piston-to-valve clearance, remember this rule! If you *do* check the part in question and it passes your scrutiny, then your time has been well spent. But if you blindly bolt together odd pieces on the belief that someone else has already done the critical measurements and blueprinting work, don't be surprised when you fire the engine for the first time and nasty chunks of piston material rain into the oil pan. And don't be beguiled by shiny new parts in fancy packages; since so many "hot rod" engine pieces are custom-made, the odds are high that some slight manufacturing variations may be present. Once you learn these facts of engine-building life, you will understand that engine blueprinting is really an art.

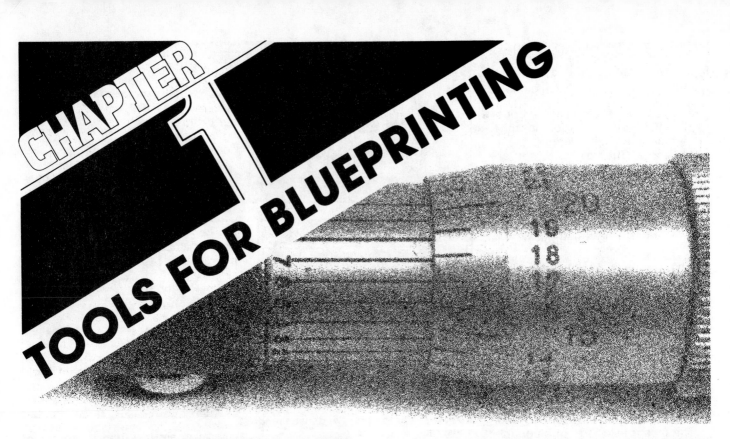

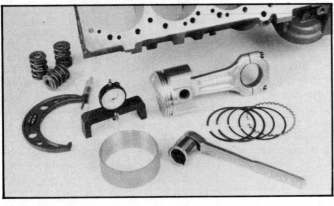

Learning how to use precision tools is an essential part of engine blueprinting. Every component should be checked and re-checked before final assembly.

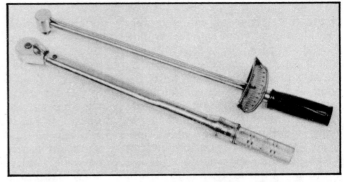

Treat your torque wrench like a dear friend—your success at engine building will depend on it. Click-type torque wrenches are convenient to use, but must be recalibrated occasionally to ensure continued accuracy. A beam-type wrench is less glamorous, but dead reliable.

TOOLS FOR BLUEPRINTING

Deep in his heart, every car enthusiast secretly lusts for a six-foot high tool cabinet, its drawers heavy with one of every item in the Snap-on catalog, its cubbyholes bursting with micrometers, gauges, and calipers. Anyone who has spent time around automobiles quickly realizes that it is impossible to have "too many" tools. But for all the appeal of a well-stocked tool chest, the fact is that a simple assortment of hand tools and a few precision measuring tools is all that's necessary for most basic blueprinting operations. Naturally, you can't expect to perform precision machine work with hand tools; but the average backyard mechanic, with modest tools

and a little common sense, can accomplish quite a bit of the preliminary preparation work, and this will better prepare you to tell your machinist exactly what you want (which greatly increases the chances of getting what you need).

If your automotive endeavors have progressed to the point that you are considering an engine blueprinting project, you have probably already accumulated a fairly complete selection of wrenches, ratchets, sockets, and screwdrivers. However, if you haven't already added a torque wrench to your tool supply, then this item should unquestionably be the first item on your shopping list.

There are two common types of torque wrenches: (1) beam wrenches,

which indicate torque loads by deflecting a flexible shaft, and (2) click-type wrenches, which produce an audible "click" when the torque resistance has reached the specified setting. Even though the click-type torque wrenches are unquestionably easier to use and "sexier" than an old-fashioned beam wrench, they have several drawbacks. First, they are several times more expensive than a beam wrench. Second, any sort of rough handling can cause them to read inaccurately—and wrenches have been known to take a tumble off a workbench. Since there is no simple way to test the accuracy of a click-type torque wrench, they must be returned to the manufacturer for adjustment. Beam-type torque wrenches, on the other hand, are dirt cheap and dead reliable. Since the beam is nothing more than a steel spring, there are no moving parts to break or go out of kilter. Probably the best solution is to own *two* torque wrenches—a click-type for tedious chores like tightening head bolts, and a beam-type for double-checking the torque readings of crucial fasteners, like rod bolts and flywheel fasteners.

PRECISION TOOLS

A revolution has taken place in the precision tool market within the past 10 years. Until recently, micrometers and other measuring tools were English, difficult to find, and expensive. Now that's all changed. Like cameras and stereo sets, the vast majority of precision tools are now imported from Japan. They can be ordered from dozens of mail-order tool suppliers, and the prices are a fraction of what they used to be. Even large department stores, such as Sears, carry a wide array of precision tools at reasonable prices. In general, the accuracy and dependability of these inexpensive measuring tools are completely satisfactory for most engine blueprinting operations.

Engine rebuilding is only an occasional pastime for most enthusiasts. In these circumstances, it makes sense to form a "tool pool" with other hobbyists. For example, you might convince the car nut next door to buy a set of micrometers, while you invest in dial indicators and magnetic stands. By swapping these tools when a particular measuring task is at hand, you can both have the equipment you need without all the expense. If you are going to need a certain tool only a few times a year, it makes sense to borrow

An accomplished engine builder quickly develops a "feel" for his torque wrench. Learn to pull the handle smoothly to prevent erroneous readings.

rather than buy.

Although a complete assortment of measuring tools is nice, it is not essential. Throughout this book, we'll point out ways to blueprint an engine *without* using anything more exotic than a feeler gauge, modeling clay, and Plastigage. In many instances, this very basic equipment can produce results as accurate as a chestful of micrometers and calipers. Then again, there are times when only the real thing will do. The important thing, however, is to know when to use which tool or technique.

BASIC MEASURING TOOLS

If you ask a professional engine builder which tools he uses most often, he will probably confess that 95% of his measurements are taken with just three tools: a 1-inch outside micrometer, a 6-inch dial caliper, and a dial indicator. With a tool budget of only $100—about the cost of an aluminum intake manifold—you can start your precision tool collection with these three essential items.

A *micrometer* is the tool that nearly everyone associates with engine blueprinting. When assembling an engine to close tolerances, there is always a need to know how thick various pieces are—and a micrometer is usually the tool that supplies the answer. For example, measuring the thickness of a head gasket, valve spring shim, or piston ring is a simple chore with a good quality micrometer. Even inexpensive

micrometers are accurate to within one ten-thousandths of an inch (0.0001-inch). Usually, though, it's not the price of the tool but the skill of the operator that determines how accurate the measurements are. Becoming proficient with a micrometer is more than learning how to read the spindle. Developing the right touch or "feel" for how tightly to turn the mike is a skill that comes with practice. Two engine builders can measure the same part with the same instrument and come up with slightly different sizes—all because of differences in the feel they have for tightening the micrometer.

When shopping for a micrometer, look for a tool that will read to one ten-thousandths of an inch (0.0001-inch). You may never need to measure anything that accurately, but the extra divisions will help you decide which way to round off a close measurement. Digital micrometers, that display the thickness of the part like a calculator are becoming more common. If you are uncomfortable reading a conventional micrometer or plan to use a micrometer very seldom, then the digital versions may be right for you. (Be warned, though, that a digital micrometer can become a crutch. Someday you will be in a shop and have to use a standard micrometer, so avoid the embarrassment of admitting you don't know how to use one by learning the basics.)

High-quality micrometers have a range of only one inch. Thus a well-stocked tool box should include five different micrometers: 0.0000- to 1.0000-inch, 1.0000- to 2.0000-inch, 2.0000- to 3.0000-inch, 3.0000- to 4.0000-inch, and 4.0000- to 5.0000-inch. This assortment will meet any measurement needs you are likely to encounter during an engine blueprinting project.

You may be tempted to buy a micrometer with interchangeable anvils. These take the place of half a

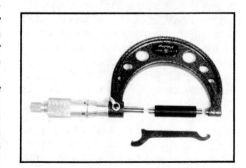

A good quality micrometer should include a setting standard to check its accuracy. Like all precision tools, micrometers should be stored and used with care.

Outside micrometers are the foundation of any precision tool collection. You can add more sizes as your engine building skills and interests grow.

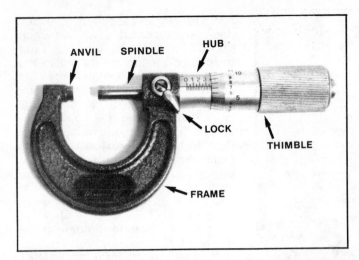

A micrometer is an indispensable tool for precision engine building. Numbered lines on the hub are exposed by turning the thimble. Each line equals 0.0125-inch.

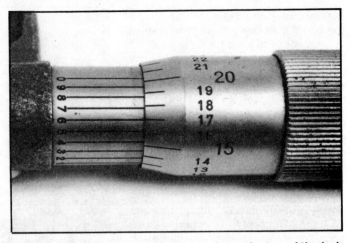

Many micrometers have a vernier scale on the top of the hub which measures ten-thousands of an inch (0.0001). To read a vernier, find the line on the hub which aligns with a line on the thimble. In this example, the "6" aligns with the "17."

HOW TO READ A MICROMETER

Mastering the art of reading a micrometer is not one of those skills that will cause rich, beautiful women to seek your company. It is, however, a talent that will greatly improve your engine building abilities. The first step is to become familiar with the parts of a micrometer, which are identified in the accompanying photos.

A screw hidden inside the thimble is what gives a micrometer the ability to make precise measurements. This screw has 40 threads per inch. This means that one full turn of the thimble moves the spindle exactly l/40th of an inch. The decimal equivalent of l/40 is 0.025-inch, so each turn of the thimble changes the micrometer reading by 0.025-inch. There are 40 lines on the sleeve, so each line that is exposed marks off 0.025-inch. Every fourth line is numbered; these larger lines are tenths of an inch (since 4 times 0.025 equals 0.l00). The circumference of the spindle has 25 equally spaced lines. Turning the thimble from one line to the next moves the spindle exactly 0.00l-inch.

To read the micrometer, first look at the large lines and numbers on the sleeve. In the example pictured here, the "3" is visible, so the indicated measurement is at least three-tenths of an inch (0.300). Three smaller lines are also exposed after the 3, so you add 0.025 for each line, which equals 0.075. So far the reading is 0.300 plus 0.075, or a total of 0.375-inch. Next, look at the thimble to see which number corresponds to the line on the sleeve. These numbers indicate one thousandths of an inch (0.001). In this example, the "7" is aligned with the line on the spindle, so you add 0.007-inch to the reading. The final measurement, then, is 0.375 plus 0.007, which equals 0.382-inch.

Many micrometers can measure to the fourth decimal place, which is one ten-thousandth of an inch (0.0001). To make this final reading, look at the top of the sleeve. Here you will find a Vernier scale, which is a series of lines and numbers. To read the ten-thousandth place, you must find a numbered line that is exactly aligned with a line on the thimble. In the example shown here, the line marked "6" is aligned exactly with a line on the thimble, so the final reading to four decimal places is 0.3826-inch (0.3820 plus 0.0006).

The first few times you use a micrometer, the procedure may seem awkward and difficult. With just a little practice, though, you will soon be taking measurements with a micrometer as easily as you read a ruler.

Most micrometers have a spring-loaded ratchet on the end of the thimble. Use this ratchet to tighten the thimble until the mike is just snug on the object you are measuring.

dozen individual micrometers, and allow you to measure anything from 0.0 to 6.0 inches. It sounds too good to be true—and it is. These wide-range micrometers are awkward to use when measuring small items, and changing the anvils is tedious. It is better to add micrometers to your precision tool collection as you find the need for them. For example, start with a 0.0000- to l.0000-inch micrometer; the next addition might be a 3.0000- to 4.0000-inch micrometer for measuring piston diameters.

Make sure that the micrometer you buy includes a *setting standard*. This is simply a bar of known length that you use to check the accuracy of the micrometer. (A 0.0000- to 1.0000-inch micrometer should read 0.0000-inch when the spindle is closed against the anvil.) You may notice that parts will measure differently at various times of the day. On a hot afternoon, for example, a piston will expand from the heat and measure slightly larger than it did after sitting in a cold shop all night. These differences are too small to affect most blueprinting work—but you should be aware of their existence. If you want to eliminate any chance of error, bring along your micrometers when you deliver parts to your machinist and compare his readings against your own.

DIAL INDICATOR

Once you own a *dial indicator*, you will wonder how you ever got along without one. It is an indispensable tool for degreeing camshafts, checking valve lift, piston deck clearances, crankshaft end play, and another

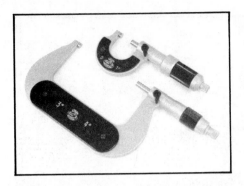

Dial indicators are indispensable in engine blueprinting. Dial indicator variations include (left to right) a Starrett "Last Word" finger indicator, Craftsman I/2-inch travel indicator, and Yuasa I-inch travel indicator.

Precision tools are available with prices that range from downright cheap to outright expensive. For occasional use, inexpensive micrometers are entirely satisfactory. If you are serious about engine building, you may want to invest in top quality tools like these Swiss-made Etalon outside micrometers.

thousand or so measurements that you will soon discover. Look for a dial indicator with at least one inch of travel, graduated in 0.00I-inch increments. Make sure you also get a good selection of extensions ranging up to 6 inches long. These extensions can be joined to allow the indicator to reach into confined areas, such as down a pushrod hole.

There are two dial indicator accessories that are essential for engine blueprinting. The first is a magnetic indicator stand. The stronger the magnet, the better. More than one dial indicator has tumbled off a cylinder head because the magnet wasn't strong enough to hold the setup securely. Look for sturdy arms on an indicator stand, and clamps that are easy to

operate even if your hands are covered with oil.

The second vital dial indicator accessory is a bridge. Dial indicators that are sold for use as depth gauges have a removable base that may be used to straddle a hole. This setup works well for measuring piston deck heights when the piston is below the block surface. A U-shaped stand is necessary when the pistons protrude above the deck. These stands are also useful for checking the flatness of a block or cylinder head.

DIAL CALIPERS

A *dial caliper* combines the measuring capabilities of a micrometer with the convenience of a dial indicator. Dial calipers are ideal for taking quick measurements when absolute accuracy is not required. Most dial calipers have both inside and outside jaws. With this setup, you can quickly determine the diameter of a hole or the size of a drill bit. Vernier calipers, which are read much like a micrometer, are much less expensive than dial calipers, but they are also much less convenient to use.

A 6-inch dial caliper, graduated in

A depth dial indicator (left) has a flat base which makes it ideal for checking piston deck heights. A U-shaped bridge (right) allows a standard dial indicator to measure dome heights and check cylinder head flatness.

This high-tech dial indicator bridge has magnets to hold it firmly in place on a slippery block.

Camshaft degreeing is easy with this modified dial indicator. It is inserted directly into lifter bore, eliminating need for stands and extensions. Rubber O-rings hold it in place.

A good magnetic stand greatly increases the versatility of a dial indicator. Select a stand with a strong magnet and clamps that can be operated easily with oily fingers.

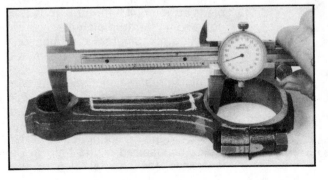

Dial calipers are ideal for measurements which don't require absolute accuracy. Dial calipers have two sets of jaws to measure both internal and external dimensions.

These dial calipers have been modified to make valvespring installed height measurements quick and accurate.

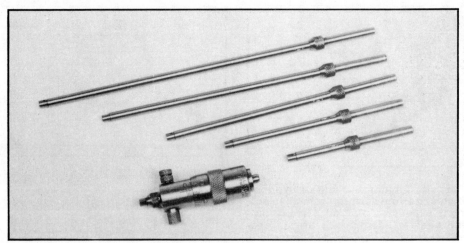

Inside micrometers are used to measure cylinder diameters and bearing bores. Extensions increase this micrometer's range from 2 to 6 inches.

0.001-inch increments, is a good all-purpose choice. Better quality calipers have a dust shield over the geared rack that turns the dial; this prevents small metal particles from jamming the mechanism. A good pair of calipers should have no play in the movable jaw. You can check this by placing a thin piece of metal in the jaws. Measure the thickness with the metal close to the rack, and then again with the metal out at the end of the jaws. If the measurements vary by more than 0.001-inch, the jaw mechanism is deflecting. Always use care when using a dial caliper—it is a precision instrument, not a clamp. And if you need a super-accurate measurement, put the dial calipers aside and get out a micrometer.

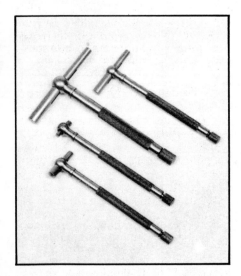

Telescoping snap gauges will reach into holes where there is no room for a conventional micrometer.

EXOTIC TOOLS

There is a large number of precision tools that fall into the category labeled "nice to have, but not essential." Because of the high cost or their limited usefulness, these tools should be considered only after you have given your precision tool collection a good foundation with an assortment of micrometers, indicators, and accessories. These more exotic tools are designed for specialized uses—but when you've got to have one, there is simply no substitute for the right tool.

An *inside micrometer* is most often used to measure the diameter of a hole. Automotive engines are full of holes to measure. Cylinder bores, main bearing bores, and the big ends of connecting rods are all likely candidates for measurement with an inside micrometer. Reading an inside micrometer is just the same as reading an outside micrometer. Using an inside mike does take more skill, however. To measure the diameter accurately, you must find the widest part of the hole. This requires expanding the micrometer while rocking it from side to side and moving it up and down. When the micrometer is adjusted properly, you should be able to pull it through the hole with just a slight drag. If the micrometer is loose in the bore or binds as you pull it through, then it is not reading the true diameter.

Inside micrometers can measure holes as small as one inch in diameter when fully collapsed. To measure larger diameters, the micrometer is outfitted with extensions or spacers. For measuring smaller holes, *telescoping gauges* are frequently used. A telescoping gauge is spring-loaded, and after it is inserted in the hole to be measured, the handle releases the gauge, which then expands to the internal size of the hole. Tightening the handle locks the expanded gauge, and after it is removed from the hole, the width of the gauge can be measured with a conventional outside micrometer.

For serious racers, a *dial bore gauge* is high on the list of desirable tools. In automotive applications, a dial bore gauge has one important function: to check the roundness of the cylinder bores. Although cylinders can be checked with a conventional inside micrometer, a dial bore gauge makes the job substantially easier and more accurate. Dial bore gauges are also excellent for checking the diameter and roundness of bearing bores in main bearing saddles and connecting rods. Most dial bore gauges can be used in holes ranging from just over 1.000 inch in diameter to 6.000 inches (and even larger) by using various

It takes practice and patience to take accurate measurements with an inside micrometer. The mike must be carefully rocked from side to side to make sure that it is recording the true diameter.

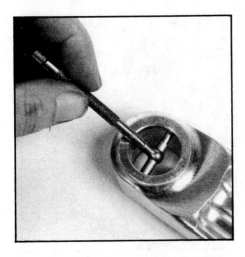

Spring-loaded snap gauges expand to fit the object being measured. Turning the handle locks the gauge, which is then removed and measured with an outside micrometer or dial caliper.

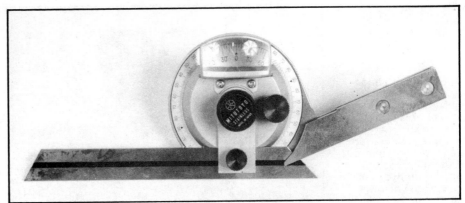

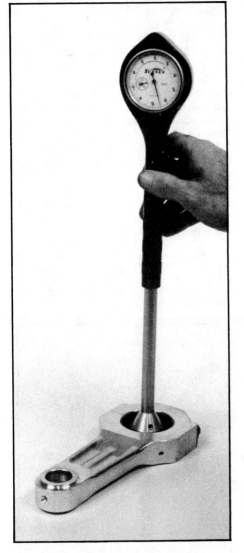

A dial bore gauge is expensive, but it is the perfect tool for checking bearing clearances and measuring cylinder bores for taper and eccentricity. This Sunnen gauge is accurate to 0.0001-inch!

A precision bevel protractor can be used to measure valve angles in cylinder heads that have been angle milled.

An inexpensive balance scale with an assortment of weights is handy when comparing piston weights.

extensions. Unlike outside micrometers with interchangeable anvils, extensions do not adversely affect the accuracy or operation of a dial bore gauge. Engine builders searching for the "Perfect Cylinder Bore" rely on dial bore gauges that are accurate to 0.0001-inch. However, these gauges are rare and expensive. Most currently available gauges are graduated in 0.0005-inch increments, and when used properly, these gauges are more

A sturdy engine stand with high quality casters is an excellent investment. This Lakewood stand disassembles for storage under a workbench between engine blueprinting projects.

than adequate.

A *bevel protractor* can be very handy if extensive piston modifications are required. Among other things, a bevel protractor can be used to determine the precise angle of the valve heads, and will help ensure that the valve notches in the piston dome are machined at precise angles. This is particularly important when using cylinder heads that have been milled on an angle, since this operation alters the valve inclination relative to the piston dome. A bevel protractor will also reveal how much material should be removed from the intake manifold surface after a cylinder head has been angle milled.

ENGINE ASSEMBLY TOOLS

One item of shop equipment in constant use during any blueprinting project is an *engine stand*. Although it's possible to bolt together a short block by wrestling it around on a workbench or the garage floor, this is definitely not the way to treat an expensive motor. If you are handy with a welding torch, you can probably knock out a home-built engine stand in a weekend. At the price of currently available commercial stands, though, it hardly pays you to buy the materials and do the dirty work. There is a wide range in quality between store-bought

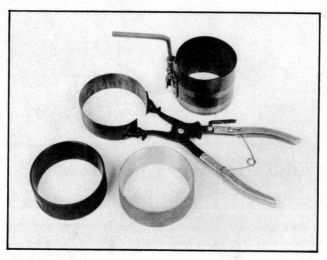

Choose your piston ring compressor carefully. Band compressor (rear) is quite inexpensive; plier-type compressor (center) is easy to use. Tapered ring compressors (foreground) are the "ultimate" piston installation tools, but you'll need a different compressor for each bore size.

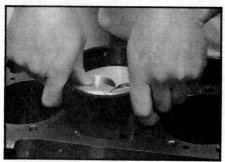

With a hard-anodized tapered compressor and low-tension piston rings, you can literally install pistons with your fingertips.

stands, however. Look for a stand that has more capacity than you think you will ever need. Even if you plan on building only smallblocks, someday you will need a stand that can hold an iron head big-block—and it better be able to stand up under the weight.

Four-wheel engine stands are more stable than the three-wheel variety. Remember, the center of grav-

ity of an engine stand is high. It is very easy to topple the whole stand when you are cinching down the head bolts with a two-foot long torque wrench. The larger the casters, the easier it will be to wheel the stand around the garage. Wheel locks are a nice refinement. If you're concerned about a place to store the stand between engine building exercises, then consider a knock-down stand that can be stashed under a work bench.

When it comes time to install the pistons in your blueprinted engine block, a *ring compressor* is essential. Ring compressors are available in several styles. The tapered ring compressors made from machined aluminum are easy to use, and present the least danger of breaking a ring. Their drawbacks: you need a different compressor for each distinct bore size, and there is little clearance for cylinder-head studs. Despite these shortcomings, tapered ring compressors are the choice of most professional engine builders.

Installing a camshaft calls for a degree wheel. This one from Mills Specialty Products has a hub that can be turned with a 1/2-inch ratchet (set screws to lock the wheel in place after locating top-dead center) and a sturdy, adjustable point.

If you're looking for a more "universal" ring compressor, the best choice is the plier-type compressors offered by K-D Tools. By inserting different compressor bands in the plier handles, these tools can be used with engines ranging from Honda Civics to Chrysler Hemis. One of the advantages of the plier-type ring compressor is that the piston can be turned with one hand while you drive it into the cylinder bore. The third type of common ring compressor is the band type. These have been around since the days of Henry Ford—but that doesn't

A good electric drill has countless uses when building a high-performance engine, from countersinking bolt holes and enlarging oil passages to honing cylinder bores.

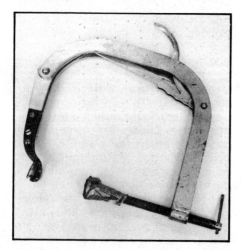

Extremely stiff valvesprings make a rugged spring compressor mandatory when assembling cylinder heads. This lever-action compressor will overcome the resistance of any racing spring.

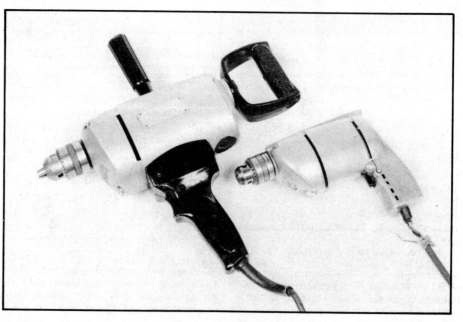

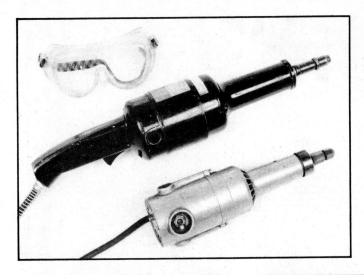

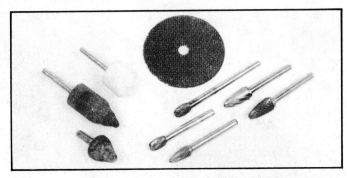

A tremendous variety of stones and cutters are available for high-speed grinders. Carbide burrs are expensive, but they will last a lifetime if used with care and resharpened regularly. Shapes include "trees," "flames," and "teardrops." Use coarse cutters for aluminum, fine cutters for steel and cast iron.

Be sure to include a high-speed grinder in your tool buying plans. A Craftsman die grinder will deburr blocks, radius piston domes, and chamfer oil holes. If you plan on doing some serious head porting, invest in a heavy duty Dumore or Milwaukee grinder. Remember to *always* wear eye protection when using a grinder!

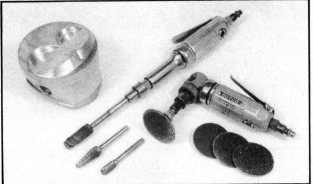

Pneumatic tools are used in production shops because of their reliablity and light weight. If you have a compressor with enough air capacity to run them, they are excellent for engine building.

make them any easier to use or less likely to snag a ring. About the best thing that can be said for band-type compressors is that they're cheap.

Sooner or later, you're also going to need a *degree wheel* to properly install the camshaft. Degree wheels can be plain or fancy, large or small, and cheap or expensive. Regardless of the other characteristics, a degree wheel should have easy-to-read numbers. The larger wheels have the advantage on this point—but a big degree wheel can also block access to the cam gear when you have to install a tiny offset cam button.

Assembling cylinder heads requires another group of specialized tools. A high quality *valvespring compressor* is a good investment. If your engine building efforts will be limited to stock-type rebuilds, a simple lever-type compressor will meet your needs. Compressing the stiff springs commonly used with racing and high-performance camshafts requires a more substantial tool, however. Several years ago, Sunnen offered an impressive spring compressor with a handle over two feet long, which really gave you some leverage. Unfortunately, these super spring compressors are no longer available. Nonetheless, the compound-leverage compressors that can be found at most tool stores or parts suppliers can handle most double and triple-coil springs.

Finding a glass *burette* may require a visit to a medical or laboratory supply house. A burette is used for such common blueprinting chores as

Speed Pro piston ring file makes short work of setting end gaps.

A piston ring expander will save your fingertips when installing rings on pistons—and reduce the chances of breaking a ring.

measuring the volumes of combustion chambers or piston domes. Buying a burette from a medical supply can be an ordeal, however. Even if you tell them what you are going to use it for, they are probably convinced that you are going to set up a backyard cocaine laboratory. In that case, your best tactic is to order a complete "cc'ing kit" from one of the mail-order tool suppliers. Ask for a burette with a capacity of at least l00cc's. A burette with a Teflon or plastic valve will be less likely to stick than one outfitted with a ground glass valve. Along with the burette, you'll need a clamp and stand.

The right way to remove a harmonic balancer is with a heavy duty puller (left)—and the correct way to put it back on is with a damper installation tool like this one from B&B Performance.

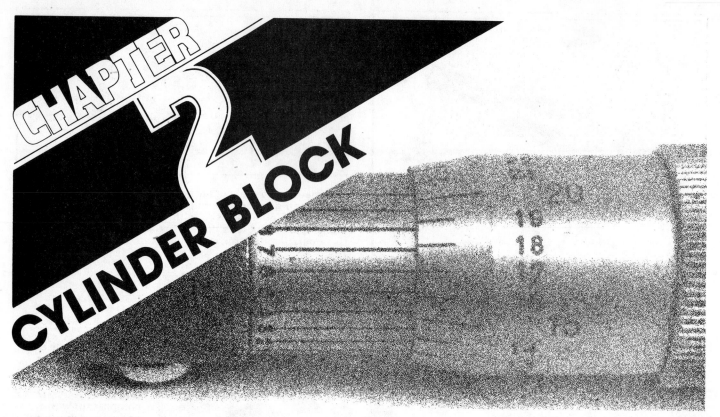

CHAPTER 2

CYLINDER BLOCK

Finding a suitable candidate for an engine blueprinting project is never easy. Approach a used motor with caution unless you are familiar with its history. Cracks and spun bearings may not be apparent until the engine is disassembled and inspected!

ENGINE BLOCK

The block is the foundation of any blueprinting project. Every other part in the engine ultimately depends on it. More time, effort, and expense is devoted to preparing the block than to any other single component. If the engine is to perform up to expectations, the block has to be *right*.

SELECTING A BLOCK

There was a time when any automotive project began with a trip to the junkyard for a suitable core. It's not that simple now. Junkyards are now called "salvage systems" or "ecological recylcing centers," and have prices that match the fancy names. More important, many of the cores now available in junkyards are less than desirable from a performance standpoint. In the "good old days," the automakers were quite liberal with their use of cast iron. When metal was cheap, the factories didn't care about the weight of their castings. Their attitude changed dramatically in the Seventies, however. The accountants pointed out that all of this cast iron costs money; and in their search for better fuel economy and mileage, the engineers were working overtime to eliminate weight from cars. The result was the arrival of thin-wall castings with flimsy cylinders, skimpy main bearing saddles, and fragile deck surfaces. The "good" castings—generally those manufactured during the Sixties—have been well picked over by now, especially in the yards surrounding major metropolitan areas. If you want a good block, it often pays to head for the country. Many of the engine rebuilding outfits that fill the car magazines with page after page of low-priced engine kits bring in trainloads of cores from Mexico and the Southwest, where there are still survivors from the Sixties.

NEW VS. "SEASONED" BLOCKS

It used to be that no self-respecting performance enthusiast would consider using a new block. This wasn't simply a matter of money. New blocks just didn't make as much power as a well-seasoned used block. Engine blocks, like football quarterbacks,

Here's evidence that the automakers are getting serious about performance again. Chevrolet has introduced Bow Tie big-block and small-block castings with all the features any racer could want; Ford and Chrysler offer similar heavy-duty pieces. For a strong street engine, however, Sixties-vintage iron is usually a better (and cheaper) choice.

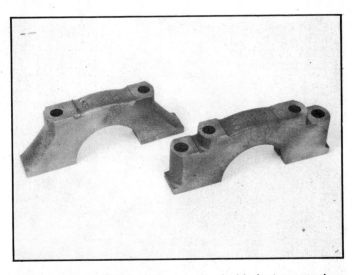

When shopping for block, look for desirable features such as four-bolt main bearing caps. Trucks, police cars, and taxi cabs are likely sources for heavy duty castings.

get better with age. In the case of a block casting, countless cycles of heating up and cooling down help to "season" the metal. When a block is first cast and then machined on the assembly line, it develops internal stresses. The heating/cooling cycle allows these stresses to "relax," until finally the block becomes dimensionally stable. In the opinion of many top-rank racers, an engine does not achieve maximum power output until it has been honed three or four times; it takes that long for the cylinder bores to settle down and hold the perfectly round shape that promotes a "tight" ring seal.

In certain applications, a used block is no longer the best choice, however. The Detroit engineers have realized that thin-wall castings are not really suitable for high-performance applications. That's why all the major automakers are now offering brand new "off-road" castings with the features that racers and performance enthusiasts demand. For example, Chevrolet will sell you both smallblock and big-block "Bow Tie" castings with extra-thick cylinderwalls, beefy main bearing bulkheads, and reinforced deck surfaces. Ford offers heavy-duty iron and aluminum blocks through the SVO division, and Chrysler makes special versions of the A-engine block available through the factory-backed Direct Connection program.

If you want the features these blocks offer, then you will have to use a "green," unseasoned casting. For a maximum effort racing engine, the advantages of thicker cylinderwalls and a beefy bottom end offset the extra effort required to rehone and rebuild the engine several times before it reaches its power potential. If a strong street

performance or moderate competition engine is in the works, then a well-used, seasoned block is probably the better bargain. Engine blocks intended for truck use tend to have more desirable features than passenger car versions. Given a choice, then, the best bet would be a mid-Sixties truck block with low mileage and no cracks—if you can find one!

PRELIMINARY INSPECTION AND DISASSEMBLY

Whether your block is packaged in a factory shipping crate or in an inch-thick layer of grime, a thorough inspection is important. You can save yourself a great deal of grief and expense by looking for fatal flaws *before* investing in any expensive machine work. Most of the points below apply to used blocks, but even factory-fresh castings deserve a careful going over.

Rebuilding an engine that you personally pulled from one of the family cars is a tremendous advantage because you already know whether the engine was basically sound. Buying an engine out of a junkyard, a swap meet, or a dark garage is a riskier proposition. In most instances, you don't have the luxury of hearing the engine run or even seeing the original vehicle from which it was removed. Was the motor simply worn out, or was it filling the oil pan full of water from a crack in a cylinderwall? It's up to you to find out whether the block is worth dragging home.

The first item on your block-inspection agenda is to decide what exactly you are looking at. Don't take the seller's word that the Chevy V-8 he's offering is a genuine 350ci high-performance LT-I. It might be, but it also could

be a $25 283 (if you don't know how to tell the difference). Your best sources of information about an unknown motor are the engine code and casting numbers. In the case of a Chevrolet V-8, the engine code is a series of letters that accompany the serial number stamped on a pad just above the water pump inlet. For example, a block stamped "DZ" is a 302ci 1969 Z/28 engine, while "FB" indicates a two-barrel 327. Be warned that these codes are not always 100% reliable, and that the same letter code is sometimes ap-

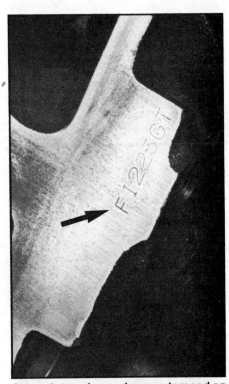

Chevrolet engine codes are stamped on a pad just above the water pump. This code may help you to identify an engine with a forged crank and big-valve cylinder heads.

15

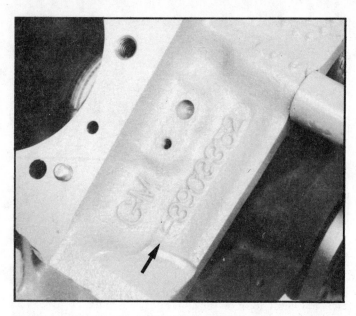

Casting numbers are clues to the identity of an unknown engine. Chevy V-8 casting numbers are located on bellhousing flange behind odd-numbered cylinder head.

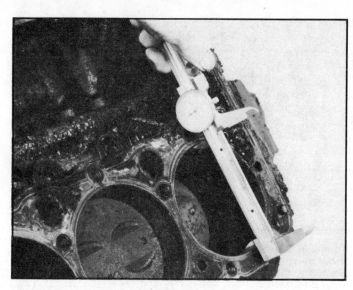

Remove the heads and measure the cylinders to determine whether the block has already been overbored. Then measure the diameter under the ridge at the top of the ring travel to see how much metal must be removed to clean up the cylinderwalls.

plied to different engines in succeeding years. If all you are looking for is a sound block, then the engine code may not be important. But if you are paying a premium price for a motor with a forged steel crank and big-valve cylinder heads, then the code is a good clue to the true identity.

Unlike engine codes, casting numbers apply to *types* of engines made over a period of years. To again cite the Chevrolet smallblock as an example, the casting number reveals the size of the main bearings and whether the block has two-bolt or four-bolt main caps. (Of course, if the engine is already disassembled, your own eyes will provide this information.) The casting number for a Chevrolet V-8 is lo-

cated on the driver's side of the block, just above the bellhousing surface. One of the several standard rebuilding references will help you decipher the casting number.

Even if the engine is encrusted with grime, a visual inspection will give you an idea about its condition. A block that looks covered with mayonnaise has been running with water in the oil. This may indicate a leaking intake manifold gasket or a serious crack in the block or cylinder heads. A valley full of "gunk" is a sure sign that the oil was changed infrequently. If this accummulation is so bad that it prevents the oil from adequately draining back to the pan, the resulting oil starvation may have caused a bearing to spin. If the oil pan

has been removed, check for a black, burned appearance around the main bearings. This will be visible even in a dirty block and indicates a bearing that was on the verge of failing. The resulting heat could have caused the bearing cap to be out of register on the block, which will require correction when the block is align honed during the blueprinting procedure.

If the heads have been removed, you can check for visible cracks in the cylinderwalls. An exceptionally rusty cylinder or a piston top with no coating of carbon is a tip-off that water was getting into the cylinder. You should also check the diameter of the cylinder bores. *Look for a block that has not already been overbored.* Scrape away

Mark the main bearing caps before removing them. Number the rods and caps with a punch.

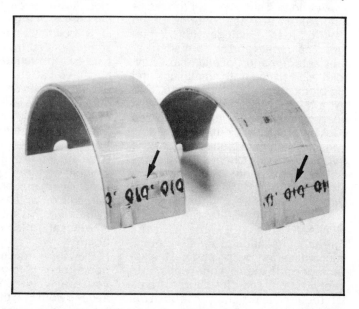

Undersize bearing inserts are a tip-off that the crankshaft has already been reground.

the carbon at the top of the bore and measure the cylinder diameter *above* the ring travel. A dial caliper is accurate enough for this measurement. If the block you intend to use has an original bore size of 4.000 inches, then a block with bores that measure 4.060 inches in diameter has already been rebuilt at least once. Boring the cylinders again may leave you with thin, fragile walls.

If the block has passed these tests, the next step is to measure the wear in the cylinders. Measure the diameter of the cylinder just under the ridge at the top of the ring travel. This is generally the point of maximum cylinder bore taper. The diameter under the ridge should be at least 0.015-inch *smaller* than your intended final bore size. This will provide enough material for the boring bar and hone to straighten the cylinderwall surface. Ideally, the cylinder bores should "clean up" with a 0.030-inch overbore.

Now it's time to invest some money in cleaning the likely candidate so that a detailed inspection can be performed. Before the block can be cleaned, it must be stripped. *Always mark the main bearing and rod bearing caps before disassembly.* You can use a fancy set of number punches or just a center punch to mark the caps—just make sure you do it. Number the main bearing caps from front to back, and mark the rod forks and caps with their respective cylinder numbers. If you forget these simple steps, your machinist will charge for the additional time he must spend sorting them out.

Used parts (like pistons, lifters, and bearings) have no place in a blueprinted engine, so special care is not required with these components. However, be respectful of the parts you will be reusing. While removing the pistons and rods, be especially careful to prevent nicks in the crankshaft journals or gouges in the cylinderwalls. A supply of coffee cans and margarine cups is essential for keeping the fasteners organized. Six months from now, you will not remember which bolt holds the oil pump in place unless you label it today. You can also get some clues to the engine's past by inspecting the back of the bearings. If the bearings are undersize, then it is likely that someone has already overhauled the engine (although the factories do occasionally "save" crankshafts that are off-spec by regrinding them and fitting oversize bearings to the block).

CLEANING

Before a used block can be carefully examined, it must be completely degreased. Most American car owners are not very conscientious about observing recommended oil change intervals, so most blocks are encrusted with grease, varnish, and sludge. There are two ways to remove this accumulated gunk: hot tanking and jet cleaning. Both methods are quite effective, and the choice will probably depend

Remove soft plugs by tapping them sideways with a blunt punch. Then lever them out with a pair of water-pump pliers or seal puller.

Kip Martin found that this Snap-on tool makes quick work of pulling old freeze plugs.

on the cleaning equipment your machinist prefers.

There are several steps that will make the cleaning procedure more effective, regardless of which technique your machinist uses. First, the freeze plugs (also known as soft plugs or core plugs) should be removed. This allows the cleaning agent to scour the water jacket, and permits a visual inspection of the outer cylinderwalls. Large flakes of rust and corrosion will be apparent in the water passages of an engine that has been used without anti-freeze protection. Although rust in the water jacket isn't cause to reject a block, you should be aware that the corroded cylinderwalls will be thinner, and therefore weaker, than unrusted walls.

There are several techniques for removing freeze plugs. Most engine builders strike the plug on one side with a dull punch, turning it sideways in its hole. Grab the edge of the plug with a pair of water pump pliers and lever the plug out of the block. Kip Martin,

Use an acetylene torch to remove stubborn oil gallery pipe plugs. Heat the plug, then spray it with WD-40.

After the plug has cooled, unscrew it with a 1/4-inch ratchet.

A length of steel rod is an ideal tool for removing soft plugs in the front of oil galleries. Drive them out with a heavy hammer.

who operates Patterson-Martin Machine in Augusta, Kansas, was our guide to the block preparation pictured here. He uses a Snap-on oil seal tool to remove old plugs quickly. Occasionally you will encounter a soft plug that refuses to cock sideways. This may be caused by a lack of clearance behind the plug, or by rust around the plug hole. In these instances, the only solution is to drive the plug into the water jacket and then fish it out with a pair of pliers. You should also remove the water drain plugs and clean out the holes with a punch or screwdriver.

The small oil gallery passages in most engine blocks are sealed with a combination of soft plugs and thread-

ed pipe plugs. If the plugs are frozen in place—and they usually are—heat from a blowtorch or welding torch will help to free them. After breaking dozens of l/4-inch drive extensions, Kip discovered a painless way to remove the plugs Chevrolet installs in the back of smallblock and big-block V-8s. He heats the plugs with a torch, using a welding tip, and then allows them to cool. After a quick spray with some WD-40 lubricant, the plugs will unscrew with the greatest of ease! After removing these threaded plugs, Kip inserts a three-foot piece of l/4-inch diameter steel into the oil galleries and drives out the soft plugs behind the camshaft gear with the aid of a small hammer.

If you want a glimpse of what hell must be like, take a look inside a hot tank sometime. Most automotive machine shops have their hot tanks located as far away as possible. They are filled with a caustic soda solution that is heated close to the boiling point. Agitators in the tank keep the solution constantly moving to scrub away the accumulated filth of years of use. The length of time that the block must be soaked depends on the strength of the solution, how hot your machinist keeps his tank, and how dirty the casting might be. Generally, a preliminary cleaning will require a couple of hours in the tank, although a really grimy block might need a stay overnight. Please note, too, that hot tanks are

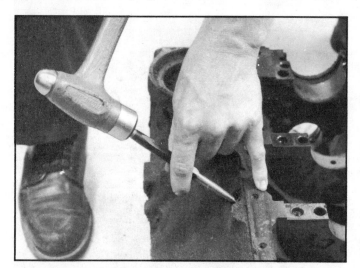

Clean out corrosion that has accumulated around water-drain holes with a tapered punch.

The hot tank is filled with a caustic solution that dislodges years of grit and grime. (Larry Hollums keeps his tank at the boiling point!) An overnight soaking will clean block so you can continue your inspection.

A jet cleaner is considerably faster than a hot tank; high-pressure nozzles will scour a used block in 20 minutes. Here Kip rinses casting after preliminary cleaning.

Bare block emerges from jet cleaner ready for final inspection and preliminary machine work.

only for iron blocks, since the solution will dissolve aluminum. Leave your Can-Am aluminum Chevy block in a hot tank overnight and it will simply disappear!

An alternative to the hot tank is a jet clean booth. As its name implies, a jet cleaner sprays the block with degreasing solution under high pressure. The block rotates on a carousel during the cleaning process to expose all its surfaces to the cleaning spray. Jet cleaning is much faster than hot tanking—even the dirtiest block will be ready for inspection in less than half an hour. Machinists who prefer the old-fashioned hot tank point out, however, that the jet cleaners aren't as effective at cleaning out the small oil passages in

the block. At this point, however, you are not trying to make the block "squeaky clean." Rather, you just want to remove the grease so that you can take a closer look at the casting surfaces.

FINAL INSPECTION

Your two eyes are the best tools for a final block inspection. Most cracks that are cause to reject a block are visible to the naked eye—providing you know where to look. If the block has been hot tanked, the soda solution will often pinpoint a cylinderwall crack by forming a white crust along the fault.

Most cracks are caused by either

overheating or freezing. These cracks are most common in the water jacket above the oil-pan rail and in the lifter valley. If the heat-riser passages in the cylinder head or intake manifold were blocked, there may be localized overheating in the valley. Stress cracks are most often found around the head bolt holes in the deck surface and nearby the oil holes in the main bearing saddles.

Dry *Magnaflux* inspection is often used to pinpoint cracks and flaws. A large U-shaped electric magnet is applied to the test area which is dusted with magnetic powder. Cracks in the block surface disrupt the magnetic field, causing the powder to form lines that highlight the flaws. A thorough

Discoloration around main bearing bores is caused by overheated bearing. Even though bearing may not have spun, localized high temperatures can foster cracks. Examine bearing saddles carefully, paying particular attention to bolt holes and oil passages.

Cylinderwall cracks are highlighted by white soda deposits when block is dried after hot tanking.

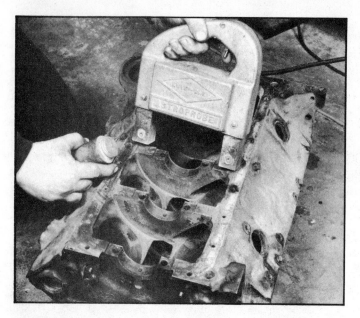

Larry Hollums begins Magnaflux inspection by magnetizing main bearing bulkheads, then sprinkling webs with magnetic powder.

Cracks in valley can be result of overheating caused by blocked heat-riser passages or inadequate coolant.

Magnaflux inspection should include both sides of the block, both sides of the lifter valley, and all the main bearing bulkheads. And don't overlook the main bearing caps while you're searching for flaws. Larry Hollums, who operates Hollums Racing Engines in Fremont, California, performed the block inspection for our camera.

If there are any suspicious cracks or evidence of water in the oil pan, then a *pressure test* is usually in order. The block is prepared for pressure testing by installing new freeze plugs, bolting steel plates to the deck surfaces, and covering the water pump inlets. The water passages are then pressurized with compressed air and the entire block is submerged in a vat of water, or sprayed with a solution of soapy water. Air escaping from the water jacket through a crack will create a telltale stream of bubbles.

You should also examine the block carefully for porosity. "Porosity" is the result of air pockets being trapped when molten metal is poured into a casting mold. When a block is machined later, the cutting tools can expose these voids, which may be as small as pinholes or as large as a quarter. Minor holes in the valley and front cover are nothing to be concerned about, but porosity in the deck surfaces and cylinderwalls is a serious problem. Blocks with excessive porosity are often repaired at the factory by welding up the offending holes. These welded areas are much harder than the parent metal, and some machinists may refuse to remachine a welded block because of the damage these hard spots cause to expensive cutting tools.

There is probably no such thing as a perfect cylinder block. The closer you look, the more flaws you will find. It's up to you to decide whether to accept the inevitable shortcomings. Stripped head bolt and main cap holes can be made better than new with Helicoil thread inserts; on the other hand, there is no sure cure for a crack in the main bearing bulkheads. A rare or limited-production block obviously requires a more forgiving attitude than a garden-variety casting.

SONIC TESTING

High-performance engine building is constantly becoming more sophisticated. Today many shops are able to *sonic test* blocks for cylinder-

If engine coolant freezes or boils, cracks in side of the water jacket are the likely consequence. Inspection powder highlights flaws by collecting along edges of crack.

wall thickness. The equipment required for this procedure costs thousands of dollars, but the importance of finding a block with thick cylinderwalls has convinced a substantial number of racers and machinists to make the necessary investment. Simply stated, the thicker the cylinderwalls, the higher the horsepower potential of the engine. Maintaining the tightest possible seal between the cylinderwalls and piston rings is essential to making horsepower. In a sense, cylinders that deform and go out-of-round under stress waste valuable horsepower.

The way the block material is distributed around the cylinder bores is also a vital concern. In most automotive engines, the thickness of the cylinderwalls is not uniform. The walls are usually thin between adjacent bores to allow coolant to circulate between the cylinders. (Exception to this general rule are the "siamese bore" blocks—such as the 400ci smallblock Chevrolet—in which the adjacent cylinderwalls are joined.) The walls are also sometimes thicker on the *major thrust surface* to withstand the stress imposed by the piston skirts. The pistons cock sideways as they travel up and down inside the cylinders; this sideways motion is called "piston thrust." These loads are highest during the power stroke, when the piston is exerting maximum pressure on the connecting rod. The highest thrust occurs on the wall opposite the big end of the rod as the piston moves down the bore. In a V-8 this is generally the outboard side of the right and inboard side of the left cylinder banks.

During the casting process, however, the molds that form the cylinderwalls can move out of alignment. This is called "core shift." A block that suffers from core shift will have cylinderwalls that are thicker or thinner than they are supposed to be.

Not all core shifts are bad. If the cylinderwalls on the side of the bores that are exposed to the major thrust axes of the pistons are extra-thick, then they will be stronger. Of course, the sides of the cylinders that bear against the minor thrust axes will be thinner, perhaps to the point of being fragile. The problem is that without a sonic tester, it's impossible to *know* how thick the cylinderwalls are and in which direction the cores may have shifted during the casting process.

Before sonic testing equipment became widely available, there were a number of signs that were reputed to indicate how badly a block had core-shifted. Examining the pad around the front camshaft bearing, checking the

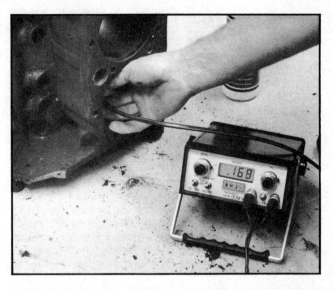

Sonic testing is the most accurate means of determining cylinderwall thickness. The BHJ Products ultrasonic tester is first calibrated with metal of known thickness, then probe is applied to cylinderwall. Readings are taken at front, rear, and both sides of bore.

relationship between the lifter bores and their bosses, and measuring from the coolant holes in the deck surface to the cylinder bores were all supposed to indicate whether a block was "good" or not. Unfortunately, sonic testing has revealed that these visual clues fall into the category of "old wives' tales." They are simply not a reliable way to determine whether a block has acceptable core shift.

A sonic tester is a high-tech instrument that measures cylinderwall thickness by bouncing sound waves through the metal, much like radar computes distances by measuring the time it takes for radio waves to bounce off a distant object. BHJ Products (Fremont, California) is the source for most of the sonic testers currently used by performance-oriented engine builders. Since the density of various cast iron alloys varies, the BHJ tester includes an assortment of calibrating standards. For example, a block with a high percentage of nickel in the iron alloy requires a different

calibration than a block with a relatively low tin content.

Most machinists make a "map" of the cylinderwalls when they sonic test a cylinder block. Each cylinder is measured in eight locations—the front, back, and each side of the bore—with readings taken both at the top and bottom of the ring travel. Machinists who have long experience with sonic testing report that there is often a substantial variation between cylinderwall thickness in the same block. In other words, you can't measure just one hole and conclude that all the bores on that side of the block will have the same wall thickness readings. Kip Martin, who performed the sonic test pictured here, reports that the number-8 cylinder tends to be the worst hole in a smallblock Chevrolet.

The question naturally arises, "how thick is thick enough?" The answer depends on both the type of engine and how it will be used. Late-model Fords and 340-type Chrysler engines, for example, tend to be thin; typical

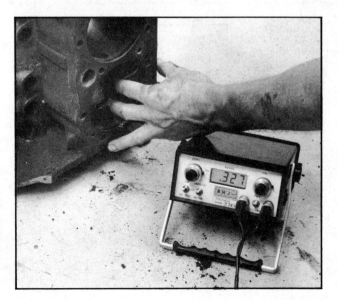

This block demonstrates how core shift can affect cylinderwall thickness. Outboard side of cylinderwall measures 0.327-inch thick; inboard wall is much thinner, with only 0.168-inch of metal.

cylinderwall thicknesses on these engines may be only 0.150-inch. A small-block Chevrolet, in contrast, may have cylinderwalls over 0.200-inch thick. Kip advises that he wants to see at least 0.180-inch of wall material on the major thrust side *after* the block has been bored to finished size. Larry Hollum concurs; his general rule is that any smallblock with a performance goal of 500 horsepower or higher should have cylinderwalls at least 0.200-inch thick.

Sonic testing a block is expensive because of the cost of the equipment involved, but it provides valuable information. It allows you to reject a block with thin cylinderwalls *before* investing a lot of time and money in machine work. Also, the wall-thickness diagram allows a sharp machinist to relocate the cylinder bores to provide the greatest possible wall thickness on the critical major thrust. It may be possible for him to adjust the bore location as much as 0.030-inch during the boring operation. Without a sonic examination, the machinist must rely on the existing bore location and hope for the best.

Is sonic testing absolutely necessary? For a high-performance street motor, sonic testing is certainly a high-cost luxury. On the street, it's not essential to extract the very last horsepower. But for a maximum-effort racing engine, sonic testing should be considered an indispensible step in the engine building procedure!

DEBURRING

If your block has passed this series of tests, it's time to get to work. The first item on the list of things to do is a thorough *deburring*. Deburring is essential for both cosmetic and structural reasons. The aim of deburring a block is to grind off all the sharp edges and casting burrs. These sharp edges are "stress risers" that can give cracks a starting point. Eliminating these flaws will also save you from collecting countless cuts and nicks on your hands while working on the engine.

Begin your deburring work with a hammer and a long punch or chisel. Usually the cam gallery and oil drain passages are full of sharp ridges and casting flash formed by joints in the block molds. Use the punch to knock off this metal residue. Then go over the main bearing bulkheads, lifter valley, and front cover, eliminating any excess metal that looks like it could break off the casting and eventually wind up in the oil pan. Before you put the punch and hammer away, it's also a good idea to take a tour around the outside of the block to knock off excess casting flash.

The next step is to break out the high-speed grinder and attack every sharp edge on the block. Plan on spending a full Saturday afternoon on this project, and remember to wear eye protection when the chips are flying. You can use either grinding stones or carbide burrs for this chore, although the carbide cutters will make less of a mess. The idea is to simply round off all the sharp edges on the internal and external surfaces. It is not necessary to meticulously radius every corner, although the finish block will *look* better if you do (possibly a consideration if

Casting process leaves numerous sharp edges and hiding places for core sand. Concentrate your deburring efforts in camshaft gallery, under oil pan rail, and alongside main bearing bulkheads.

A hammer and a long punch are essential for removing casting flash from cam gallery and other inaccessible areas.

Smooth edges along pan rail will help oil return to sump, reducing windage and improving lubrication.

Casting flash is common around oil drain holes in lifter valley. Ridges can break off and cause damage by scuffing piston skirts or jamming oil pump; remove them with a high-speed hand grinder.

the engine is destined for a street rod or ski boat).

You should also concentrate on chamfering the oil drain holes. These passages are often full of casting flash that can break loose and find its way into the oil pump. By gently rounding the edges of these holes, you'll encourage the lubricant to return quickly to the sump.

It's possible to get carried away with this operation. Some novice engine builders don't stop until the entire lifter valley is practically polished. These misdirected efforts may actually cause more harm than good, since cleaning out all the grit left from grinding the engine is virtually impossible. The slightly rough surface of the block casting helps transfer heat to the oil, which can account for almost 60% of the engine cooling.

Deburring outside of block denies cracks a starting place, and saves your hands from cuts and scratches.

Before you hang up the hand grinder, radius main oil passage on Chevy rear bearing cap.

Deburr lifter bores with extra-fine-grit brake-cylinder ball hone.

ALIGN HONING AND BORING

Align honing or *align boring* the main bearing saddles should be the first major machine operation. All the block machine work that follows will be based either directly or indirectly on the main bearing saddles, so it is crucial that this first step be done properly.

As a matter of course, the main-bearing bores of every high-performance engine should be align honed or align bored. On the assembly line, engines are routinely fitted with specially selected main bearings to make up for imperfections in the main bearing saddles. Once these bearings are replaced, the alignment is lost. Also, as a block ages and the cast surfaces relax, the main bearing bulkheads can distort. Since this is a slow process, the bearings and crankshaft wear to accommodate this movement. But when new bearings or a blueprinted crankshaft is installed on misaligned bearing saddles, rapid failure can result. Many of the standard backyard tests, such as placing a straightedge on the main bearing saddles or installing a crank to see if it turns freely, are not reliable. For example, these checks will not reveal whether the main bearing bores have become egg-shaped as a result of the main bearing caps distorting. Of course, if a main bearing has spun or if special steel main bearing caps are being installed, the main bearing saddles *must* be realigned.

There is still considerable controversy about the advantages of align *honing* versus align *boring*. In align honing, the main bearing bores are straightened with self-centering abrasive stones. Align boring uses a steel pilot with a single-edged cutting tool. In theory, align boring has the advantage of allowing the machinist to remove the majority of material from the main bearing caps, which leaves the relationship between the crankshaft and camshaft undisturbed. (Only the heavy-duty Tobin-Arp machines have this capability, however. The small, block-mounted boring bars frequently found in machine shops work much like an align hone, removing material equally from both the cap and block saddles). In practice, however, the skill of the machinist counts for more than the type of equipment he uses. In skilled hands, an align hone can produce results that rival align boring.

Sunnen is currently one of the major manufacturers of align-honing machines, and the wide-spread popularity of Sunnen brand equipment means

Kip Martin begins align honing operation by cleaning main cap parting lines with fine file.

File marks highlight irregular contact between caps and block. Align honing increases area of block-to-cap contact.

Shiny spots on main bearing caps are evidence of "cap walk," or movement, between caps and block under load.

Sunnen precision grinder removes small amount of metal from cap parting line. This trues cap surface and reduces vertical diameter of main bearing bore.

Most critical part of align honing Chevrolet V-8 is cutting wide rear main bearing cap. If this cap is cocked, thrust bearing will be overloaded on one edge.

After grinding, mating surfaces of main bearing caps are flat and uniform.

Main cap bolt holes are chased with undersized tap to clean threads without removing any metal.

Parting line of main caps is deburred by drawing cap across fine file.

Caps should fit tightly in block. If caps are loose, Kip peens block with blunt chisel to improve register.

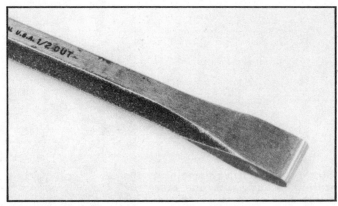

Chisel point is rounded with bench grinder for peening chores.

Main cap fasteners are cleaned, lubricated, and torqued to recommended specifications before align honing begins.

Long honing mandrel is centered in bearing bores with aligning pins. Martin prefers greater precision provided by dial indicator.

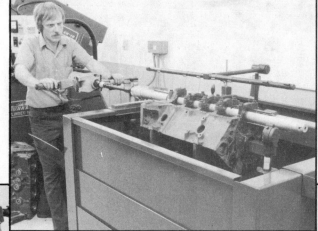

With all the preliminaries finished at last, actual honing can begin. Stones are constantly flushed with honing fluid to carry off block material and abrasive. Drill motor rotates hone as operator strokes mandrel back and forth in bearing bores.

Discarded oil pump housing bolted to rear main cap simulates distortion that occurs when pump is installed; credit Larry Hollums for this refinement.

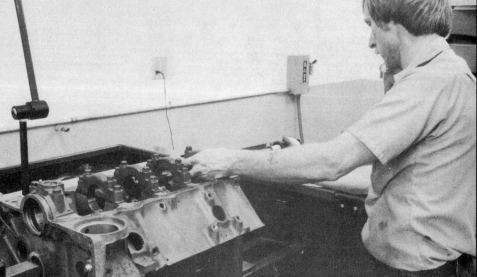

Kip constantly checks diameter of bearing saddles with dial bore gauge. Size of bores is critical if bearing inserts are to have proper crush.

that most automotive shops can now align hone blocks. And since most align hone operations are performed on similar equipment, *the difference between a first-rate job and a mediocre effort usually lies in the setup and the preparation.* Few performance enthusiasts have the opportunity to witness the align honing procedure from start to finish. That's why you are now invited to follow along as Kip Martin takes us step-by-step through an align honing job.

Kip begins by running a file over the parting surfaces between the caps and block. This spotlights the high spots on the surfaces and underlines the fact that many main bearing caps are not flat when they leave the factory. Before returning the file to the tool box, he deburrs the sharp edges on both the cap and saddles. The main-cap bolt holes are then chased with an undersized GH-3 tap. This small tap cleans the threads *without removing any metal,* which would weaken them. The bolts are put aside in a can of carburetor cleaner while Kip readies the caps.

Preparing the caps properly is critical to the success of the align honing operation. The caps *must* be square when the parting-line surface is being prepared. This is especially important on the thrust bearing (the rear main on Chevrolet V-8's). If the cap surface is not ground on a true plane that is parallel with the crank axis, the cap will be cocked when it is reinstalled on the block and this will cause the thrust bearing to wear unevenly. In severe cases, the thrust loads are concentrated on a small part of the bearing surface area, which causes the bearing to fail prematurely. (This is extremely critical if the engine will be used with a manual clutch that has very heavy spring pressures.)

A special Sunnen main-cap cutter precisely grinds material from the parting surface of the cap. Kip removes only enough metal from the cap to produce a smooth, flat finish. (This is one of the overlooked advantages of align honing, since resurfacing the main caps increases the block-to-cap contact.) Trimming several thousandths of an inch of metal from the main caps means that the bearing bores will *not* be round when the caps are reinstalled on the block. Thus, the hone also resizes the portion of the main bore that lies in the block main webs, much like a connecting rod is reconditioned.

The main caps should fit tightly in the alignment notches. If the fit is sloppy, Kip peens the block alongside

the main cap register with a blunt chisel. He also lightly chamfers the parting-line edge of the cap bore by drawing the edge across a fine file. This breaks the sharp edge, which can scrape material off the backside of the bearing shells when they are inserted. The clean main cap bolts are retrieved from the carb cleaner, washed in solvent, and lightly oiled. The caps are then bolted to the block and the fasteners tightened to the recommended torque reading.

Kip prefers to set up the align hone with a dial indicator instead of the usual centering pins. This helps ensure that the bearing bores will be perfectly round. He adjusts the dial bore gauge (which measures the diameter of the bearing holes) to the nominal size listed in the manufacturer's specifications. Undersize bearing bores are to be avoided, since they will cause the bearing clearance to be too tight. A bearing bore that is *slightly* larger than the manufacturer's specifications is acceptable—as long as the bearing still has the proper "crush"—because performance engines are generally set up with generous bearing clearances. The Sunnen align hone has a built-in lubrication system that bathes the stones with honing oil to carry away worn abrasive. After several strokes with the hone, Kip checks to make sure that the bearing bores are being cut evenly. If not, the caps are removed and trimmed slightly in the cap grinder.

DECKING

Decking the cylinder block accomplishes several important results. First, it makes the block "square." This means that if you measure from both deck surfaces to the crankshaft centerline at the front and rear of the block, all four dimensions will be equal. If a BHJ Blok-Tru is used, decking will also "index" the block. In most V-8s the decks should be exactly 90° to

each other. If you imagine a line between the crank centerline and the camshaft centerline, it should divide this 90° angle between the decks into two equal 45° angles. In the real world of engine building, it's not unusual to find that the decks are slightly cocked, and that the camshaft is somewhat off-center.

The third aim of decking a block is to establish the *deck height.* Deck height is measured when the installed piston is at exact top dead-center (TDC) and is defined as the distance from the flat quench area of the piston to the deck surface of the block. Deck height is a critical dimension in engine building. If the deck height is too small, the pistons can hit the cylinder heads; if it is too large, the compression ratio may be reduced considerably.

Unfortunately, there is no "ideal" deck height. The thickness of the head gasket must be considered when computing the total clearance between the piston and cylinder head. For example, if the flat part of the piston is 0.020-inch *below* the deck surface at TDC and a head gasket with a compressed thickness of 0.020-inch is installed, then the final piston-to-head clearance is 0.040-inch.

This is only a static measurement; when the engine is running, the actual operating clearance will be much less. In fact, the goal of most engine builders is to have the piston-to-head clearance as close to zero as possible *under actual operating conditions.* When an engine is running at high rpm, the connecting rods stretch, the pistons rock, and the wrist pins flex slightly. All of this reduces the actual clearance between the pistons and cylinder heads.

Engines that operate at very high rpm require more deck height and more piston-to-head clearance than low-rpm motors, since the loads on the engine components increase greatly with speed. Also, the connecting rod material must be considered; aluminum rods stretch more than steel rods. Finally, the clearance between the pistons and the cylinder walls has to be considered. When the pistons are fitted loosely (as is common in high-rpm engines) they will, in effect, tip over more sharply at the top of the stroke—when the crank stops pushing the piston upward and begins to pull it down. This causes the piston decks (along the major thrust axis) to approach the cylinder heads more closely. And, if any of the pistons accidentally tap the cylinder head, the top ring groove can collapse and pinch the piston ring, greatly reducing the

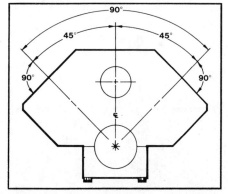

The cylinder head decks of most V8's should be machined 90° to each other.

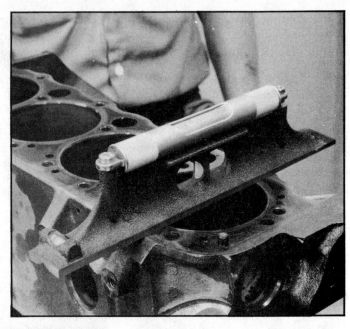

BHJ Blok-Tru fixture centers on main bearing bores and camshaft bearings. It provides accurate reference points when surfacing block to correct factory machining mistakes. Conventional V-8 decks should be at precisely 90 degrees to each other.

Machinist's bubble level is used for preliminary block setup. Bubble level is not accurate enough for final alignment, however.

Two-inch diameter steel bar supports block on main bearing saddles; this ensures that deck surfaces will be parallel to crankshaft. Screw jack supports bar to prevent weight of block from deflecting bar. Block is securely clamped to work table before surfacing.

Head dowel pins must be removed from block before surfacing. You can use Vise Grips or a punch; Kip prefers this slick Kent-Moore dowel puller that yanks them out in seconds.

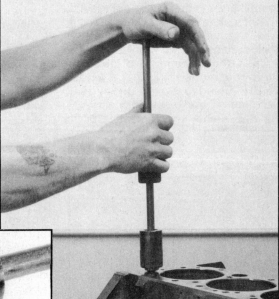

ring seal and power output.

Determining the absolutely correct piston-to-head clearance can be a long trial-and-error process. For most applications, however, the following recommendations can be followed with reasonable confidence. For a high-performance street engine with steel connecting rods, 0.035-inch piston-to-head clearance is the absolute minimum. For a racing engine with steel rods, 0.045-inch clearance is required; aluminum rods require increasing the clearance to at least 0.060-inch (and even more if there is evidence of the pistons contacting the heads). Remember, these are *total* piston-to-head clearances; *the thickness of the head gasket must be subtracted to arrive at the desired deck height.* In some instances, the block may not be tall enough to produce the desired deck height; in this case, the pistons must be milled.

So how much should the block be milled to arrive at the desired deck height? Well, if your machinist happens to own a BHJ Products Blok-Tru fixture, the answer is easy. A Blok-Tru is a precisely machined steel plate that provides consistent reference points for block machining. Once registered in the main bearing saddles and camshaft bore, the Blok-Tru gives an automotive machinist two flat surfaces that are precisely 90° apart. This allows him to set up his mill or grinder

so that the block will be indexed perfectly, regardless of how slanted or cocked the deck surfaces might be as they came from the factory. Also, since the height of the Blok-Tru fixture is fixed, the machinist can measure from the deck surfaces of the block to the top of the fixture to determine just how much metal must be removed to produce the desired deck-height dimension.

It works like this. To compute the block height from the crank centerline to the deck surface, use the following formula:

deck height + piston compression height + center-to-center rod length +

$$\frac{\text{crank stroke}}{2} = \text{BLOCK HEIGHT}$$

If you fill in the blanks using the typical dimensions of a 350ci Chevrolet, the numbers look like this:

$$0.015 + 1.560 + 5.700 + \frac{3.48}{2} = 9.015$$

This means that the block should measure 9.015 inches from the center of the crank to the deck surface. The BHJ Blok-Tru fixture measures 7.500 inches from the center of the bearing bores to its deck reference point. Subtracting this 7.500-inch figure from the desired block height of 9.015 inches leaves 1.515 inches. The machinist simply measures from the Blok-Tru to the deck surface, then mills the block until a micrometer reading taken from the deck to the fixture reads 1.515 inches. The result? The right deck height on the first try!

Final leveling adjustment is made with dial indicator attached to cutter wheel. Needle must not move as indicator travels across top edge of Blok-Tru. By milling both sides of block parallel to fixture, decks will be at desired 90 degree angle.

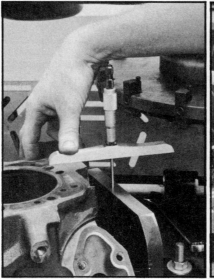 

If the block height dimension—the distance from crank centerline to deck surface—has already been finalized, then depth of cut is easy to calculate. Fixture plate measures exactly 7.500-inch from crankshaft centerline to top edge. If depth micrometer reads 1.500-inch from deck to fixture plate, then total block height is 9.000-inch. Machinist can then compute how much material to remove to produce required piston-to-head clearance.

Final step in decking Chevrolet V-type block is to trim intake manifold mating surface after both decks have been cut.

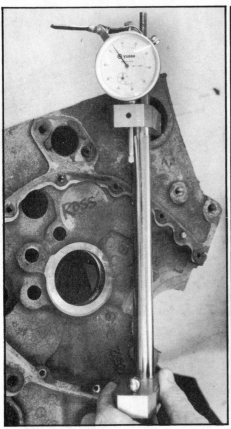

Block height can also be measured with a large micrometer or a specialized tool like this one. After setting gauge with a standard, distance from main bearing saddle to deck surface is measured as shown. Round ball provides accurate reading against curved main bearing bore.

The Blok-Tru is a "state of the art" machining fixture, and not every shop has one. Don't despair; there are other ways to come up with the right block height. A large micrometer can provide the answer. The desired block height dimension is computed as in the example above. Then the block is measured from the main bearing saddles to the deck surface. Adding one half the diameter of the main bearing bore gives the existing block height dimension. Subtract the desired block height from the present block height and you

Record final deck height dimension on block with number punches. You can refer to this dimension years later when selecting head gaskets to provide the necessary piston-to-head clearance.

are left with the amount that must be machined off the deck surface. The only shortcoming of this method is that it does not allow the machinist to correct the angle of the decks if they are not at 90°—although that may be a problem that only concerns the most fanatic engine blueprinters.

Finally, there is the do-it-yourself method that has been used by generations of engine builders. All it requires is a dial indicator or depth micrometer. First, the short block must be preassembled, using the same pis-

tons, connecting rods, and crankshaft that will be installed in the engine. (If oversized pistons are used, the cylinders will have to be bored before the deck height can be checked.) Each piston is brought up to TDC, then the distance from the deck surface to the piston top is carefully measured and recorded.

If the pistons have flat tops, this measurement should be taken at the center of the piston. Domed pistons require a little more effort, since the domes usually interfere with the depth micrometer. You'll have to measure the deck height on the flat part of the piston, which is called the *quench area*. To obtain an accurate deck height figure, rock the piston all the way over to one side and note the deck height. Then rock the piston to the other side and take a second measurement. The *average* of these two readings should be used as the piston deck height dimension.

Even if you don't have a depth micrometer or dial indicator, you can still check the piston deck heights with an acceptable degree of accuracy. Simply place several small balls of modeling clay on the piston quench surface, put a drop of oil on the clay to prevent it from sticking to the head, and rotate the crankshaft until the piston is halfway down its cylinder bore. Place a head gasket with the same thickness as the one you intend to use for final assembly on the deck surface; then install the head, and torque down the bolts. Rotate the crank through two revolutions, then remove the cylinder head. The measured thickness of the compressed clay indicates the *actual piston-to-head clearance*.

The precise thickness of the head gaskets can be measured using a similar technique. It is important to know the *compressed* thickness of the particular type of head gasket you intend to use. Composition "sandwich" gaskets must be clamped between the head and block before the *true* compressed thickness can be determined. Similarly, the embossed beads on steel shim gaskets add slightly to the thickness, even after these gaskets have been compressed. To determine the compressed thickness, place the gasket on the block deck surface and then position a BB-size piece of lead shot on the block wherever a hole in the gasket exposes the deck surface beneath it. If there are no places where the deck surface is visible around the gasket, then cut a hole in the gasket. Install the cylinder head, torque the fasteners, and then remove

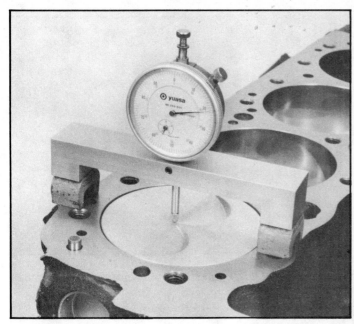

the head. Measure the thickness of the compressed lead ball with a micrometer to learn exactly how much the head gasket will compress under actual conditions.

After all the piston deck heights have been measured, you may notice a pattern. For example, the deck heights may increase from one end of the block to the other. This indicates that the deck surface is tapered. Another possibility is that the deck heights for two pistons that share the same crank throw may be noticeably higher or shorter than the other pistons; the crankshaft stroke on that particular throw may be the culprit. Occasionally one or two random pistons may be higher or lower than the rest. This usually means that the wrist pin holes were bored inaccurately, or that the center-to-center lengths of the corresponding connecting rods are too long or too short. Often these problems can be corrected by swapping connecting rods and pistons until the deck height readings are consistent.

After you have come up with a good match of pistons and rods, you can decide how much metal should be machined off the deck surfaces. For example, if the goal is a minimum deck height of 0.020-inch, and the existing heights range from 0.030- to 0.033-inch, then you would ask your machinist to mill 0.010-inch off the deck of the block. And remember, the stock deck heights of the right and left cylinder banks of a V-type engine will vary somewhat, so both must be measured and correspondingly larger or smaller cuts may be required.

You should expect some variation in *piston deck heights*. Most conscientious engine builders will accept a

Piston deck height and compressed head gasket thickness determine total piston-to-head clearance. Measure deck height with dial indicator and bridge as close to center of piston as possible. Then, take measurements at several points around circumference of piston as shown. Rock piston back and forth to obtain average deck height dimension.

spread of 0.002- to 0.003-inch between the highest and lowest deck heights. It is difficult to get perfectly accurate deck height readings when rocking a piston, so this much variation falls within the range of normal measurement errors. It's important,

however, that none of the pistons have *less* than the minimum deck height needed for your particular engine. If you are cutting the piston-to-head clearance close, it is better to give away a little compression than risk letting the pistons hit the heads. Also remember that head gasket thicknesses can vary several thousandths of an inch over a period of time (due to manufacturing tolerances).

Block surfacing machines fall into two general categories: mills and grinders. These types of equipment differ considerably in the way they remove material from the engine block. The mills have a large rotating wheel that is outfitted with several

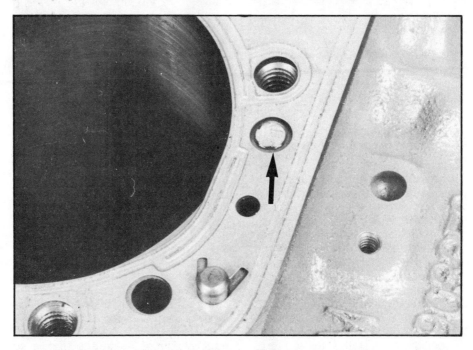

To measure thickness of compressed head gasket, crush lead shot or modeling clay between head and block with gasket in place, then measure with micrometer.

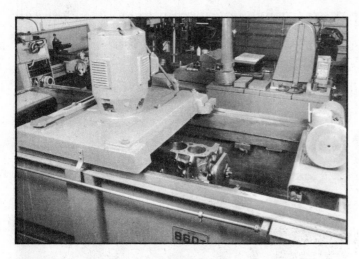

Although grinders are not as common as mills, they can also produce good results. This Kwik-Way 860 surfacer is about the size of a small car, and considerably heavier.

Adapter rings allow block fixture to be used with various main bearing diameters.

Block is leveled by measuring from top of grinder to bar at both ends of block.

Next step is to level block from side-to-side. Grinding stone is perfectly parallel to Blok-Tru when indicator reading remains constant as it is moved across top edge of fixture plate.

As with mill, amount of metal to be removed is determined by measuring from fixture to top of block. Grinder removes only a few thousandths of material with each pass, leaving extremely smooth surface.

dozen sharp cutting tools. The grinders, in contrast, use a heavy abrasive stone that literally wears away the deck surface. The weight and mass of the machinery is important in both types of surfacers. Making a perfectly flat cut over the two-foot span of an engine block demands an extremely rigid and precise tool. Among machinists, the Storm-Vulcan Blockmaster is generally the top-rated mill, while the Kwik-Way 860 gets the high marks among grinders. Both of these impressive machines are pictured here. You may encounter other types of milling

machines in your search for a good machinist, but beware of lightweight surfacers. The small equipment simply can't produce the consistent, high-quality results that careful blueprinting demands.

Mills and grinders produce distinctive finishes on the deck surfaces. Assuming that the cutting bits of a mill are sharp and properly aligned, the surface finish left by the cutting wheel will be slightly rough. A grinder, in contrast, produces a surface that is so smooth it seems to be almost polished. The grinder removes material very

slowly, typically only 0.002-inch or so of metal on each pass. Mills can take much larger cuts, although the final pass is usually a clean-up run that removes only 0.002- to 0.005-inch of metal. There is some controversy about which is the "better" surface finish. Machinists who prefer mills point out that the slight texture left by the cutters gives the metal microscopic "teeth" to grip the head gasket. Advocates of grinding contend that the smooth finish left by their technique maximizes surface contact between the block and head gasket.

After block has been surfaced, it must be leveled in boring stand. Dial indicator must move across deck surface without change in reading.

Patterson & Martin Machine uses this block-mounted boring bar. Since deck surfaces have already been milled parallel to crank, block-mounted bar will bore cylinders perpendicular to crankshaft centerline.

BORING

Overboring the cylinders is one of the most common automotive machine operations. It is also the task most often bungled. During a typical "quickie rebuild" the machinist sets up a boring bar on the block, centers the cutter on the existing cylinder bore, and then quickly enlarges the cylinder diameter to within a hair of its final size. In engine blueprinting, however, each one of these steps must be done carefully and thoughtfully. After all, *it is the "roundness" and the "straightness" of the bores that determines how well the cylinders will be sealed.*

There are two common types of boring equipment. The first mounts on the deck surface of the block, while the second attaches to the main bearing saddles of the block. Regardless of which kind of machine is used, the objective is to bore the cylinders exactly perpendicular to the crankshaft centerline. In theory, if the deck surfaces have been machined parallel to the crankshaft centerline, then a block-mounted machine should bore the cylinders perpendicular to the crankshaft. As with many machining operations, the skill and care of the operator counts as much as the type of equipment he uses.

This Kwik-Way machine at Hollums Racing Engines supports the block by the main bearing saddles; boring head mounts on flat work table above block.

Hollums inserts brass shims between block and support bar to level block under boring bar.

Three equally spaced pins align tool spindle with center of existing cylinder bore.

Micrometer gauge sets diameter of cutting tool. Cylinder is bored to within 0.010/0.006-inch of final bore diameter; remaining material will be removed with hone.

When a cylinder is bored, the cutting tool leaves a rough surface on the cylinderwall. Even the sharpest machine tool produces tiny rips and tears in the metal. This is why the machinist does not bore the cylinder to the final finished diameter. Instead, he intentionally bores the cylinder slightly smaller than the desired final diameter. For example, if a block is to have a finished cylinder diameter that is 0.030-inch oversize, then the machinist would bore the cylinders only 0.024-inch oversize. The remaining 0.006-inch of material will be removed during the honing operation. This effectively eliminates the tiny pits and

Semi-finished heavy-duty blocks have rough-bored cylinders when they leave the factory. Since these bores are not accurately located, a fixture like this BHJ Bor-Tru must be used to position the boring bar when preparing one of these racing blocks. Bor-Tru plate properly locates dowel pins and cylinder bores in relation to other critical block dimensions.

gouges left by the tool bit of the boring machine.

The traditional way to overbore an engine block is to center the cutting tool in the existing cylinder bore. This is not always the best location for the cylinder, however. A block with core shift (the casting cores were misaligned slightly when the block was cast) may have thin walls on one side of the cylinders, as described in the section on sonic testing. In these instances, you may want to instruct the machinist to *offset bore* the cylinders. Using the "map" of cylinderwall thicknesses produced during sonic testing, a sharp machinist can actually

If sonic testing reveals that cylinderwall is thin on one side of bore, cylinder can be offset bored by placing shim under boring bar centering pin. Amount of offset is limited by how much the bore is being enlarged, since boring tool must remain in continuous contact with cylinderwall.

relocate the centerline of the cylinder slightly. Inserting a shim between the cylinderwall and the centering pins of the boring machine can cause the cutter to remove more metal from one side of the bore than the other. Naturally, there are limits to how far the bore can be moved; but in building a maximum-effort engine, no advantage can be overlooked.

The arrival of "racing-only" blocks from the automakers presents a new challenge to machinists. The Chevrolet Bow Tie (high-performance) small-and big-block castings, for example, have rough-finished cylinder bores. This allows the engine builder to bore/hone to stock or over-size bore diameters and still maintain the thickest possible cylinderwalls, but it also presents some problems. The cylinder bores in these semi-finished Bow Tie blocks are *not accurately located*, so a special fixture is required to put the holes where they belong when the block is finished. Most shops use BHJ Products' Bor-Tru for this important chore. The Bor-Tru plate bolts to the deck surface, providing an accurate reference point for locating the cylinder bores and head-dowel holes. This fixture locates the cylinders from the crankshaft thrust surface, ensuring that the cylinders are precisely centered over the crank throws.

The final step in boring a block is to lightly chamfer the tops of the cylinder bore. This can be done with either a conical sanding drum or a 60° cutting

Final step in boring operation is to lightly chamfer top of cylinder with 60-degree tool or sanding drum. This makes piston ring installation easier and eliminates bloodshed caused by sharp edges of cylinder.

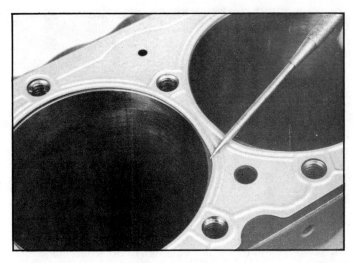

Sharp edge at top of block can disrupt airflow in combustion chamber. Cylinder bore should be notched or chamfered to match chamber contour.

tool inserted in the boring machine. Breaking the sharp edge at the top of the bore prevents damage to the honing stones, and allows the piston rings to slip into the bore more easily during final engine assembly.

HONING

Honing is both an art and a science. Certainly a great deal of the credit for recent improvements in engine performance is due to advances in cylinderwall preparation. The engine produces power because of the pressure exerted on the piston tops by the expanding gases in the cylinders. If less of this pressure escapes past the piston rings, more usable power will be pro-

Before honing block, chamfer top thread of head bolt holes with 60 degree countersink.

duced. *This means that the cylinder bores must be as round and as straight as possible.* Careful honing makes the difference.

If you examine a cylinderwall under a microscope, after it has been bored, you will find hundreds of jagged peaks and valleys left by the boring tool. During honing, these irregularities are cut away, leaving a smooth, uniform finish. During the honing process, radial pressure is exerted against a series of rotating abrasive "stones" that are continuously passed back and forth through the bore. The bonding agent in the stones breaks down, exposing fresh abrasive, and a constant stream of honing oil flushes away particles of the cylinderwall and worn abrasive.

If the stones simply skim across the surface of the metal without cutting, they will lay over the tiny peaks of metal left by the boring tool. This is called *burnishing*, and it should be avoided at all costs. A cylinder that has been burnished will wear out piston

rings very quickly and can destroy the piston skirts in short order. But a competent machinist can easily avoid this problem by selecting the proper grade of abrasive stones and correctly adjusting the pressure applied to the stones.

The optimum surface finish on the cylinderwalls depends on the type of piston compression rings that will be used. The two most common ring face materials are chrome and molybdenum. Chrome-plated compression rings have an extremely hard surface that is resistant to abrasion caused by dirt. The chrome plating is uniform (microscopic cracks account for only about 2% of the surface area); and the hard, smooth surface of a chrome compression ring requires a *relatively rough* cylinderwall finish. Most piston ring manufacturers specify 280-grit

Block threads should be cleaned with bottoming tap to insure accurate torque readings.

Install freeze plugs in block before honing cylinderwalls; socket and short extension work well to drive soft plugs into place.

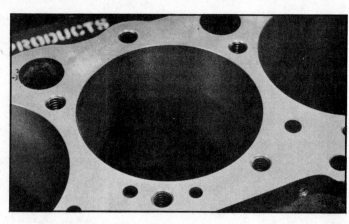

Examined under a microscope, freshly bored cylinderwall has jagged, torn surface left by boring bar bit. Honing operation must remove enough material to reach undisturbed block metal.

finishing stones for use with chrome-plated rings. The small grooves left in the cylinderwalls by these relatively rough stones provide important oil reservoirs that lubricate the ring face.

Compression rings faced with molybdenum can use a much finer wall finish. Approximately 20% of the surface area of a moly-coated ring is made up of tiny voids that effectively trap lubricant; and because of this "micro-porous" surface, it is possible to use very fine finishing stones. Also, moly rings are lapped in long metal cylinders during manufacturing, so they require virtually no break-in period. For these reasons, cylinderwalls are often finished with 400-grit honing stones when moly rings will be installed. In fact, many builders of all-out racing engines prefer "mirror finish" cylinderwalls for moly rings. To produce these extremely smooth finishes, the final honing passes may be made with cork-bonded stones designed for honing aluminum cylinder blocks (linerless) or

with 400- or 600-grit wet-or-dry sandpaper wrapped around the hone stones.

HONING WITH TORQUE PLATES

Even though an engine block seems to be a rigid mass, in fact it is quite elastic. A decade ago, engine builders discovered that they could increase engine output by honing the block with *torque plates* bolted to the deck surfaces. A torque plate is simply a two-inch thick slab of metal that simulates the distortion created when the heads are torqued down. The force exerted by the cylinder-head fasteners (whether bolts or studs) pulls the bores out-of-round when the heads are mounted to the block. For example, a cylinder surrounded by five head bolts will be pulled into a pentangle shape when the heads are torqued up tight. The effect isn't great, but it is measurable. And since the top of the bore is where the cylinder seal is

most important during the compression and power strokes, anything an engine builder can do to improve the effectiveness of the seal will increase horsepower.

When a block is honed with torque plates, a head gasket should be used between the block and plate. If you plan on using a composition head gasket, then make sure that you (or your machinist) installs the same type and thickness of composition gasket between the torque plate and cylinder head. The same goes for steel shim gaskets—use the same type and thickness that will be installed when the engine is assembled for the final time.

The goal of plate honing is to recreate the conditions which are present when the heads are torqued on the block. Stands under head bolts allow fasteners to stretch just as they do when clamping head in place. Bolts should be tightened to recommended torque specification.

Any block destined for racing or high-performance applications should be honed with torque plates. Thick steel plates simulate distortion of bores which occurs when cylinder heads are installed. Use the same type of head gasket when plate honing which you intend to use when assembling the engine.

Remember, the object is to duplicate the same stresses and distortions during honing that will be present when the engine is running.

Some engine builders go to elaborate lengths to simulate these forces. For example, they will bolt engine mounts to the side of blocks, water pump housings to the front, and bell-housings to the back. Some even circulate hot water through the coolant packages while honing the cylinder bores! In some classes of competition, such as Stock Eliminator drag-racing where attention to detail separates the winners from the losers, such practices may be somewhat justified. For most applications, though, these efforts are probably overkill.

HAND HONING

We mentioned earlier that honing was partially an art, partially a science. The artistic side of honing is most apparent when a cylinder block is honed by hand. Before automatic honing machines were developed, all cylinder blocks were finished with hand-held hones. And it takes a lot of practice and a sensitive touch to *feel* a slight taper in a cylinder bore. This human element is precisely why some engine builders prefer to hone by hand. The results can rival anything done by a high-dollar automated hone!

The equipment required for hand honing is not elaborate. A hone is a necessity, obviously, and so is a honing tank. The honing tank can be any container large enough to accommodate an engine block—old bathtubs and sheetmetal basins have been used with success. The tank is filled with several gallons of honing oil, which a pump circulates through a fil-

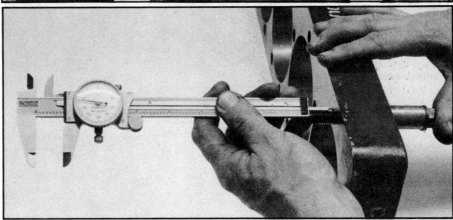

Since different types of bolts have different elasticity, use the same bolts when plate honing which you plan to use when assembling the engine. Bolts should extend as far through torque plate as they do through cylinder head. Thread engagement is adjusted by adding and removing washers under fasteners.

ter and sprays into the cylinder during the honing procedure. A selection of fine- and medium-grit stones will also be required, and a dial bore gauge is needed to check the results.

However, honing a block by hand is a tedious task. If the block was bored properly, there will be 0.004- to 0.006-inch of metal left to remove from each

cylinder to reach the final bore size. The usual progression for conventional moly-faced piston rings would be to use 280-grit (AN 500) stones to enlarge the cylinder to within 0.0015-inch of the final diameter. The next 0.001-inch of metal would be removed with 400-grit (M27-J85) stones, and the last 0.0005 with 500-grit (M27-

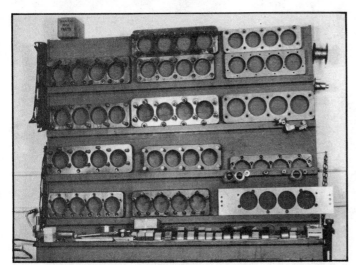

Torque plates are now available for nearly every make of high-performance engine. Larry Hollums is ready for any honing job with this assortment.

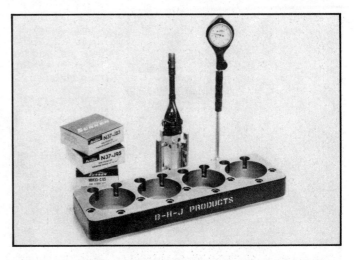

A 1/2-inch drill, a Sunnen hand hone, and a selection of stones are all that's required to hone a block at home. An accurate dial bore gauge will make it easy to check the progress of your work.

A sheetmetal box, plastic shipping crate, or even an old bathtub can be pressed into service as a honing tank. Electric pump circulates and filters five gallons of Sunnen honing oil. Cylinders should be constantly flushed with oil to wash away abrasive grit as stones wear.

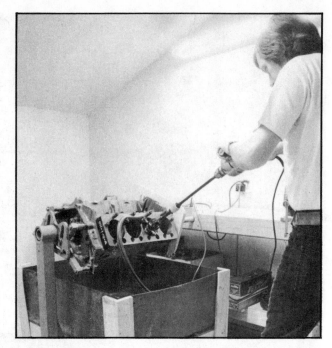

Sunnen CK-l0 Cylinder King automatic hone has become standard equipment in high-performance machine shops. Here Kip adjusts pressure applied to the stones and sets length of the hone stroke.

J95) stones. The final passes with 600-grit (MM33-CO5) extra-fine stones—or with sandpaper wrapped around the stone set—remove a neglible amount of material, but do provide the desired mirror finish on the cylinderwalls. At several points in the process the cylinder must be measured carefully with the dial bore gauge to check for taper (from top to bottom) and for any signs that the cylinder is not finishing to a perfectly round shape. It's no wonder that precision honing a V-8 block can be an all-day job!

Very few professional machinists can justify devoting this much time to a customer engine, which is why close-tolerance hand honing is becoming a lost art. The cost of a complete hand honing setup (including a l/2-inch or larger drill motor to spin the hone) is a tiny fraction of the price of an automatic hone. Depending on the going rate for a professional hone job (with torque plates and all), it may pay you to invest in the equipment needed for honing at home, especially if you plan on blueprinting engines regularly.

Automatic hone eliminates tedious hours of hand honing. Metal bar inserted through main bearing saddles clamps block in place; block can be raised and lowered with hand crank. Note stepped torque plate which eliminates need for spacers under long head bolts.

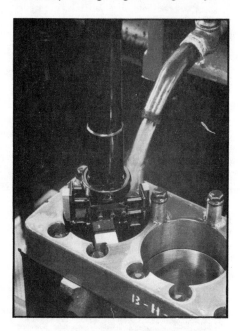

Sunnen CK-l0 floods stones and cylinderwalls with filtered honing fluid to carry away grit and metal particles as bore is enlarged. Hone automatically strokes up and down to produce desired cross-hatch pattern.

This fixture allows hone operator to quickly select shims which adjust stones to bore diameter.

Stone selection is essential for proper cylinderwall finish and good ring seal. Molybdenum piston rings work best with super-fine finish, while chrome plated rings require a relatively rough surface. Like sandpaper, honing stones are available in a variety of grits. Progressively finer stones are used as bore size approaches final diameter.

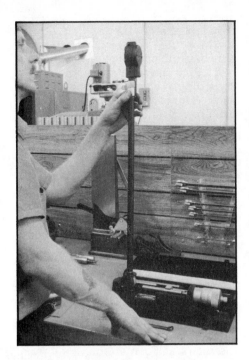

Micrometer fixture adjusts dial bore gauge to read zero when cylinder bore is at desired final diameter (including piston-to-wall clearance).

Bores are constantly checked for "taper" or "bellmouthing" during honing operation by measuring diameter at top and bottom of cylinder. Sunnen dial bore gauge is marked in 0.0005-inch increments; this hole has no measurable taper.

AUTOMATIC HONING

It is unlikely that many readers will rush out to purchase a $20,000 automatic hone after digesting this section, but understanding the honing procedure may give you an insight into what your machinist is doing with your precious engine block. The Sunnen CK-10 Cylinder King is the standard of the industry, and the machine you are most likely to encounter in a well-equipped shop. The CK-10 gives its operator complete control over the stroke and pressure of the honing stones. By watching a load meter on the machine he can quickly detect whether the bore is bell-mouthed on the top or tight at the bottom. The CK-10's recirculating pump provides a virtual flood of honing oil to wash away block material and used abrasive, and there is an enormous selection of stone sizes and grits available. An important feature for a professional machinist is the speed with which a complete engine block can be honed on the CK-10. A cylinder bore that may demand an hour to hone properly by hand can be finished in a matter of minutes on a Sunnen machine.

As with hand honing, the stone grits become progressively finer as the cylinder bore is made larger. For example, Kip Martin, who is pictured here with his trusty CK-10, starts by bringing the bore to within 0.00l- to 0.00l5-inch of the final diameter with EHU-525 stones, maintaining a 40% reading on

If cylinder bore is too small at the bottom, CK-10 operator can press "Dwell" button, which signals hone to make an extra revolution at bottom of bore on each stroke. The load meter on automatic hone indicates pressure against stones. By reducing pressure on final strokes, machinist can produce an extremely fine surface finish—but he must be careful not to "burnish" cylinderwalls by applying too light a load.

Slight cross-hatch pattern should be visible in finished cylinderwall surface. These microscopic grooves retain oil to lubricate ring faces during break-in.

Wrapping 400/600 grit wet-or-dry sandpaper around honing stones for final strokes produces super-fine wall finish. This last step is usually reserved for maximum effort racing engines.

the load meter. Then he switches to finer JHU-625 stones and hones at slightly less pressure until the cylinder is within 0.0005 of the intended diameter. The last bit of bore stock is removed with a JHU-800 stone, at a relatively light 20% load. If the customer has specified a mirror finish, the last six strokes are made with ultra-fine cork-bonded stones normally used for finishing Vega silicon/aluminum blocks. Our second consulting machinist, Larry Hollums, follows the same general plan, although his choice of stones varies slightly. Also, when the engine will be used in a racecar or when extra effort is invested to gain maximum ring life and seal, he prefers to use an assortment of 400- or

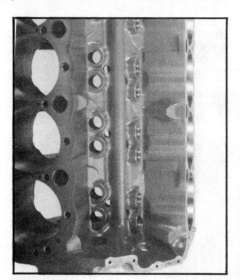

Block surface must be scrupulously clean before painting. Paint seals pores in metal and may speed oil return to sump.

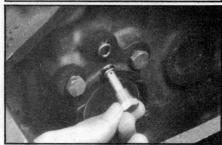

Restrictor plugs limit oil reaching lifters and rockerarms in Chevrolet V-8s; they should only be used with solid lifters and roller rockerarms.

600-grit wet-or-dry sandpaper for the final finish.

BLOCK PAINTING

Painting the inside of an engine is strictly a matter of personal preference. On the plus side, painting the block helps to seal the surface and trap any tiny particles of grit that might have escaped the cleaning process. Also it is easier to spot small metal flakes in a painted block, and picking up bits of used gasket material is simpler. A painted block may help the oil return to the pan more quickly, although this is a

It takes a tough paint to survive inside an engine block. Glyptal and armature winding paint are highly resistant to acids and oils. Rubber plugs for metal chair legs are useful for masking lifter bores.

debatable point.

There are, however, two definite drawbacks to painting the inside of the block. First, the metal surfaces must be *scrupulously clean* or the paint will not stick. Paint chips can clog an oil pump pickup or oil filter element, so it is important that the paint stay where it belongs. Also, painting an engine block properly is quite time-consuming. To do the job right, all the machined surfaces—lifter bores, main bearing saddles, cylinders, etc.—must be carefully masked. Currently most professional engine builders feel that the minor advantages of painting the interior of a block hardly justify the considerable work required to do the job correctly.

RESTRICTING OIL PASSAGES

An engine block that is destined for the race track can often benefit from restricting certain oil passages. Racing rockerarms outfitted with roller-bearing trunions require much less lubrication than conventional rockers. The oil that would normally be pumped to the rockerarms can be redirected to the main bearings, where it will do a lot more good. There are several ways to accomplish this in Chevrolet V-8's. In production big-block and smallblock Chevys, the oil passages that feed the lifter galleries are 0.250-inch in diameter. Moroso and other manufacturers sell oil restrictor plugs to limit the flow of oil to the top end. These are 0.3125-inch (5/16) socket head set screws with 0.060-inch holes drilled through the centers. If you have a drill press, you can make similar restrictor plugs in five minutes.

This modification is quite simple. The oil passages leading from the rear cam bearing are tapped and the restrictor plugs can be inserted through the gallery openings in the block. Or, you can buy special gallery plugs (Moroso type shown here) that have extensions that seat inside the gallery passage, restricting the amount of oil admitted to the gallery. These restricters can simply be screwed into the block in place of the standard 0.250-inch pipe plugs.

Please note that this is a modification intended only for engines equipped with roller-mounted rockerarms and solid or roller lifters. Since the amount of oil reaching the lifters and rockers is cut to the bare minimum, there is *not* enough lubrication supply for hydraulic-type lifters or stock ball-pivot rockerarms.

Even if you have limited the oil

reaching the top end, there is still a significant volume of oil that eventually must find its way back to the pan. In a smallblock Chevrolet, much of this lubricant drains back through holes drilled alongside the lifter bores. It drips onto the spinning camshaft, which in turn flings the droplets onto the rotating crank assembly. While splash lubrication is useful, it is to be discouraged in a racing engine because all those oil droplets slinging around cause *windage losses*, which is a fancy name for less horsepower. Fortunately, Chevrolet drilled these oil drainback holes just the right size to accommodate a 0.250-inch pipe tap. Simply thread the holes and screw in a handful of pipe plugs. Forever after, the oil will have to return to the crank via the front cover and rear oil drain.

DEBRIS SCREENS

One fact of life for everyone who builds or races engines is that eventually something is going to break. It is unavoidable—or you're not going to win many races—and the best way to prepare for this certainty is to make sure that whatever fails does not take the rest of the motor with it. Valvetrain components are usually the most fragile pieces inside an engine. When springs, rockers, or pushrods give up, the debris can circulate throughout the engine, causing further damage. Many engine builders epoxy wire screens over the oil drainback holes to catch broken pieces before they can reach the oil pump or crankshaft assembly. You can buy kits that include pre-formed screens and epoxy, or you can make them yourself in an afternoon. Just be certain that the block surface is absolutely clean before applying the epoxy. If the screens break loose they can cause as much damage as the pieces they were meant to catch!

ROD & CRANK CLEARANCE

If the engine will be assembled with a stock-stroke crankshaft and the original factory connecting rods, then interference between the rods, crank, and cylinder block will not be a problem. If, however, you have opted for a stroker crank or aftermarket connecting rods, chances are that they are going to hit the block someplace. The most likely locations for this collision are the oil-pan rail and the bottom of the cylinder bores. The only way to find out with certainty exactly where there is insufficient clearance is to install the crank assembly. Of course, if you plan

Drain holes in smallblock Chevy lifter valley are blocked with l/4-inch pipe plugs to prevent oil from splashing on spinning crankshaft assembly. Note debris screens over drainback holes behind cam gear.

Wire screen epoxied over webs in big-block Chevrolet lifter valley catches broken valvetrain parts before they can cause further damage.

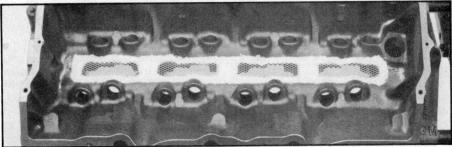

to use oversize pistons, this will have to wait until after the block has been bored. But, hold off on honing the cyliner bores until *after* the crank and rod clearance has been checked. This will prevent ruining the cylinderwall finish if you should slip with the hand grinder!

The amount of metal to be ground away depends on how far you have strayed from the stock components. Aluminum rods, for example, are much bulkier on their big ends than most steel rods, and will require more grinding before the crank can turn without interference. Usually the rod bolt heads are the biggest offenders.

When you need more operating clearance the best approach is to grind just enough material off the block so the crank assembly can rotate without interference. Then go back over the areas you have ground and cut away enough metal to allow a 0.050-inch drill bit to slide between the block and the connecting rods or crankshaft. This provides enough "running clearance" to prevent collisions when the pieces start whipping around at high rpm.

Whenever you are cutting on a cylinder block, there is always the

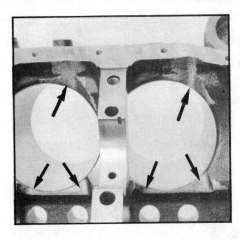

Long stroke crankshafts and racing connecting rods may require extra block clearance at bottom of cylinder bores and oil pan rail. Grinding marks should be polished out to remove stress risers.

If you can slide a 0.050-inch diameter drill bit between block and connecting rods, clearance is adequate.

danger of hitting water. Some heavy-duty castings, like the Chevrolet Bow Tie blocks, have coolant passages relocated to reduce the chances of breaking through into the water jacket. With a standard production block, though, you are on your own. The problem becomes most acute when using a long-stroke crankshaft with aftermarket connecting rods. In these instances, you may need to direct some of the metal-removal efforts to the rotating assembly. For example, the bolts on the connecting rods can be ground down slightly, and the bottom of the connecting rods can be profiled to reduce interference problems. These tactics can be risky, though, since you may be weakening highly stressed components. When Chevrolet engineers expanded the smallblock V-8 to 400 cubic inches, they were forced to redesign the connecting rods to accept shorter bolts. The 400's poor reputation for durability was one result of this decision. You can learn from this, and use caution and common sense when it comes time to make all the parts fit in the engine.

OIL HOLE ALIGNMENT

The block preparation regimen must include a thorough check to ensure the proper alignment between the oil holes in the block and the main bearing inserts. In most engines, the oil passages in the bearing saddles are

Make sure that all oil passages in block are unobstructed. Use a long drill bit to remove burrs and open up undersize holes.

larger than the holes in the bearing inserts, which helps compensate for any small mismatch. The rear main bearings on Chevrolet V-8's deserve special attention, since the oil holes intersect the bearing bores at an angle. You may need to elongate the hole in either the block or the bearing shell to gain an unimpeded flow of oil. Some engine builders advocate enlarging the oil holes in the bearings to match the passages in the block. Although this is not really necessary in most applications, make sure that you thoroughly deburr the bearings if you decide to open up these holes. Also, check that the oil passages are not blocked by machining chips or other obstructions. In some early Chevy smallblocks, the holes between the main oil gallery and the camshaft gallery are only 0.1875-inch (3/16) in diameter; use a long 0.250-inch drill bit to open these passages until they match the size of the holes connecting the camshaft gal-

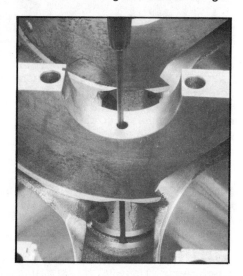

lery to the main bearings.

BLOCK CLEANING

When all the machining, honing, and grinding is finally done, it's time to wash the block. The object of this exercise is to remove all the grit, dirt, and machining chips that have accumulated in the block during the blueprinting process. To do the job properly you must scour the block with solvent and hot, soapy water. This is definitely a chore that is best left for a hot afternoon, because you are going to be drenched by the time the job is completed.

Throughout the block washing process, care must be taken to prevent the machined surfaces from rusting. It is extremely important to protect the cylinder bores against corrosion. When the walls have been scrubbed clean, they can develop a layer of oxidation in an instant unless they are immediately sprayed with a rust-inhibiting agent (like WD-40). If you can enlist an assistant, the block washing chores are more likely to be successful. One member of the cleaning team can spray the metal surfaces with the rust inhibitor, while the other follows up with paper towels and compressed air.

A large, paved driveway is an ideal place to wash the engine block. You'll need access to a supply of hot water. Attach a garden hose to a laundry sink or kitchen faucet. Open the cold water tap, then increase the flow of hot water until it reaches the desired temperature. Be careful. Hot tap water may exceed 160°F! Hot water is good for washing, but tap water can be hot

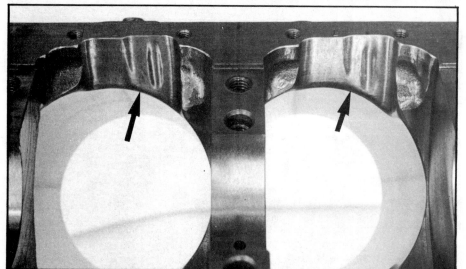

Here's an example of the extreme block clearancing required to build a 600 cubic inch Pro Stock motor! Water passages are relocated in Chevrolet heavy-duty engine block to allow such extensive grinding.

Enlarge holes in bearing inserts if they are not aligned with oil passages in block.

enough to scald human skin. An air compressor, although not a necessity, will make drying the block much easier. In a pinch, you can even use a vacuum cleaner with the hose attached to the exhaust so that it blows hot air. You will also need a bucket, laundry detergent, an assortment of scrub brushes, paper towels, and a spray can of rust inhibitor. A solvent gun or a high-pressure sprayer designed for washing cars is helpful for blasting out the oil passages.

The local do-it-yourself car wash is a good place to wash a grimy block. These car washes usually have high-pressure sprayers that do a fine job of blasting away machining grit. However, the one drawback to cleaning your block at a car wash is the lack of compressed air to dry it thoroughly. Unless you have a portable air compressor and a source of electricity, you must spray down the cleaned block with rust inhibitor oil or automatic-transmission fluid to prevent it from rusting until you can get it back home to your garage.

Both Mr. Gasket and Moroso Performance sell brush kits specifically designed for cleaning engine components. A selection of brushes with various bristle diameters is useful for dislodging dirt from the nooks, crannies, and oil passages. Long-handled rifle cleaning brushes are well suited for cleaning out deep oil galleries. Interchangeable brushes are available for bore sizes ranging from 0.22 caliber rifles to huge shotgun barrels.

Begin the cleaning by dousing the block with solvent. Using a stiff brush, scrub every part of the block that you can reach to loosen the metal filings and grinding dust that has accumulated. If you have a solvent sprayer, blow out the oil galleries, lifter bores, and cylinder bores. Don't scrub the cylinders yet, since the grit may scratch the wall finish. If you are cleaning the block on an asphalt driveway, protect the pavement with a drip pan to prevent the solvent from breaking down the asphalt.

The next step is to scrub the block with soap and water. Dissolve several cups of laundry detergent in a pail of hot water, and prepare to get wet. Once you begin scrubbing an iron block, you must keep it constantly wet to prevent rust from forming on the machined surfaces. While your partner directs a steady stream of hot water on the block, you should scour the block with stiff brushes. Then clean out the lifter bores and oil passages with the small diameter brushes. After the rest of the block has been cleaned, wash

It takes gallons of solvent, soap, and hot water to scrub a block clean before assembly. Pressure sprayers and stiff brushes will help dislodge grit and machining chips.

the cylinder bores with a soft rag soaked in soapy water. When you have cleaned the entire casting, rinse off the soap and get ready to start drying.

Rust will begin to form the instant that your partner stops spraying the block! Immediately begin coating the cylinderwalls with oil or a rust inhibitor. The oil solution will cause the water to bead up and run off the wall surface. Flip the block over and spray the main bearing saddles and the lifter bores. Once these machined surfaces have been protected, you can start drying the block with compressed air (or your reverse-flow vacuum cleaner.) Spray the remainder of the block with rust inhibitor to prevent rust from forming on the rough casting.

After you have blown off all the water droplets, check your work by running your finger over the block surface. Pay special attention to the places where dirt and grit can hide, such as underneath the oil pan rail and in the corners of the cam gallery. If you can still find casting sand, abrasive, or grinding dust on your fingertip, the block must be cleaned again. It may require two or three sessions before a freshly machined block will pass the fingertip test.

After the block has been cleaned to your satisfaction, the cylinderwalls still

require further attention. Removing the last traces of honing abrasive is an important step in ensuring long ring life and good cylinder seal. Saturate a paper towel with automatic-transmission fluid and scour each cylinderwall thoroughly. The ATF will loosen tiny particles of abrasive, they will be apparent as dark spots on the towel. Keep scrubbing until a fresh paper towel wetted with trans fluid shows no traces of dirt when it is rubbed against the cylinderwall. When all the cylinders pass this test, coat them with clean motor oil to prevent rust, and cover the block with a plastic trash bag while you work on the other engine components.

Scour new block surfaces with stiff wire brush to loosen casting sand.

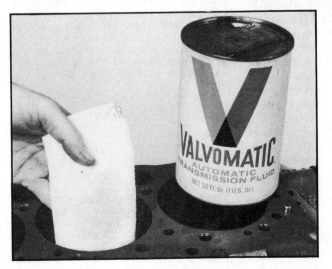

Cylinder bores should be absolutely spotless before assembly. Protect them from rust while washing, then clean them with auto trans fluid and paper towels.

CRANKSHAFTS

The crankshaft is the most highly stressed component in an engine. It converts the frantic up-and-down motion of the pistons into a rotating force that can be readily harnessed to move the car forward. Every ounce of torque travels through the crankshaft, while the pistons do their best to alternately push the crank out through the bottom of the oil pan and pull it toward the cylinder heads. Is it any wonder that the crankshaft warrants your attention during a thorough engine blueprinting?

SELECTION & INSPECTION

During the Sixties, you could be almost certain that any high-performance engine had a *forged steel*

You may have to go on a scavenger hunt to find a suitable crankshaft core. Shops that specialize in crankshaft repairs are usually good sources, since they buy used cranks in quantity. Most late-model motors are equipped with cast iron cranks because of the higher production costs of forged cranks. You're more likely to find a steel crank in an engine manufactured during the Sixties.

This before-and-after comparison illustrates how a sound core can be turned into a race-ready crank. The finished crank (right) has been inspected, cleaned, deburred, shotpeened, reground, polished, and straightened.

crankshaft. This is no longer the case. Because of manufacturing and raw material costs, the automakers have adopted *cast iron* crankshafts. A forging has a much denser molecular structure and a grain pattern that flows through the crank much like the grain in wood. A casting, in contrast, has a random pattern of molecules, and may have microscopic holes or "voids." Obviously for high-performance applications, a forged steel crankshaft is superior. If forgings are available for your engine, it's worthwhile to hunt one down.

So how do you spot a forging when you find one? Simple. Look for the forging marks. As the accompanying photos point out, a cast iron crank has a very distinct *parting line*. This is formed where the two halves of the mold meet. A forging, in contrast, is created by compressing the metal under extreme heat and pressure. The die marks left by this process are typically 0.375- to 0.500-inch wide, and appear as a slightly raised surface. Look for these telltale marks on the front and rear crank throws.

Forged cranks are not available for all engines. Don't despair; many high-performance street motors have led long and productive lives with cast cranks. If you plan on 10,000 rpm engine speeds, then you should also plan on buying a crankshaft carved out of a *solid steel billet*. Production cast iron cranks often have extra-large bearings or other features that compensate for the reduced strength of the crankshaft material.

Once you have found a likely crankshaft candidate, measure the rod and main bearing journals to determine if they have already been turned *undersize*. Many crankshaft grinders mark the front counterweight with a notation such as "M20-R20," which would indicate that both the rod and main journals have been ground 0.020-inch undersize. There's nothing inherently wrong with an undersize crank; providing, of course, that the work was done properly and that bearings are readily available. In fact, some racers in the Stock classes (drag racing) have their crankshafts turned 0.040- or .050-inch undersize as a matter of course. They feel the smaller bearing diameter creates less drag, which in turn frees up a few more horsepower for the rear wheels.

The evidence of a spun or burned bearing will be quite obvious. The journal in question will usually turn dark blue, and the bearing surface will be pockmarked and scored. Even though such damage looks irreversible, many

The front counterweight will sometimes indicate the crank's past history. Most shops stamp the rod and main bearing journal diameters on the counterweight when they grind a crank for undersize bearings.

It's easy to spot the difference between a cast and a forged crank. If there is a distinct parting line on the rod throws and counterweights, the crank is made of cast iron. A wide, raised die mark indicates a forged steel piece.

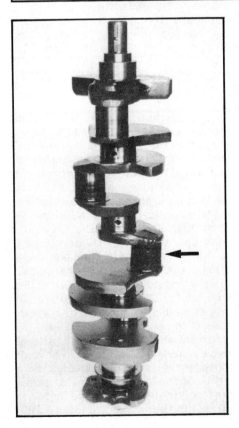

crankshafts with spun or burned bearings can be saved. If the gouges are not too deep, and if the crankshaft is not cracked, turning the journals undersize or adding new material by *welding* or *chroming* can restore the crankshaft to better-than-new condition. These repairs are not cheap, of course, and you will have to decide whether it is worthwhile to repair a damaged crank. If you are using a common crank like a 283 Chevy forging, it would be foolish to try to rescue a damaged crank when you can probably find another core for $15.

If the crank passes your visible inspection, then have it hot tanked or jet cleaned to remove all varnish and grease. The next step is absolutely essential: have the crank *Magnaflux in-*

A quick visual inspection will reveal obvious problems such as spun or burned bearing journals. A discolored journal is a sure sign that a bearing has overheated, usually from a lack of lubrication. Unless the crank is cracked, such damage can usually be repaired by grinding, welding, or chroming the journals.

The first step in crank preparation is to strip away the layers of varnish and grime with a pressure cleaner or hot tank. After cleaning, examine the core for stripped bolt holes, broken or chipped counterweights, and other flaws.

spected! Do not pass go, and do not spend another dime on the crank, until it gets a clean bill of health from the Magnaflux man. Unlike the dry Magnaflux powder used to detect cracks in an engine block, a crankshaft is saturated with a magnetic solution. This florescent *Magnaglo* liquid reveals any cracks or imperfections in the metal when the crank is examined

under an ultraviolet black light. Cracks show up as a bright green line, but it takes a sharp eye to spot them. Small stress cracks around the oil holes are nothing to be concerned about, but cracks in the fillets between the bearing journals and the throws are usually fatal. To put it as bluntly as possible, there are no effective repairs for a cracked crankshaft. Throw it away and go look for a replacement.

DEBURRING

If the crankshaft core is sound, then the next step is to detail and *deburr* it. A crankshaft must be deburred for the same reason that blocks and cylinders are detailed: sharp edges are stress risers that foster cracks and catastrophic failures. If you intend to use the crankshaft without regrinding the bearing journals, then these surfaces must be protected from the metal particles flung off the abrasive wheel when you are grinding off the sharp edges and casting flash. Wrap heavy masking tape or duct tape around the journals to protect them from pits. A body grinder or an abrasive wheel attachment on a hand drill will make quick work of die marks and parting lines. Crankshafts are both heavy and awkward to work on, so a work stand fabricated from scrap lumber can be helpful when you are working over a forging.

Take the time to clean out all the crankshaft threads. Chase the holes in the flywheel flange and the front snout with a tap, checking carefully for stripped or cross-threaded holes.

SHOTPEENING & STRESS RELIEVING

Shotpeening and stress relieving are two operations that can improve the life expectancy of a high-performance crankshaft. Both jobs must be performed by a crankshaft service, but you should know what you are paying for. When a crankshaft is *shotpeened*, it is bombarded with small steel balls—somewhat like a sandblasting process, only with tiny ball bearings. This compresses the metal on the surface of the crank, depriving potential cracks of a starting point. Both the size of the steel shot and the air pressure used to propel them are important to the success of the shotpeening process.

Stress relieving is a technique that helps a crankshaft to "relax." The forging process is very traumatic for a crank. Almost all domestic V-8 cranks are forged flat, with all the rod throws in one plane. Before the crank can cool, it

is literally twisted to place the rod journals at 90° angles. Naturally, this only adds to the stresses already created by the hammering and heat of forging. When a crank is stress relieved, it is heated in an oven to a temperature that permits the molecules of metal to rearrange themselves. This "baking" process is similar to what occurs as a new engine block becomes seasoned with use, since it helps stabilize the

Magnaflux inspection is mandatory for any used crank. It is pointless to invest money in crank work until you know that your core is free of cracks in critical areas.

The first step in the inspection procedure is to magnetize the crank, as demonstrated here by Larry Hollums.

metal structure. Stress relieving is not a necessity for most street and drag-racing crankshafts, although it is a lifesaver for cranks intended for circle-track and heavy-duty marine applications.

CRANKSHAFT GRINDING

When the bearing journals of a crankshaft are reground, several things happen simultaneously. First, of course, the diameters of the rod and main bearing journals are reduced. How much material is removed depends on the condition of the crank-

The magnetized crank is then saturated with Magnaglo solution, taking care to cover all the main and rod journals.

Under a black light, cracks appear as bright green lines. A deep crack is easy to spot, but smaller fissures in the journal fillets require a sharp eye to detect. Experience and patience help when inspecting a crank core.

If the crank passes inspection, the next step is to deburr and detail the rod throws and counterweights. Crank shops often use a body grinder and coarse abrasive discs for this chore. Use caution when grinding near the journals!

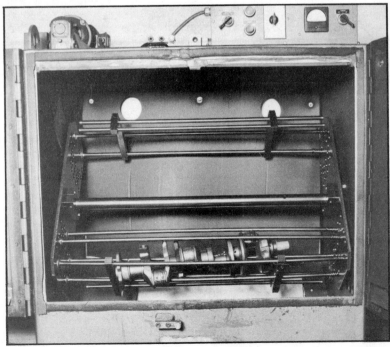

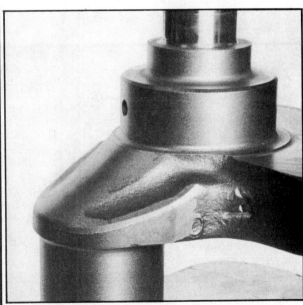

Shotpeening compacts the surface of the metal by bombarding it with small steel balls. A smooth, uniform surface denies cracks a starting place.

47

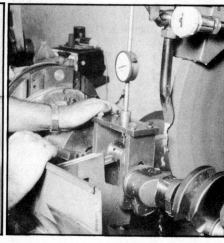

Grinding a crankshaft is not a job for beginners. It takes expensive machinery and skill to do the job right. Here a technician at Chrome-A-Shaft (Memphis, Tennessee) regrinds the rod journals on a small-block Chevrolet crank. This operation simultaneously indexes the rod throws and equalizes the strokes on each journal.

shaft core. If the crank has had only normal wear, and if the journals are not badly pitted or scored, then a "clean up" grind of 0.010-inch will usually restore the bearing surfaces to like-new condition. In cases where the journal has been badly scored by a spun or burned bearing, the crank grinder must remove more material to produce a smooth surface.

When the rod bearing journals are reduced in size, they are also indexed and stroke equalized. *Indexing* simply means that the interval between throws is brought into spec. In a conventional V-8 engine, for example, the rod throws should be exactly 90° apart. Although it is relatively rare to encounter a production crank that has misindexed rod throws, mistakes do happen. Factory cranks with unequal strokes are much more common.

While checking piston deck heights, an engine builder will often find a piston that is noticeably higher or lower in the block than the others. If the compression height of the piston and the center-to-center length of the rod are all right on spec, the culprit is the crankshaft stroke for that particular piston, and if throw is way off spec, the only solution may be to have the the crank reground with all of the stroke lengths equalized.

A high-performance crankshaft should have the largest possible radius between the bearing journals and the crank cheeks. This is an area of extremely high stress where most crank failures originate. Most performance-oriented crankshaft services use grinding stones with generous radiuses to form this critical junction. Beware of cranks sometimes included

with cheap rebuild kits; the journals may have sharp edges or distinct corners. The only drawback to a crank with extra-large fillets is the necessity of checking for *interference* between the bearing inserts and the journal radius. If the edges of the bearing contact this radius, the flow of oil across the bearing surface can be cut off. Further, the load on the bearing is concentrated on the outside edges. Both conditions contribute to early bearing failure.

CROSS-DRILLING

Cross-drilling is a modification that provides "fulll time" oiling to the rod bearings. In most stock crankshafts, a single oil passage connects the main and rod bearing journals. Although this system works well for a low-rpm powerplant, it may not meet the lubrication needs of a high-performance engine. When a crankshaft is cross-drilled, two intersecting holes are bored through the main bearing journals at right angles. When used with a standard half-grooved main bearing, this modification guarantees that the rod journal oil passage is *always* exposed to full oil pressure.

Cross-drilling the crank has several advantages over other schemes intended to provide failsafe rod oiling. It is superior to grooving the main bearing journals or using full-groove bearing inserts. When either the crankshaft or bearing insert is grooved, the load carrying capacity of the bearing is reduced considerably. Instead of distributing the loads evenly across the face of the bearing, these loads are concentrated in two narrow bands.

Some engines—notably the small-block Chevrolet V-8—do not require cross-drilling except for endurance-racing applications. In other instances, the factories have taken the initiative and cross-drilled the main

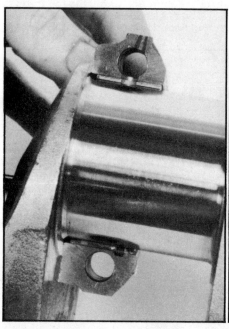

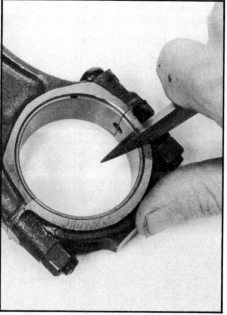

Large fillets between the journals and the crank cheeks make a crankshaft stronger. If this radius is too generous, though, it can interfere with the rod and main bearings. The edges of the bearing inserts must not contact the fillets; if there is minor interference, chamfer the bearings with a sharp deburring knife.

bearing journals—high-performance big-block Chevrolet cranks, for example, are cross-drilled on the assembly line. Cross-drilling the mains is a modification that can never hurt—and it can definitely help.

CHAMFERING OIL HOLES

Chamfering the oil holes on the rod and main bearing journals is a simple procedure that can be done on your garage workbench. When these passages are drilled at the factory, the bits often leave sharp, ragged edges where they break through the surface of the journal. A small grinding stone will readily deburr and radius these openings. Don't get carried away; all that's needed is a gentle depression around the oil hole. This will act as a small reservoir to help distribute the oil across the bearing and journal surfaces, while also denying cracks a starting point. To complete the deburring process, the journals should be well polished after this chamfering operation.

COUNTERWEIGHT MODIFICATIONS

During the early Seventies, *windage* became a trendy theme among engine builders. Windage is simply the drag on the spinning crankshaft assembly caused by the whirlwind of oil droplets inside the crankcase. If you have ever ridden a bicycle in a rainstorm, you are certainly aware of the impact that a million tiny drops can have. Most of the attention was devoted to keeping this oil mist under control. Windage trays, oil pan screens, and exotic dry-sump oil systems all helped reduce the volume of oil suspended in the crankcase. Then engine builders started looking at ways to reduce horsepower losses by streamlining the crankshaft counterweights. And with that, the "knife-edged" counterweight was born.

A knife-edged counterweight is ground to a sharp Vee on the leading edge. To our knowledge, no one has ever tested whether sharpening the counterweights provides any real benefits (aside from the obvious advantage of lightening the rotating assembly). On the face of it, it seems doubtful. As any textbook on aerodynamics will point out, it is the *trailing* edge of an object, not the leading edge, that accounts for most of the drag. In fact, the "perfect" counterweight shape from an aerodynamic standpoint would be a teardrop, with a blunt leading edge and a long, taper-

Cross-drilling the main bearing journals is a better way to achieve constant oil flow to the rod bearings than grooving the mains or installing full-groove bearing inserts.

Chamfer the oil holes in the crank journals with an abrasive hard roll or a small grinding stone. Don't dig a hole with the grinder—just break the sharp edges.

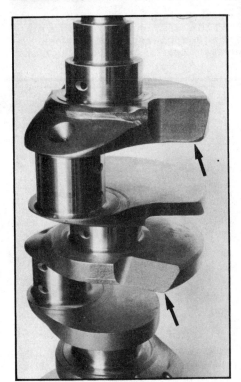

These counterweights have been "knife-edged" to reduce drag as the crank spins in a heavy oil mist. There is some controversy about whether streamlining the counterweights is really beneficial.

ing tail. So, if you really want to spend time shaping the counterweights for a racing engine, it might be wiser to concentrate on the back ends of the counterweights.

Smooth balancing is another trick that developed from the preoccupation that racing-engine builders have for windage losses. A smooth-balanced crank is one that has had all of the balancing holes in the counterweights covered. Freeze plugs or thin metal straps are welded over the

49

holes, then ground down so that the circumference of the counterweights is perfectly smooth. Again, the idea is that this will eliminate turbulence and drag as the crankshaft slices through a fog of oil droplets. Does it make a difference? Who knows—but it probably doesn't hurt.

Among all the counterweight treatments for a racing engine, the most useful and practical is to *reduce* the diameter of the weights. If you are using lightweight pistons and connecting rods, it is almost certain that a great deal of metal will have to be removed from the counterweights to balance the engine. (See the section on balancing for a full explanation.) Instead of drilling the counterweights full of holes, it is just as effective to set up the crankshaft in a large lathe and turn down the diameter of the counterweights. This has several benefits. First, it eliminates the need for numerous holes in the counterweights. Second, it reduces the inertia of the crankshaft assembly, which in turn can

translate into quicker engine response (a feature that is especially important in oval-track competition and road racing). Use restraint, though, when cutting down the counterweights. If you go too far, you may have to add weight with expensive heavy metal.

HARD CHROMING & TUFFTRIDING

There are several ways to improve the surface hardness of the bearing journals. The most popular methods are nitriding (Tufftriding) and hard chroming. The goal of both these processes is to produce a tough, wear-resistant finish on the bearing surfaces. For most street and drag racing engines, the untreated steel or cast iron surface is perfectly satisfactory. An engine that will see long hours of severe-duty service can, however, benefit from these treatments. Some of the premier performance engines of the Sixties, such as the high-winding

Chevrolet Z/28 smallblocks, were equipped with Tufftrided cranks when they left the factory, which indicates the engineers' high regard for this process.

When a crankshaft is *Tufftride* heat treated, it is heated to 800°F and dunked in a bath of cyanide salt. Ideally, the treatment should penetrate approximately 0.200-inch into the metal—but in fact, the hardening can be very shallow in spots. In some areas, the hardening may be so thin that simply polishing the crank can remove it! Crankshaft shops may be reluctant to work on Tufftrided cranks because of this inconsistency in hardness. Also, the equipment required for the process is quite elaborate, so few shops offer this service.

Chroming, in contrast, is much easier to obtain. Chrome is an extremely hard metal. When a crankshaft is chrome-plated, the aim is not to improve the appearance, but to improve the durability. Chroming can also be used to repair a damaged crank by building up the journals with a layer of chrome. This makes it possible to use standard bearings even with a crank that has suffered a spun or scored journal.

The initial steps in preparing a crank core for chroming are similar to regrinding a crankshaft. The journals are first ground and indexed, then covered with masking tape. The crank is immersed in a vat of hot wax, which coats the counterweights and all surfaces that will not be chromed. The tape is removed, exposing the journal surfaces. The crank is then placed in the chroming tank, with an anode resting on each bearing journal. It remains in the tank for several hours (or several days, depending on the thickness of

Hard chrome is an industrial plating process that makes the crank journals extremely resistant to wear. Chrome-A-Shaft chromes hundreds of cranks every year for fuel-burning engines, sprint car motors, and super-speedway engines. The first step in the process is to mask the journals and coat the crank with a thick layer of wax.

After the masking tape is removed, anodes are placed on each crank journal. Chrome will not be deposited on the parts of the crank that are covered with wax.

The crank is then lowered into the chroming tank and slowly rotated. The crank remains in the solution for hours or days, depending on how thick a layer of chrome is desired.

When the crank is removed from the chroming tank and the wax stripped off the counterweights, the chrome that has been deposited on the journals is quite apparent. If a damaged crank is being repaired, it's possible to chrome a single bearing journal.

the chrome to be plated). During this time the crank is constantly rotated, building up layer after layer of chrome molecules.

After the crank is removed from the chroming tank, the journals are again ground and polished. This leaves a super-hard surface. If the chrome has been applied properly, there is virtually no danger of it peeling off. However, a chromed crank cannot be checked for cracks using the Magnaflux inspection procedure. Also, the chroming process may cause *hydrogen embrittlement*, a condition that further increases the problem of surface cracking. For these reasons, hard chroming is generally reserved for crankshafts that will be used briefly in high-load situations and then replaced. Many fuel-burning engines, for example, are equipped with hard chromed cranks.

PILOT BEARINGS

Pilot bearings are usually ignored—ignored, that is, until the transmission will no longer shift. That's when these seemingly insignificant items take on major importance.

Most factory crankshafts rely on bronze pilot bushings. These are pressed into a relief in the rear of the crank whenever a manual transmission will be used. When pilot bushings wear, the inside diameter becomes galled or egg-shaped. Occasionally the pilot bushing will spin inside the crank. Any of these conditions can prevent the clutch from releasing cleanly. At the very least, you should replace the stock pilot bushing with a new one during the blueprinting procedure. If you don't have a pilot bushing puller, you can remove the old bushing by packing the relief behind it with heavy grease. When you hammer on the end of an old transmission input shaft inserted in the bushing, the grease will force the bushing out of the crank.

For racing and high-performance applications, there are alternatives to the standby bronze bushings. For example, many racers bore the back of Chevrolet crankshafts to accept a roller bearing. Chevy also carries a roller-type bearing for 6.2L diesel engines, which is a direct replacement for the standard bronze bushing.

STROKE CHANGES

There is no reason to limit your choice of engine displacements to the stroke dimensions that the factories happen to offer! There are several common ways to change the stroke of a crank. *Offset grinding* is now a popular and quite common practice. When a crankshaft is offset ground, the diameters of the rod bearing journals are reduced, while the centerlines of the crank pins are moved closer to or farther away from the centerline of the main bearings. Small-block Chevrolets are particularly good candidates for this procedure, since two different rod bearing diameters (2.00- and 2.100-inch) have been used in this engine. By reducing the bearing journal diameter 0.100-inch and regrinding the throw with the maximum possible offset, the stroke can be changed a total of 0.090-inch. Through

After chroming, the journals are ground and micropolished. If the chrome is applied properly, it becomes part of the crank, and should never peel or chip.

OFFSET GROUND CRANK

NEW CRANK PIN O.D.

ORIGINAL CRANK PIN O.D.

1/2 STROKE INCREASE

MAIN JOURNAL

Offset grinding the rod journals is an effective way to change the stroke length. The stroke may be increased or decreased by grinding down the rod journal while simultaneously moving the centerline of the rod throw.

the miracle of offset grinding, a Chevy smallblock crank with a factory stroke of 3.00 inches, for example, can be reground with any stroke between 2.9l0 and 3.090 inches!

Of course, this modification requires connecting rods with the proper bearing bores to accommodate the smaller diameter rod bearings. In the case of smallblock Chevrolets, the use of pre-l968 connecting rods solves this dilemma—although in the vast majority of engines built with offset ground cranks, specialty connecting rod are installed. Remember, too, that a change in crankshaft stroke requires a change in the piston compression heights or the center-to-center length of the connecting rods.

An intriguing variation of the offset ground cranks are the so-called "cheater cranks." In certain racing classes that demand stock engine specifications, the rulebooks spell out allowable tolerances on certain dimensions. In NHRA Stock eliminator classes, for example, the allowable deviation on stroke measurements is 0.0l5-inch. Naturally, racers who want to take advantage of everything the rulebook allows have their crankshafts stroked exactly 0.0l3-inch. The difference in final engine displacement amounts to less than two cubic inches, but in these categories, attention to such minute details can mean the difference between winning and losing. A stroke change of only 0.0l3-inch can easily be compensated for when the block is milled to establish the piston deck heights.

The amount of metal that can be safely removed from the rod journals by offset grinding does limit an engine builder's stroke choices. In instances where a more radical change in crank stroke is needed, *welding* is the only alternative. The welding process adds material to the outside of the rod throw—in the case of a *stroker crank*— or the inside of the journal—if a *destroked crankshaft* is the goal. If the welding is done correctly, the additional material is virtually indistinguishable from the parent metal. Crankshaft welding is usually performed with an automatic wire welder—using a "submerged arc" process, in which the electrode is covered by a constant shower of iron particles. After welding, the crankshaft journals are ground and micropolished just like an unmodified crank. Using this technique, it is possible to increase the stroke of a suitable core by as much as 0.625-inch (5/8-inch)—although the cost of this operation quickly becomes prohibitive for all but the most

An old shoelace or a leather thong will put you in the crank polishing business. Cut a piece of 600 grit wet-or-dry sandpaper to match the journal width. Wrap the sandpaper and shoelace around the journal, then polish by pulling the ends of the lace back and forth. Lubricate the abrasive paper with solvent.

dedicated advocates of big-displacement engines.

MICROPOLISHING

The surface left by the crankshaft grinding stones must be smoothed and polished before it is suitable for bearings. *Micropolishing* performs this important function. A motor-driven abrasive belt is used to dress the bearing surface to a mirror finish. Minor

Chrome-A-Shaft uses this special "submerged arc" welder to repair or add material to a crank journal. Radical stroke changes can be made by building up the rod throws with welding rod and then offset grinding the journals.

touch-ups can be done at home with nothing more elaborate than a shoe lace and a sheet of extra-fine wet-or-dry sandpaper. Cut the sandpaper into strips that are as wide as the bearing journals. Saturate the sandpaper with solvent, wrap it around the journal, and then make one full loop with the shoe lace. By "sawing" the shoe lace back and forth, the paper will be pulled across the bearing journal. This technique is an ideal way to polish out the minor nicks and imperfections that inevitably result from assembling and disassembling the short block. However, if the crank has been Tufftrided, you must remember that even a light polishing can cut through the shallow spots in the surface treatment, so don't get carried away!

CRANKSHAFT STRAIGHTENING

Internal stresses, a fall from a workbench top, high engine loads, and heat treating can all cause a crankshaft to *bend*. After investing considerable time and money in align honing a block, it stands to reason that the crankshaft should be as straight as possible. Checking crankshaft straightness is a simple procedure. Install the crank in the engine block with only the front and rear main bearing inserts in place. Torque down the front and rear bearing caps, and then set up a dial indicator to read the runout (rotational eccentricity) of the center main

To check crankshaft straightness, install the crank in the block on the front and rear main bearings. Read the crankshaft run-out on the center journal as you rotate the crank

Straightening a bent crank is fairly simple if you have the right equipment. Cranks are surprisingly flexible; a hydraulic press and a heavy hammer will straighten a crank quickly.

This stroke checking fixture uses a long-travel dial indicator to detect differences between rod throws. The stroke is measured by noting the difference in the indicator readings when the rod journal is at the highest and lowest positions.

To determine the bearing clearances, first measure the diameter of the crankshaft journals. Check each journal at several points to make sure that it is not tapered or out-of-round.

Then measure the inside diameter of the bearings with the rod cap or main bearing cap torqued in place. Measure the bearing inside diameter at 90 degrees to the parting line. The difference between the journal diameter and the inside diameter of the bearing inserts is the actual clearance.

bearing. Ideally there should be zero runout—but as a practical matter, readings as high as 0.002-inch are acceptable.

Suppose you discover that your prize crankshaft is bent—then what? While a crank might seem to be a rather formidable mass, straightening a crank is a fairly straightforward procedure for a competent crankshaft shop. The crank is set up in a fixture and then preloaded with a hydraulic jack. When the crank is struck sharply with a heavy hammer, it will yield. A skilled technician can usually bring a bent crank into spec in short time.

STROKE CHECKING

The most accurate way to check crankshaft stroke is with a gauge similar to the one pictured here. This fixture has a long-travel dial indicator mounted on an aluminum bridge that straddles the main bearing journals. Of course, few backyard engine builders have such an instrument at their disposal. Don't despair, though. There are other ways to check the accuracy of the individual rod throws.

The perfect time to check crankshaft stroke is when the engine has been preassembled to measure piston deck heights. A dial indicator, a depth micrometer, or even a pair of dial calipers can be used. Simply run the piston up to TDC and measure from the deck surface of the block to the quench flat on the piston. Then rotate the crank until the piston is at BDC; you may have to rock the crankshaft forward and backward to find this exact point. Measure again from the top of the block to the piston. The difference between the two readings is the crankshaft stroke.

The accuracy of your measurements will be improved if you take readings as close to the center of the pistons as possible; this helps minimize the problem of piston rock. Also, if you know that the block is perfectly square, you can check the deck heights in every cylinder using only one piston/rod combination; different readings from one cylinder to another will indicate variations in the crankshaft stroke (but remember this technique is only valid if the block decks are perfectly square and parallel to the crankshaft bore centerline).

BEARING CLEARANCES

Proper bearing clearances are critical to engine life. The clearance between the crankshaft journals and the

You can adjust bearing clearances by using thicker or thinner bearing shells. To accurately measure the thickness of a curved bearing, you'll need a ball bearing adapter for your micrometer spindle.

bearing inserts permits a constant flow of oil to pass across the bearing surface. This oil flow is essential for both lubrication and cooling. If the clearances are too small, the oil supply is choked off; if it is too large, the oil simply washes across the bearing without forming a wedge to support the crankshaft and without carrying heat away from the bearing insert. Just a few seconds of metal-to-metal contact between the bearing and crankshaft can be fatal to an engine!

The most accurate way to measure rod and main bearing clearances is by comparing the outside diameter of the crankshaft journals to the inside diameter of the bearing inserts. This procedure requires both inside and outside micrometers—or, better yet, a dial bore gauge. As you check the bearing clearances with this method, you will soon discover that bearings are not perfectly round. Rather, they are slightly elliptical, with the diameter across the parting line somewhat larger than the diameter at 90° to the parting line. The *vertical diameter* is the critical dimension, since the high-

est crank loads occur in this direction. The increase in diameter at the bearing parting line provides an oil reservoir that lubricates the rapidly spinning crankshaft.

There is an alternative way to measure bearing clearances without precision tools: Plastigage. Although professional engine builders frown on this method, the truth is that thousands of engines have been assembled using this simple technique.

Plastigage is a waxy plastic string. To measure a clearance, a short piece of Plastigage is first placed on the crankshaft journal. The main cap and bearing are installed and torqued. The cap is then removed, exposing the flattened Plastigage. Comparing the width of the smashed string with a chart on the Plastigage package indicates the bearing clearance.

In order for the Plastigage to give an accurate reading, the bearings and journals must be clean and free of oil. The crank must not be turned while the Plastigage is in position. And don't forget to remove all traces of the compressed wax before starting final engine assembly.

Most high-performance and racing engines are content with bottom end clearances ranging between 0.0025- and .0035-inch. There are exceptions, however, and you should find out if your particular engine is one of them. Crankshafts that are particularly susceptible to flexing may require larger clearances, as will engines with inefficient oiling systems.

If the bearing clearances are within the specified range for your particular engine and intended usage, then you

Common Plastigage will provide a fairly accurate indication of the bearing clearance if you don't have access to a set of micrometers. After the waxy string has been compressed between the bearing and crank journal, its width is compared to a chart on the package to determine the bearing clearance.

can get to work on other blueprinting projects. But if the bearings are too tight or too loose, you have several options. The first is to buy bearing inserts that will produce the desired clearance. Bearings are commonly offered in 0.001-, 0.002-, and 0.010-inch undersizes. It is more difficult to find bearings that are slightly *oversize* to increase the clearance (although Chevrolet does offer a limited selection of these bearings for smallblock V-8's).

Another alternative is to try a different brand of bearing. If, for example, Clevite bearings don't produce the exact clearance you are seeking, try a set of Vandervell or Federal Mogul bearings. Just be certain that the bearings you audition are really made by different manufacturers. Just because they come in different packages doesn't necessarily mean that they are made by different companies.

Minor adjustments in bearing clearances can be made by "half-shelling" the bearings. As an example of half-shelling, you might combine the lower halves of a set of standard bearings with the upper halves from a set of 0.001-inch undersize bearings. Even though this solution commits you to buying two sets of bearings for a single engine, you will have enough inserts left over for another complete engine.

The final cure for tight bearings is to reduce the diameter of the crankshaft journals. This can be a risky business, since it is very difficult to polish small amounts of metal off a crankshaft without causing the bearing journals to become crowned. Many crank grinders prefer to grind the crank a full 0.010-inch undersize to produce the correct clearance, since grinding the journals allows much greater control over the amount of material actually removed.

THRUST CLEARANCE

The *thrust clearance* limits the

To check thrust clearance, set up a dial indicator parallel to the crankshaft axis and pry the crank forward and back.

On some engines, you can measure crank end play by inserting a feeler gauge between the crank thrust flange and the thrust bearing.

front-to-rear motion of the crankshaft. The thrust bearing, like the other bearings in the crankshaft assembly, requires clearance to allow for thermal expansion and to permit oil flow across its surface for both cooling and lubrication. The correct clearance varies between engines, but generally a figure between 0.005 and 0.010-inch is acceptable.

To determine the existing clearance, the crankshaft is installed in the block and the main caps torqued in place. In most automotive engines, the rear or center main bearing controls crankshaft thrust. Before the main cap for the thrust bearing is tightened down, the bearing should be *seated* by smacking the crank snout and flywheel flange with a soft-headed hammer or mallet. After all the main caps have been tightened, set up a dial indicator with the plunger parallel to the crankshaft axis (as shown). Pry the crankshaft forward and backward with a long screwdriver and note the indicator readings. The total travel is the crankshaft thrust clearance.

On some engines it may be possible to measure thrust clearance with a feeler gauge. Pry the crank as far forward as it will go, then select the largest feeler strip that will slide between the bearing and the crankshaft thrust surface.

If the thrust clearance is too small, it can be increased by carefully sanding the thrust bearing. A piece of heavy, flat glass is a good low-buck surface plate for this operation. Place a piece of 600-grit wet-or-dry sandpaper on the glass, then saturate the abrasive with solvent. Carefully sand the thrust surface of the bearing on the abrasive,

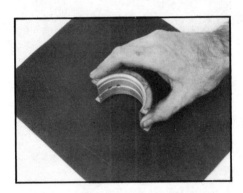

If the crank end play is too small, it can usually be increased by carefully sanding the thrust bearing. Use a piece of thick glass for a surface plate, and move the bearing in a figure-8 as you sand it.

using a figure-8 motion to remove material evenly across the bearing face. Concentrate your efforts on the front side of the bearing, which is only lightly loaded when the engine is running.

Occasionally you may find a crank with too much thrust clearance. Usually this is caused by a thrust surface that has been previously damaged and repaired. In extreme cases, the thrust clearance is so large that the entire crank assembly can move far enough to allow the rods or crankshaft counterweights to hit the block. The only practical cure for this condition is to have a competent crankshaft service build up the thrust surface by welding additional material onto the thrust bearing flange.

Thrust bearing problems are, unfortunately, quite common in high-performance engines. In many instances, it is the torque convertor or clutch that is at fault, not the thrust bearing itself. If the pressure plate has excessively high

You can check for a cocked or misaligned thrust bearing by painting the bearing with machinist dye and noting the contact pattern after rotating the crank. An alternate method is to check crank end play before and after the cap is installed; if the end play changes, the cap may be cocked.

spring pressure, or if the convertor "balloons," the load exerted against the thrust bearing can cause it to gall or burn. The life expectancy of a thrust bearing can be increased by making sure that its thrust surface is exactly parallel to the thrust flange of the crank. To check this, paint the bearing with machinist's dye or a felt-tip pen. Rotate the crank while prying against the end of it with a large screwdriver. Then remove both halves of the thrust bearing and examine the contact pattern where the dye has been worn away. The dye should be worn evenly around the entire circumference of the bearing. If the contact is concentrated in one area, the main bearing cap may have been cocked slightly when the block was align honed.

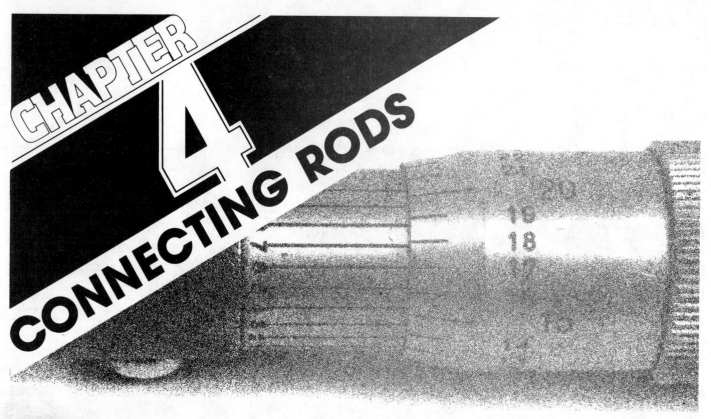

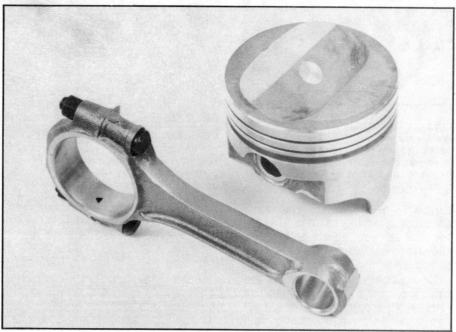

Stock connecting rods can be reworked to perform perfectly in street and certain limited racing applications.

CONNECTING RODS

Life is never easy for a connecting rod. With every turn of the crankshaft, it is alternately stretched and compressed. The motion of the crank and pistons tries to snap the beam in half, while the big and little ends are baked with intense heat. Considering the environment they live in, the survival rate among connecting rods is remarkably high. Of course, there are steps you can take that will extend the lifespan of any connecting rod used in racing or high performance.

SELECTION & INSPECTION

The type of connecting rods you choose will depend on how the engine will be used. If you are assembling a high-performance street engine, then it is likely that you will be using production connecting rods. Drag-racing engines are usually outfitted with aluminum rods, when the rulebook allows a choice, while road racing, marine, and circle-track motors depend on specialty steel rods. (Exceptions to these general rules, of course, would be those "limited" classes that restrict competitors to original factory parts.) Each type of connecting rod has distinct advantages and shortcomings that make it best suited for certain applications.

On the street, low cost and ease of installation tips the scales in favor of stock rods. The horsepower levels attainable even with supercharged street engines will not overtax a good forged steel factory rod. Since these rods are designed specifically for the engines in which they are installed, clearance problems between the rods, cam and block are eliminated (as long as a stock-stroke crankshaft is retained.)

In highly modified drag-racing engines, aluminum rods make more sense. Although the fatigue factor disqualifies aluminum for endurance racing, these rods are brutally strong for short periods of time—a characteristic that is ideal for high-rpm drag engines. The price of aluminum rods is not much higher than the cost of preparing a set of stock rods. Also, most manufacturers can supply virtually any combination of rod length and bearing size, which suits drag-

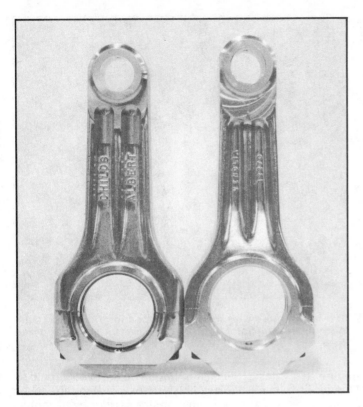

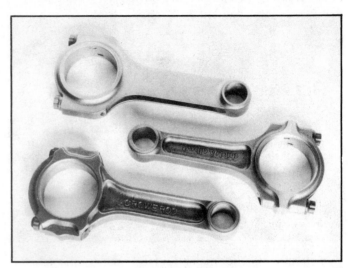

Aluminum rods are ideal for drag racing. They are reasonable in price, very strong, and available with a variety of lengths and bearing bore diameters. Remember that the low fatigue strength of aluminum demands regular rod replacement.

Growing popularity of oval-track racing has prompted aftermarket manufacturers to introduce new steel connecting rods. Differences in beam sections and big ends are apparent.

racing engine builders who are constantly juggling strokes, pin heights, and bearing diameters in search of a competitive edge.

Until recently, the choices in specialty steel connecting rods were quite limited. For many years the famous Carrillo forged, premium-steel connecting rod had a virtual monopoly on this market. The growing popularity of oval-track racing has enticed a number of companies into manufacturing their own steel rods. Also, the factories have stepped up with their own off-road rods, like the Chevrolet "Bow Tie" forgings. If you are racing a smallblock Chevrolet, you have at least six alternatives when selecting steel connecting rods. Of course, if you are planning on running a Morris Minor at Daytona, your choices will be somewhat more limited. The going rate for specialty steel rods is around $1000 a set—a big check, to be sure, but a bargain when you consider how much damage a broken rod can cause. A top quality specialty rod requires virtually no preparation. You inspect them (for shipping damage), clean them, and install them.

Getting a set of stock rods ready for assembly is not so easy. The first task is to do a bit of research to determine exactly what you've got. For example, Chevrolet has produced several different versions of the venerable smallblock rod, just as Chrysler and Ford have offered various grades of connecting rods for their respective performance engines. It makes little economic sense, though, to pay more money for features that you won't use. The difference between a premium Chevy LT-I connecting rod and an ordinary smallblock rod, for example, is simply the extra operations performed at the factory. But if you are already planning on polishing, shot-peening, bushing, resizing, and installing new bolts in your connecting rods, then the high-dollar cores offer little, if any, advantage.

Most connecting rod cores come

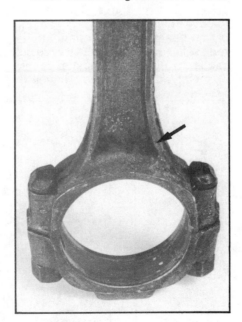

Black carbon deposits around big end of used connecting rod are warning sign that overheated bearing was on verge of spinning.

out of well-used engines. Although there is no way to knowing how many cycles a rod may have endured, the instances when a rod simply breaks are rare indeed. Almost all rod failures are caused by either the fasteners yielding or the bearing spinning because of a lack of lubrication. Black, baked-on carbon around the big end of the rod indicates that the bearing had overheated and was on the verge of spinning. If your rod cores are still in one piece and they show no signs of spun bearings, then you can proceed with the inspection procedure.

The surest way to find flaws inside a connecting rod is to have it X-rayed. For most applications, however, a

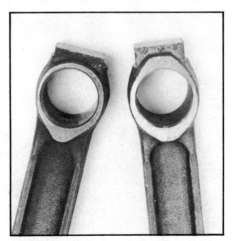

If you have a number of stock rods to chose from, favor rods with small balancing pads. They are likely to have more metal in the crucial beam section!

Larry Hollums begins Magnaflux inspection by magnetizing connecting rod candidate.

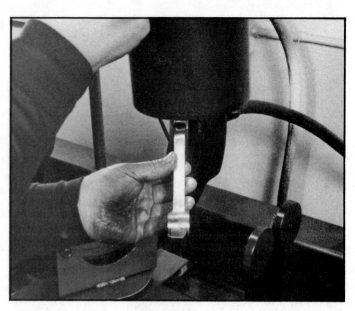

Rod is saturated with magnetic inspection fluid and examined under ultraviolet light. Flaws show up as bright green lines.

simple Magnaflux inspection will reveal surface cracks that could cause problems later. The procedure for Magnafluxing connecting rods is similar to checking a crankshaft. Each individual rod is magnetized, saturated with magnetic fluid, and then examined under a black light. Cracks show up as bright green lines under the florescent lamp. Our connecting rod advisor for this section, Larry Hollums, notes that relatively few rods are rejected during Magnaflux inspection. He prefers to grind the die marks off the rod beams *before* inspecting them. This reveals any "cold lap" flaws that might otherwise be concealed.

POLISHING & SHOTPEENING

Polishing the connecting rod beams is cheap insurance for any high-performance engine. It's a task you can easily do at home with a minimal investment in time and equipment. In some racing classes (notably certain Stock categories) it is not legal to grind away the die marks on the connecting rods. But unless the rulebook prohibits these efforts, your time will be well spent if you clean up the rod forgings. You will deny cracks a starting point, while also reducing the reciprocating weight.

If the beams are particularly rough, you may want to start by cutting off most of the forging flash with a carbide burr mounted in an electric or pneumatic die grinder. The goal is to remove only the raised forging marks on the beam without cutting into the rod itself. You can also use a wide belt sander to grind off the nastier chunks of metal on the beams. No matter which method you use, you should always finish up by polishing the beam with an abrasive cartridge roll *parallel to the long axis of the beam*. Don't bother trying to polish the rod to a mirror finish. Instead, concentrate on removing all the grinding marks left by the carbide burr or belt sander.

Most stock connecting rods have a machined shoulder under the bolt head. Remove the rod bolts—you'll be replacing them anyway—and carefully deburr and smooth this area with a small hand file. This is a highly stressed part of the rod; nicks and gouges left here by machine tools can give cracks a place to start.

After the rod has been polished, it is ready for *shotpeening*. As noted in the crankshaft chapter, shotpeening compacts the metal surface by bombarding it with steel balls. This closes up the

Forging marks on side of connecting rod beams are removed with carbide cutter.

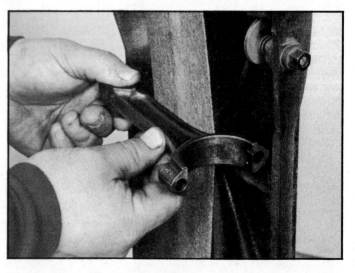

Rod beams are then smoothed with coarse grit belt sander.

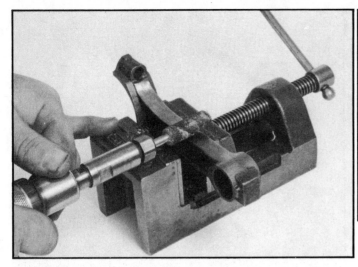

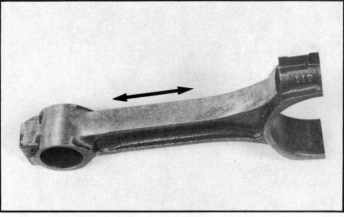

Final polishing is done with abrasive cartridge roll. Polish beams parallel to long axis of rod.

grain structure, preventing stress cracks from developing. The detailed technical procedures recommended by Chevrolet engineers for shotpeening is to use number 230 cast steel shot to obtain an Almen 0.012/0.015 arc height. Good luck finding a shop that can meet these specs! Most shops have a favorite type of shot, a favorite air pressure for the blasting gun, and let it go at that.

ROD BOLTS

The absolute best investment you can make in a high-performance engine is to replace the stock connecting rod bolts with high-strength fasteners. There are many sources for super-quality rod bolts, including Mr. Gasket, Moroso, B&B Performance, and similar racing suppliers. Fasteners made by the SPS Company are highly regarded because of their superior material, close quality control, and unique thread angle. If there is a shortcoming to the SPS fasteners, it is the nuts, which should never be

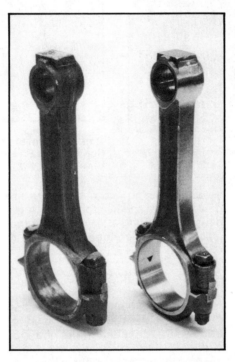

Carefully prepared stock connecting rod is slightly lighter than original forging and significantly more durable.

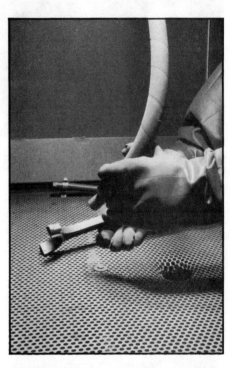

Shotpeening compacts surface of connecting rod to deny cracks a starting place.

Radius between beam and rod bolt shoulder is dressed with small round file and then polished with sandpaper to eliminate stress risers.

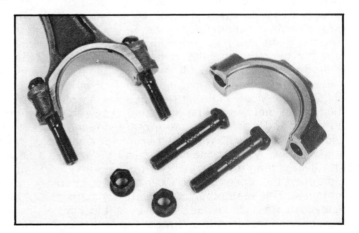

High strength aftermarket connecting rod bolts are a worthwhile investment for any engine. The unique fasteners made by the SPS company have special asymmetrical threads and diamond knurled shanks.

59

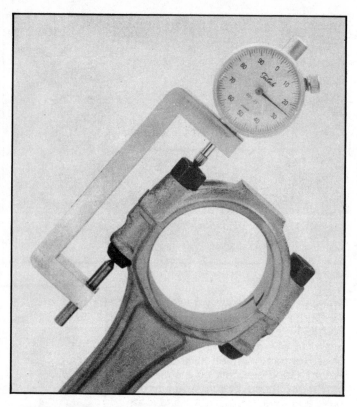

Hydraulic press prevents damage to rod when installing new bolts. Bolt head must be fully seated on shoulder of rod.

Rod bolts develop their maximum clamping force at specified stretch. Stretch gauge provides more accurate readings than torque wrench.

torqued more than five times. The SPS nuts are available individually, but you can eliminate this hassle by using stock nuts during the many mock-ups, saving the good SPS nuts for the final assembly.

In a pinch, you can install new rod bolts yourself. Support the rod with soft jaws in a vise and drive the new bolts into place with a brass hammer. However, a hydraulic press does a much neater job, and you can be sure that the bolts are seated properly if you apply 3000 pounds of pressure.

Rod bolts are designed to stretch. It is this carefully controlled spring action that keeps the nut tight and provides the clamping force. A torque wrench measures this stretching indirectly by recording the force required to turn the nut. A better way of determining bolt stretch is to measure it directly. Most high-performance bolts have dimples on the head and threaded end to accommodate an outside micrometer with a pointed anvil and spindle. By noting the changes in the overall length of the bolt as it is tightened, the proper "stretch" can be obtained. This method also makes it easy to spot a bolt that has been over-tightened, because the bolt reaches the yield point and suddenly stretches alarmingly. Since it is difficult to get an accurate micrometer reading inside the narrow confines of a crankcase,

several precision tool suppliers are now offering special rod-bolt stretch gauges, featuring a dial indicator that quickly records changes in the length of the rod bolt.

ROD RESIZING

When the big end of a connecting rod distorts, the rod bearing is in for trouble. The constant, rapid changes of direction can cause the big end to become egg-shaped, unless the mass around the bearing bore is substantial enough to resist these forces. If the bore does distort, the bearing clearances change dramatically. The edges of the bearings at the parting line can actually become metal "squeegees," shearing off the oil film that protects the bearing surface. Without a wedge of oil between the bearing and the crankshaft journal, the bearing quickly seizes, and another engine is ready for the scrap pile. Resizing the big end of a rod can help prevent these disasters.

When a production connecting rod is originally forged and machined, it has internal stresses that cause it to be dimensionally unstable, just as a new block goes through a seasoning period during initial use. Combine these internal stresses with the constant loads imposed by the reciprocating mass of the piston and small end of the rod, and the need for rod resizing be-

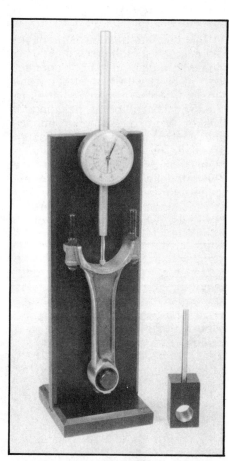

Patterson Racing uses this gauge to measure center-to-center length of connecting rods. It is significantly more accurate than dial calipers.

First step in rod reconditioning is to trim rod fork and cap with precision grinder. Minimum material should be removed to prevent shortening center-to-center distance.

This is how Kip Martin intentionally finishes big end of rods out-of-round. Shims are punched out of typing paper, then inserted between rod fork and cap.

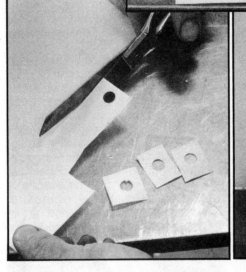

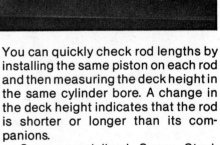

comes clear. Like align honing a block, resizing stock connecting rods is an essential part of engine blueprinting.

Connecting rods are resized on a reconditioning machine. The procedure is very similar to align honing a cylinder block. The rod caps are trimmed slightly on a cap grinding machine, and reinstalled on the rod fork. The bearing bore is then honed, restoring it to a perfectly round circle with a diameter matching the manufacturer's specifications.

When the big end of a rod is resized by this method, the minimum amount of metal should be ground off the rod caps, which will allow the bore to be restored to the correct diameter. As the caps are trimmed and the bearing bore honed round again, the center point of the big end is effectively moved closer to the small end. Usually a 0.003-inch cut is sufficient. If a cap requires more trimming, then the center-to-center length of the connecting rod will be changed significantly. This can cause inconsistency in the piston deck heights.

Measuring the center-to-center length of a connecting rod is difficult without the proper equipment. Dial calipers can give a ballpark figure. Measure the distance between the bores on the big and small end. Then measure the diameter of the pin hole and the bearing bore, and divide both of these dimensions in half. Add all three numbers and you have the center-to-center length of the connecting rod.

Most engine builders are more concerned with the consistency of the connecting rod center-to-center lengths than the actual dimensions.

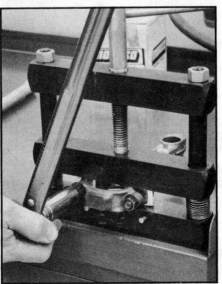

Rod and cap are held in special vise while bolts are torqued. Never hold rod by shank when tightening fasteners.

You can quickly check rod lengths by installing the same piston on each rod and then measuring the deck height in the same cylinder bore. A change in the deck height indicates that the rod is shorter or longer than its companions.

Some specialized Super Stock (drag-racing) engines require factory connecting rods with big ends that are intentionally finished "out-of-round." Machinist Kip Martin explains that by increasing the bore diameter at the bearing parting line, the bore will become round *under actual operating conditions*. Just as a torque plate is used to stress the cylinder bores to duplicate the conditions that exist when a head is torqued down, Kip's out-of-round Super Stock rods assume the proper shape only under a load.

Rod bearings inserts, like main bearings, are not perfectly round when

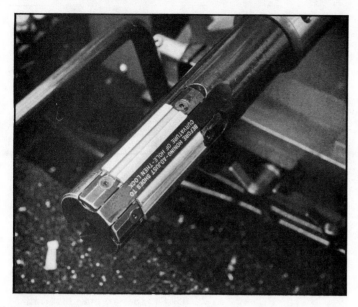

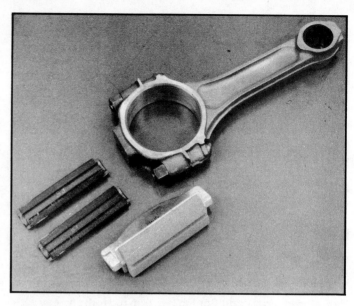

Reconditioning machine resizes big end of connecting rod with precision hone.

Kip reserves one set of finishing stones for each rod bore size so stones will always have proper arc.

installed; the inside diameter is larger at the parting line than at the vertical axis (the axis parallel to the beam of the rod). This slightly eccentric shape allows the bearing to pick up lubrication as the parting line passes over the oil hole in the crankshaft journal. When the big end of the connecting rod stretches under a severe load, the bore *draws in* at the sides, cutting off this vital oil supply. But if the diameter of the bearing bore is intentionally increased 0.0025-inch at the parting line, the oil flow will not be cut off even when the bore distorts. In fact, Kip reports that the rod bearing clearances can be reduced 0.00l-inch with

this technique, since the *effective* clearance is adequate even when the bore distorts under the stress of racing.

In order to produce a bearing bore with the proper eccentricity, Kip places 0.004-inch shims between the cap and rod. The bolts are then torqued and the rod resized normally. Kip hones the bearing bore to within 0.00l-inch of the finish size with a set of roughing stones, then switches to special finishing stones for the final passes. Each set of finishing stones is reserved for a single bearing bore size. This means that Kip has one set of stones for smallblock Chevy rods with

2.125-inch bearing bores and another set for rods with 2.225-inch bores. Thus the honing stones always have the proper arc for the rod bore they are sizing. This produces bearing bores that are smooth and straight, with no trace of "bellmouthing" at the sides of the rod. When the shims are removed and the cap reinstalled, the bearing bore has the desired eccentricity.

PIN FIT

Up to this point, the big end of the connecting rod has received most of our attention. It is the small end of the rod that takes care of the important business of supporting the piston, however. There are two ways to hang a piston on a connecting rod: with *pressed pins* or with *full-floating pins*. Floating wrist pins have a racier image than pressed pins, a reputation that may not be completely warranted. The real reason that racers prefer floating pins is convenience. By their very nature, racing engines are overhauled frequently. Full-floating pins make it easy to assemble and disassemble piston and rod pairs. Most production-line engines, in contrast, rely on the less glamorous press-fit pins. In an engine that may go over l00,000 miles before a rebuild, ease of disassembly simply is not a consideration.

More and more racers are beginning to recognize the virtues of pressed pins, however. In a well-equipped shop, having to press apart the pistons and rods is not a great hardship. Pressed pins eliminate the constant worry that free-floating pins will start floating too much! None of the pin retaining devices—Tru-Arcs, Spi-

Jets spray inside diameter of bore with honing fluid as operator strokes rod back and forth on mandrel. It takes skill to prevent bore from becoming "bellmouthed" or "tapered."

rolox, and buttons—is totally reliable. In contrast, when you press a pin into a rod with a 0.0015-inch interference fit, you *know* that pin is going to stay put.

Very few press-fit pins are actually pressed into rods these days. The preferred installation method is to heat the rods in a special oven. This expands the pin hole and allows the pin to slide through easily. As the rod cools and contracts, it grips the pin tightly. The mismatch in the diameters of the pin and the small end of the rod is critical. Although an interference fit of 0.001-inch is adequate for a stock engine, a high-performance motor requires at least a 0.0015-inch difference in diameters to lock the pin firmly in the rod. Piston pins are commonly available in 0.0015- and 0.003-inch oversizes to provide the proper interference fit in rods with larger-than-normal pin bores.

Unless your connecting rods were

Gauge measures diameter of resized rod bearing bore to 0.0001-inch.

Semi-finished connecting rods are manufactured with blank small ends. Reher-Morrison Racing Engines uses this special machine to bore pin hole while maintaining correct center-to-center distance.

originally designed to accommodate floating pins, they will have to be modified if full-floating pins are part of your engine building plans. Some smallblock Mopar and big-block Ford connecting rods have factory-installed bronze bushings in the small end. This is an ideal bearing material for floating pins. Stock smallblock Chevrolet rods, in contrast, were never offered with pin bushings. Chevy rods intended for use with floating pins had a microscopic layer of babbitt plated inside the pin bore. For years it has been a common engine building practice to bore the small end of the rod and install a bushing when floating pins are used. This also allows the engine builder to correct minor differences in center-to-center length by offset boring the small end bushing. Unfortunately, this practice leaves the wall thickness surrounding the pin bore very thin. That is why many Chevy engine builders now eliminate the bushings altogether. Instead, they hone the pin bore to provide 0.001-inch clearance and assemble the pin and rod combination "steel-on-steel." As long as the pin has adequate lubrication, this method works well.

Regardless of whether the small end of the connecting rod is bushed, a floating pin requires constant lubrication. The "correct" way to oil the pin is always a matter of controversy. Cur-

Very few press fit pins are actually pressed into connecting rods. Instead, an electric oven heats small end of rod, expanding the bore diameter. Pin is pushed through small end, then locked in place as rod cools.

Small end of connecting rod is honed on rod reconditioning machine to provide clearance for full-floating piston pins.

of the rod—and probably safer as well.

ROD-TO-CAM CLEARANCE

When you combine a long-stroke crankshaft with specialty connecting rods and a radical high-lift camshaft, what do you get? Sometimes you get a collision between the rods and the cam lobes. Providing clearance between the rods and engine block requires grinding some strategic reliefs in the block, but ensuring that the rods and cam lobes don't come together is a little more difficult. Specialty aluminum and steel connecting rods are generally stronger than stock rods because they are *bigger* than stock connecting rods. The extra material makes them more resistant to distortion, but it also makes them more likely to interfere with other parts inside the engine. This isn't just a problem with V-8 engines; inline sixes and fours that have their cams mounted in the block also have to be checked for interference between the cam and connecting rods. In general, any small-block Chevy equipped with a 3.48-inch or longer stroke and non-stock connecting rods should be checked. And if you are using the 3.750-inch stroke (400cid) crank, don't even dream of not checking.

What makes this procedure tricky is the fact that the cam rotates at half crankshaft speed. In other words, it takes *two* revolutions of the crank for

rently most engine builders prefer to drill a single 0.125-inch hole through the top of the rod with a generous 45° chamfer around the hole, which acts as a funnel to channel oil to the wrist pin. Until recently, however, Chevrolet recommended drilling *two* holes un-derneath the wrist pin, angling toward the rod centerline. Carrillo and other specialty connecting rods use this type of pin oiler, but it has been blamed as a contributing cause of rod failure in stock connecting rods. Certainly it is easier to drill oil holes through the top

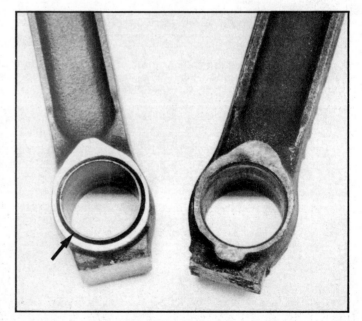

Super Stock drag-racing engine builders often bush small end of Chevy connecting rods to accept light 0.875-inch wrist pins in place of stock 0.927-inch diameter pins.

Floating wrist pins need 0.001-inch clearance in connecting rod.

Chamfered oil hole in top of connecting rod supplies lubrication for floating pin.

Clearance between small end of connecting rod and piston pin bosses must be checked when engine is preassembled. Not all connecting rods are centered under pistons; rod must be narrowed or pin bosses relieved to eliminate rubbing.

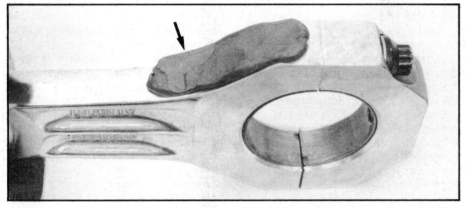

Long crankshaft strokes and bulky big ends may cause interference between rod and camshaft lobes. Impressions left in clay on rod shank indicate where lobes are too close.

every *one* revolution of the camshaft. Thus there can be adequate clearance on one stroke—but on the next cycle, the cam lobes may hit the cam. In fact, the cam lobes that operate the valves for adjacent or opposite cylinders may be the cause of interference problems, depending on the particular engine layout and the relationship between the lifter bores and the rod centerlines.

The easiest way to check for rod-to-cam clearance is to cover the rod shanks with a 0.125-inch thick layer of modeling clay. Preassemble the engine with the pistons, rods, and crank in place. Install the cam and timing chain you plan to use—it's not necessary to degree them in precisely, although the cam should be reasonably close to the final phasing. Then rotate the crankshaft at least four full revolutions. If the engine stops turning, don't force it. Get an inspection light and find the problem. Even if the crank turns freely, you are not finished yet. Re-

move the piston and rod assemblies, and then look closely at the clay on the rod shanks and around the bolts for impressions left by the cam lobes. If you find marks in the clay left by the lobes, carefully section the clay with a sharp knife or razor blade. If the clay is at least 0.050-inch thick, there is enough clearance to keep the rods and cam from colliding when the engine is at full speed.

If the thickness of the clay reveals that the cam and rods are too close for comfort, there are two solutions—neither of which is totally painless. You can either relieve the rod and bolts with a grinder, or install a cam with a smaller base circle. If you choose the first alternative, remove the minimum amount of metal that will provide the required clearance. Remember, the rod shank and fasteners are highly stressed in a performance engine, and they may fail if the grinding weakens them. Always deburr and polish the areas where you have removed metal

to prevent stress risers from forming.

If the cam-to-rod clearance problem is severe, a cam with a smaller base circle may be the only alternative. These specially ground cams have a smaller minor diameter than a standard cam. This means that the lobes are smaller, even though the lift and duration figures are unchanged. Small-circle cams have their drawbacks, however. These cams usually have to be custom ground, which adds expense and limits your selection. The smaller base circle requires longer pushrods to restore the proper valvetrain geometry. Finally, the tappets project farther out of the bottom of the lifter bores. In extreme cases, this can cause a massive internal oil leak when the reliefs in the lifters unmask the oil gallery passages. Certainly part of the art of blueprinting is solving the problems that your other "solutions" may have created.

PISTON-TO-ROD CLEARANCE

If you are using stock pistons and stock rods, you can skip this section. But if you have changed either or both of these components, then you must check the clearance between the small end of the connecting rods and the underside of the pistons. Make sure there is room between the top of the rod and the underside of the piston deck to allow the rod to pivot freely. Aluminum rods require careful scrutiny, because they generally have a greater wall thickness around the pin bore than steel rods. The balancing pads on the top of factory rods can sometimes hit the underside of non-stock pistons, especially when the pistons have a relatively short compression height.

You should also check the clearance between the small end of the rod and the pin bosses. Just because the rod has room to slide back and forth between the bosses when it is on the workbench does not mean that the clearance will be adequate when the rod and piston are installed in the engine. In many engines, including the Chevy V-6 and big-block Chevy V-8, the connecting rod beam is *not* centered under the piston. If the small end of the rod rides against the pin boss, it will cock the rod and overload one edge of the rod bearing. The usual result is a spun bearing and a broken rod. Again, aluminum rods are most likely to have extra-wide small ends, which can create these problems.

Check the rod-to-piston clearance when the engine has been preassembled. Turn the motor upside down

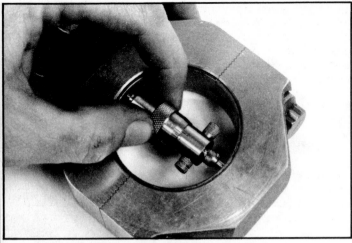

To check rod bearing clearance, mike crankshaft journal diameter, then measure vertical diameter of bearing shell after fasteners are torqued. Clearance is the difference between these two dimensions. Bearing diameter will be larger at parting lines.

on the stand and watch the small end of the rod move back-and-forth between the piston-pin bosses while the crankshaft is rotated. You should be able to move the small end of each rod from side-to-side without contacting the pin bosses. If the rods are rubbing against the pin bosses, you have a problem that must be corrected before final assembly. The pin bosses can be milled or the small end of the connecting rod narrowed. If the rods are offset slightly in the engine, only one of the piston pin bosses or one side of the rod may need to be machined to provide enough clearance.

ROD BEARING CLEARANCE

The rod bearings are often the last to receive lubrication, yet they operate under the most adverse conditions. Providing plenty of cool, clean oil at the correct pressure and with the proper clearances is the secret to rod bearing survival.

Rod bearing clearance is measured just like main bearing clearance. The diameter of the crankshaft journal is measured with an outside micrometer. Next, the bearing shells are inserted in the rod and cap, the fasteners are torqued, and the inside diameter of the bearing is determined with a micrometer or dial bore gauge. The difference between the two readings is the bearing clearance.

Whenever the rod bolts are tightened, the cap and rod should be held in alignment with a vise. Engine shops have special rod clamps for this purpose, but a standard workbench vise works well if you protect the rods with soft jaws. Clamp both the rod fork

and cap in the vise when you torque the fasteners; *never* hold the rod by the shank. A long torque wrench provides considerable leverage, and you may inadvertently twist the rod beam.

Rod bearings, like main bearings, are not always perfectly round. The diameter is generally largest at the parting line, where the bearing picks up oil as it rotates around the crank journal. When measuring the bearing clearance, it is the *vertical diameter* (90° from the parting line) that is important. The highest loads occur in this direction, caused by both combustion pressure and the stretching forces as the piston changes direction at the top

of the stroke. If precision tools are unavailable, rod bearing clearance can also be measured using Plastigage, as described in the crankshaft chapter.

The rod bearings should also be checked for interference with the crankshaft fillets. When a crankshaft is reground for performance or racing use, the radius of these fillets is often increased to add strength at this critical area. In some instances, however, the radii extend into the bearing surfaces on the journal. This can be checked by installing a bearing insert in the rod and pushing the rod firmly against the crank cheek. Usually the amount of interference is minor and

Rod bearing clearance is adjusted by selecting thicker or thinner inserts. Ball bearing is used on micrometer spindle when measuring curved bearing shell.

can be corrected by chamfering the outside edges of the rod bearing with a deburring knife. In extreme cases, however, the rod bearings will have to be narrowed. The usual procedure is to make a fixture from a discarded rod; and when the bearing shells are mounted in this makeshift fixture they can be precisely chamfered in a lathe.

ROD SIDE CLEARANCE

Connecting rod side clearance is a factor in controlling the amount of oil circulating through the engine. If the rod side clearance is too small, the flow of oil across the bearing surface is restricted. This oil flow is vital, since it both cools and lubricates the bearing. Further, the centrifugal force of the spinning crankshaft throws the oil onto the cylinderwalls, piston skirts, wrist pins, cam lobes, and other moving components. This "splash system" is the only source of lubrication for many parts, so it is vital that the rod side clearance be correct!

Rod side clearance can be checked by measuring the width of the rods and then comparing this dimension with the distance between the crankshaft cheeks on both sides of the journal. An alternative method is to assemble the rod (or rods, in the case of engines in which a pair share the same journal) and then measure the side clearance with a common feeler gauge. Make sure the rod caps are aligned squarely with the rod fork, and then tighten the fasteners. Keep trying progressively thicker gauges until you find the one that will just slip between the rod pairs or between the rod and crank cheek. The thickness of this feeler gauge equals the rod side clearance.

If the side clearance is tighter than the recommended specification for your engine, there are several ways to increase it. First, you may be able to correct the clearance by swapping rods between journals, or by pairing up different sets of rods. For example, you may have two rods that are slightly larger than the rest installed on a rod journal that is slightly narrow. By rearranging the rods, you may be able to gain the required side clearance.

The second alternative is to sand down the sides of the rods. This is actually easier than it sounds. You will need a thick piece of plate glass to use for a surface plate, and several dozen sheets of emery paper. Place the abrasive on the glass and sand the side of the rod by moving it in a figure-8. This technique works well if you need to remove only a few thousandths of metal; taking a larger cut will require

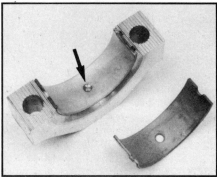

To check rod side clearance, measure combined width of connecting rod pairs—if two rods share a common journal—then subtract this dimension from width of crankshaft journal.

Dowel pins in aluminum connecting rods must not protrude above bearing surface or they will score crankshaft journal.

dozens of sheets of sandpaper and hours of arm work. When the rods must be cut substantially to correct the side clearance, they will have to be machined or the crankshaft reground to widen the journal (an expensive and sometimes impractical solution).

Occasionally you may find that the rod side clearance is larger than the recommended specification. Unfortunately, there is no easy solution to this problem, short of obtaining new rods or a replacement crankshaft. Excessive rod side clearance increases the amount of oil flying around in the crankcase, which can lead to higher windage losses and oil control problems on the cylinderwalls. Neither of these conditions is necessarily fatal to performance, however. As long as the rods are not banging around on the journals, a little extra side clearance is acceptable.

For reasons known only to rod manufacturers, most aluminum rods are much narrower than factory steel rods. Consequently, many engine builders discover that the side clearance may be in excess of 0.040-inch (for a pair of aluminum rods). Although aluminum does expand at roughly

Rod side clearance can also be checked by inserting feeler gauge between rods bolted to crank throw.

twice the rate of steel, these enormous clearances are not necessary. In fact, many successful racers run aluminum rods with side clearances more often associated with steel rods, ranging from 0.016- to 0.020-inch. They report no detrimental effects, and note that the combustion chambers have noticeably less oil contamination than before they reduced the side clearances.

TYPICAL TEMPERATURE DISTRIBUTION

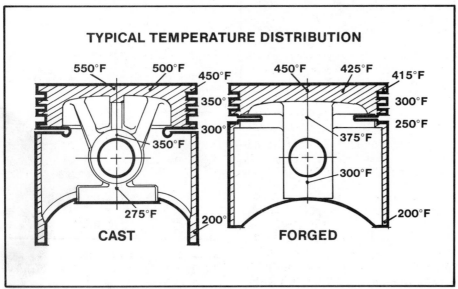

This diagram illustrates the heat distribution in cast and forged aluminum pistons. The densely packed molecules in the forging allow it to conduct heat away from the piston top quickly.

PISTONS

Aluminum pistons are really rather amazing. They are alternately seared by the heat of combustion, then blasted by a jet of cold air with every intake stroke. They are accelerated and decelerated at tremendous speed with every turn of the crankshaft, while withstanding side loads that try to weld the piston skirts to the cylinderwalls. Everything that an engine builder does to increase performance, from installing a hot-rod cam to porting the heads

to bolting on a blower, is intended to do just one thing: increase cylinder pressure. And, of course, the more pressure there is in the cylinders, the higher the loads the pistons must endure.

Much of the work devoted to piston preparation is required by the special characteristics of aluminum. Since aluminum expands at approximately twice the rate of steel, clearances that are correct at room temperature can change dramatically when the piston tops are heated to over 500°. Forged

aluminum pistons have a much denser molecular structure than cast pistons, so heat transfers through the forged material more quickly. Also, different parts of the piston expand at different rates. There is more metal around the pin bosses than in the skirts, so these two areas grow to different sizes when heated. This is why an engine that is noisy when first started on a cold morning can run quietly after it has warmed up. As the pistons are brought up to operating temperature, they expand to create the proper clearances.

PISTON-TO-WALL CLEARANCE

The right clearance between the piston skirts and the cylinderwalls is absolutely essential. If the *piston-to-wall clearance* is too large, the pistons rock back and forth in the bore. This prevents the rings from sealing the cylinder properly, and can crack the skirts as the piston slaps from side to side. If the clearance is too small, the piston will literally stick in the bore, scuffing the skirts and destroying the wall finish. There's a thin line between too much and not enough, but providing the correct running clearance pays dividends in both durability and horsepower.

There are two piston characteristics that affect the clearance. The first is the *cam grind*. All good quality pistons have skirts that are not perfectly round. If you were to cut a piston in half horizontally through its pin bore and then examine the skirts, you would discover that the skirts are slightly elliptical or oval. The eccentricity is hardly noticeable—usually between 0.020- and 0.040-inch—but it's important. The skirt diameter perpendicular to the pin bore is the widest part of the piston, becoming smaller as you move around toward the pin axis. Why? The answer again lies in the different expansion rates of various parts of the piston.

The second piston characteristic that must be considered is *taper*. If you measure that skirt diameter at several places between the top and bottom, you will probably discover that the average piston is wider at the bottom of the skirt tangs than it is at the piston pin hole. The amount of taper is very slight, typically between 0.005- and 0.010-inch. Since the range of piston-to-wall clearances for high-performance pistons runs from 0.0015-inch all the way up to 0.015-inch, piston taper can have a tremendous impact on the actual clearance. Some pistons have an even more complex skirt shape called a *barrel grind*. Barrel-ground pistons have skirts that bulge outward beneath the oil ring groove, then taper back inward as you move toward the tangs at the bottom of the piston. Regardless of how the piston is shaped, it is extremely important to know *where* on the skirt the manufacturer wants you to measure the clearance!

Most piston makers call for measuring the piston diameter perpendicular to the wrist pin when setting the piston-to-wall clearance. There are exceptions, however. Some racing pistons are measured just below the oil

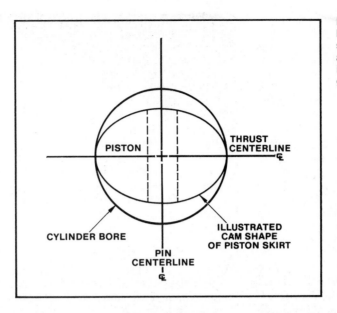

PISTON — THRUST CENTERLINE ℄

CYLINDER BORE

ILLUSTRATED CAM SHAPE OF PISTON SKIRT

PIN CENTERLINE ℄

Piston skirts are slightly elliptical when measured at room temperature. This oval shape is the piston's "cam grind."

A "barrel face" piston has a skirt that bulges outward in the center. Because of this complex shape, it is essential to follow the piston manufacturer's instructions when setting piston-to-wall clearance.

ring groove, while others are miked at the tangs. These differences depend on the particular cam and taper that the manufacturer has chosen.

Other factors also affect the clearance. There are several different aluminum alloys commonly used by piston manufacturers. Although aluminum is the primary ingredient, the amounts of silicon, magnesium, manganese, nickel, copper and other elements vary between the different alloys. These differences in turn affect the expansion characteristics and wear properties of the piston.

The design of the piston skirts also must be considered. Stock cast aluminum pistons, for example, often have steel struts inserted in the pin bosses. These struts hold the skirts in a permanently expanded position, so the piston-to-wall clearance can be greatly reduced. Also, slots behind the oil rings in these pistons effectively isolate the piston head from the skirts, creating a heat dam that prevents the transfer of heat below the ring band. These features produce a very quiet engine, which is ideal for an everyday commuter motor. Forged pistons, in contrast, do not have struts, so the piston-to-wall clearance must compensate for thermal expansion. Also, high-performance pistons frequently rely on holes drilled in the back of the bottom ring groove (instead of a wide slot) to drain oil away from the cylinder-walls. Thus the heat at the top of the piston can travel downward to the skirts, where it causes the aluminum to expand.

Engine speed also determines the optimum piston clearance. High-rpm racing engines require more piston-to-wall clearance than street motors. Piston noise is not a consideration when you are running with wide-open

Proper piston-to-wall clearance is essential to protect skirts from scuffing. Measure piston diameter at point specified by manufacturer.

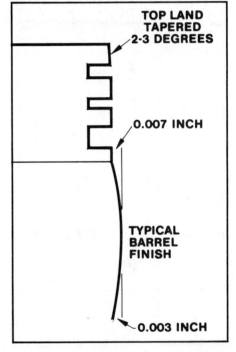

TOP LAND TAPERED 2-3 DEGREES

0.007 INCH

TYPICAL BARREL FINISH

0.003 INCH

Piston-to-wall clearance can also be checked by inserting feeler gauge between skirt and cylinder bore.

exhaust headers, so racing engines have decidedly looser piston clearances to prevent skirt scuffing under the heat and pressure of competition.

With so many variables to consider, the best advice is simply to follow the piston manufacturer's recommendations—*precisely*! The piston maker will be familiar with the expansion characteristics of his piston material and skirt design. Measure the piston diameter exactly where the instructions tell you to take the readings. And don't talk yourself into believing that a "little extra" skirt clearance is a good thing. More clearance than is necessary simply makes the engine noisier, oilier, and less reliable.

RING GROOVES

The vast majority of automotive pistons have three ring grooves—two for *compression rings* and one for an *oil ring*. Although some racing engines pare this assortment down to a single compression ring, and some heavy-duty diesels add an extra one, three seems to be the magic number for piston rings.

Ring grooves are machined with great precision. The top and bottom of the grooves must be as smooth as possible to provide a sealing surface for the rings. Whenever the engine is preassembled or the pistons are being worked, the ring grooves should be protected by wrapping masking tape around the ring band. This protection is crucial if the pistons are glass beaded; unprotected ring grooves will be pitted, destroying the smooth surface that is essential if the rings are to seal tightly to the piston grooves.

Unlike piston skirts, the ring lands have no cam grind—they are always perfectly round. The diameter of the lands, however, is somewhat smaller than the diameter of the piston. This prevents the lands from contacting the cylinder walls when the piston "rocks over" at top-dead center. Reducing the diameter of the ring lands ensures that the thrust loads will be handled by the skirts alone. The diameter of the ring lands may be stepped, with the land between the top and second ring slightly smaller than the land separating the second ring from the oil ring. On some pistons, the land diameters are tapered, with a constant 2° cut from the oil ring upward.

VALVE POCKETS

Almost all overhead valve engines require *reliefs* or *notches* in the piston tops to provide clearance for the valves. Without these notches, the valve lift would be severely limited. Installing a camshaft with longer duration and higher valve lift increases airflow through the engine, allowing the engine to produce more power. As the valves move farther off their seats and are held open longer, the location and depth of the valve pockets in the piston tops become more important.

The valve notches found in stock pistons are usually the wrong sizes and in the wrong places. Factory flat-top pistons for a smallblock Chevrolet, for example, have four equal-size valve reliefs—even though each combustion chamber has only two valves with unequal head diameters. With four notches, however, the pistons are "universal"—they can be installed in any hole on either bank of cylinders, and there will always be a valve pocket where it's needed. High-performance and racing pistons yield more compression by eliminating the two "extra" valve reliefs. And once the size of the pockets is reduced to fit the exhaust and intake valve heads precisely, then each piston must be assigned to a cylinder with the same valve layout.

If you are using a high-perfor-

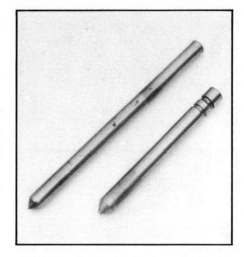

Punch made by sharpening valve stem or length of drill rod is perfect tool for locating center of valve relief on piston.

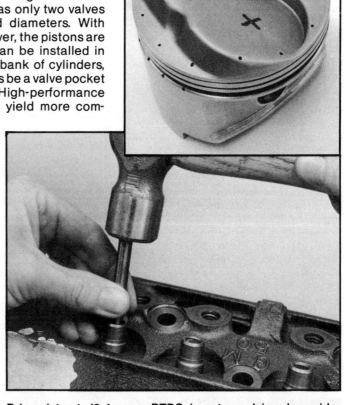

Bring piston to 10 degrees BTDC, insert punch in valve guide, and then lightly tap piston to mark exact valve location.

Flat-top pistons with four valve notches may be installed in any cylinder, since two notches always correspond to valve location. The "extra" notches reduce compression, however.

Check valve relief size with compass set at valve head diameter (plus required safety margin). Center compass in punch mark and scribe around valve notch.

mance camshaft, specialty pistons, or oversize valves, the location of the valve reliefs must be checked. This requires a sharpened punch that you can insert through the valve guides. (A tool can be made by cutting the head off a discarded valve and sharpening the stem to a point in a lathe or drill press.) Preassemble the crank, rods, and pistons in the block, then attach a degree wheel to the crank snout and adjust it to indicate top-dead center for the number-one piston. (See the camshaft chapter for a full explanation of this procedure.) Place head gaskets of the same type that you intend to use on the block, then bolt down the bare heads (without valves). The point when the exhaust valve is closest to the piston generally occurs at 10° *before* TDC; intakes are closest at 10° *after* TDC. To mark the exact centerpoint of the valve pockets, bring the number-one piston to 10° before TDC. Insert your punch into the exhaust valve guide and tap the end with a hammer. Remove the punch, rotate the crank to 10° after TDC, and mark the centerpoint of the intake valve, following the same procedure. Repeat this process on the remaining cylinders, marking the valve locations at 10° before and after TDC. (If your particular cam grind differs greatly from the norm, then you may have to adjust the point at which you punch the pistons.)

You will find a pair of punch marks on the top of each piston when you remove the cylinder heads. These punch marks correspond to the exact center of the valve stem when the piston and valve are closest. To determine if the valve notches are large enough and in the correct location for your engine combination, scribe the valve head diameters on the piston top, using the

punch marks as the center of the circle. When scribing these circles, add 0.080-inch to the radius of the valve heads to allow for piston rock and valve float. If the circles you have scribed are within the existing valve notches, then the location of the valve reliefs is correct. If not, the valve notches must be machined to provide clearance. But before you start cutting on the piston tops, the *depth* of the valve notches must also be checked.

How brave are you? That's a question you will have to answer before deciding how much *piston-to-valve clearance* is enough. Surprisingly, determining the right piston-to-valve clearance for a full-on racing engine is easier than settling on the clearance for a high-performance street engine. This is because racing engines usually have stiff valve springs, rigid valve trains, and solid or roller lifters. Street engines, in contrast, often have heavy valves, weak springs, and hydraulic tappets—all of which contribute to *valve float*. When you decide how much valve clearance is enough, you are really trying to estimate the worst case of valve float that your engine could encounter.

If you had an ideal engine in which the valves always followed the camshaft lobes exactly, the piston-to-valve clearance would never have to be larger than the dimension you used for piston-to-head clearance. This clearance would be enough to allow for *rod stretch* and *thermal expansion* of the pistons. But in the real world, piston-to-valve clearance always has to be larger than the piston-to-head clearance—usually two or three times greater. The reason is that the valves

don't always do exactly what the cam profile tells them to do. Valve float is a danger that cannot be ignored. Even if you are so skillful with a four-speed that you never miss a shift, or have an automatic transmission that never allows the engine to over-rev, there will still come a day when the engine rpm goes sky high. Maybe a universal joint will break, or the tires will simply lose traction. On that day, you will be thankful that you took the possibility of valve float into consideration.

The exhaust valves are usually the first to hit. If you ever have an opportunity to see one of the cutaway engines that cam makers always display at the shows, you can see why the exhaust valves have such a tough time. The piston is "chasing" the exhaust valve as it closes. If the exhaust valve motion is no longer controlled by the cam lobe, it is quite likely that the piston will smack the valve as it floats freely in the chamber. Valve action is more controlled on the intake side, though. Here the intake valve follows the piston down the cylinder bore. Since the intake valve is opening when it is closest to the piston, the valve spring exerts greater control over the valve motion. This is why cam manufacturers frequently recommend more clearance for the exhaust valves than for the intake valves.

There are several ways to check piston-to-valve clearance using dial indicators and light tension springs, but the best method is still the old-fashioned clay technique. When you check with clay, you eliminate questions about how much the pushrods might deflect against stiff valve springs or whether the rockers will bend as they

Clay method may not be the most glamorous way to check piston-to-valve clearance, but it is the easiest and most reliable. To be accurate, you must use the same springs and valvetrain that you intend to use when the engine is assembled. Coat clay with oil or talcum to prevent it from sticking to valve, then measure thickness with calipers after turning crank several complete revolutions.

overcome the valve spring resistance. What you see when you check valve clearance with modeling clay is exactly what you've got.

Once again, the engine has to be preassembled, with the camshaft degreed in and the heads assembled with the correct valves and springs. Before bolting the head onto the block, place a 0.125-inch thick layer of modeling clay in the valve notches. Dust the clay with talcum powder or a few drops of oil to prevent it from sticking to the valves. Tighten down the heads on the block, install the rockerarms and pushrods, and adjust the valve lash to the recommended setting. (If you are using a hydraulic cam, you must substitute solid lifters when checking piston-to-valve clearance. Adjust the valves to zero clearance when checking the clearance with a hydraulic cam.) When all these preparations are finished, rotate the crank through four complete revolutions. Remove the cylinder head. The impressions left in the clay by the valve heads will tell you how much piston-to-valve clearance you have.

Section the clay with a sharp knife or razor blade. Measure the thickness of the clay with a dial caliper, or assemble a stack of feeler gauge strips that equal the height of the clay left on the piston. Although every engine and camshaft design differs, the general rule is that *you must have at least 0.080-inch clearance for the intake valve and 0.100-inch clearance for the exhaust.*

There are several tactics that will increase the piston-to-valve clearance. You can install a cam with shorter duration and/or less valve lift. You can

change the *phasing* of the cam by *retarding* or *advancing* it; this will increase clearance for one valve while decreasing it for the other. You can regrind the valve seats to sink the valve seats deeper in the chamber (which, unfortunately, hurts airflow). You can also make the valve heads thinner by taking a cut across the faces in a lathe. Finally, you can have the pistons machined to deepen the valve notches.

Among these possible solutions, deepening the valve pockets is usually the best choice. The compression ratio will be reduced slightly, but that is a small sacrifice to keep the pistons and valves from colliding. When the valve notches are machined, you can add enough clearance to accommodate future cam changes and to compensate for the inevitable timing changes that occur when the timing chain stretches.

Deepening and enlarging the valve notches requires a vertical mill, which means that most amateur engine builders will have to pay a machinist for these services. There are several do-it-yourself tools to cut valve pockets, but the results generally are not as good as paying a professional to do the job right. The most common way to deepen valve notches is with a *fly cutter.* A fly cutter has a single bit that can be adjusted to the diameter required to provide clearance for the valve head. In racing engines, where every last bit of compression counts, the valve

reliefs are sometimes *plunge cut.* In this method, a cutter of the correct size is plunged straight downward into the piston dome, leaving an eyebrow of piston material around the valve relief.

Occasionally the angle of the valve pockets must be corrected as well. This is usually required if the cylinder heads have been angle milled, since this modification changes the relationship between the valve heads and the piston tops. If the clay impression produced during the piston-to-valve clearance check measures thicker on one side of the valve notch than on the other, this indicates that the angle of the valve relief does *not* match the angle of the valve heads. This can be checked with a bevel protractor, and the angle corrected when the valve reliefs are machined.

DOME FITTING & RADIUSING

The best piston dome is no dome at all! A lump of aluminum projecting into the combustion chamber does raise the compression ratio, but it also disturbs the flame front as the flame spreads through the chamber. Almost without exception, it is better to cut the chamber volume in a wedge-type engine in order to increase compression than to increase the size and height of the piston dome.

There are times, however, when a dome is unavoidable. Racing engines, particularly those that burn alcohol, thrive on compression. In these situations, it is important to maximize the benefits provided by the dome, and to minimize the shortcomings. This means that the domes must be fitted carefully to the chambers, contoured

Valve relief in piston must match valve angle in cylinder head. Protractor bevel provides precise measurement.

to promote flame travel, and shaped to prevent the creation of pockets and dead areas that can promote detonation.

Most "TRW-type" pistons have universal domes. That is, the domes are small enough to fit most combustion chambers without interference, as long as the cylinder heads have not been milled unmercifully. With these mass-produced pistons, all that is required is some hand work with a grinder to radius the edges of the dome. By blending and rounding the dome contours, the flame front has an easier time of reaching the far corners of the chamber as the piston parks momentarily at TDC at the start of the power stroke.

Custom pistons will require more work. It is usually a struggle to coax maximum compression from a small-displacement drag-racing engine. First, the *swept volume* of the cylinders is small in this type of engine, which limits the available compression. Second, these engines are generally fitted with high-lift, long-duration cams that demand deep valve reliefs in the piston tops. These notch-

To mark bore location on cylinder heads, paint around combustion chambers with machinist dye, then bolt head to block and scribe around cylinders.

es reduce the effective dome volume, so again the final compression ratio suffers. The result is.that most "universal" custom-made pistons have very large domes, that must be *individually fitted* to the combustion chambers.

To fit the domes to the chamber by hand, you must first mark the exact location of the cylinder bores on the deck surfaces of the heads. Paint the head with machinists' dye, then bolt it onto the bare cylinder block. Reach up into the cylinders and mark the location of the bores with a long, sharp scribe. When the head is removed, you will have a circle around each chamber that corresponds to the exact bore location.

Lay the head on a workbench with the chambers facing you. Select the piston that you have assigned to the first chamber, turn it upside down, and position it inside the circle scribed on the head. Take care to align the piston pin holes so that the piston is in the same position relative to the chambers as it will be when it is installed in the engine. Hold the quench area of the piston flat against the deck surface of the head and slowly move it around inside the scribed circle. If the piston moves freely within this circle, there is no interference between the dome and the combustion chamber. Since the top ring land is slightly smaller than the cylinder bore, you can be reasonably sure there will be adequate clearance between the dome and chamber when the piston rocks over at top-dead center.

If the piston cannot be moved to the edges of the scribed circle, the dome and chamber are hitting. To pinpoint the interference, paint the dome with dye, and then attempt to fit it inside the scribed circle. As you move the piston within the circle, the dye will be rubbed off where the dome is too close to the chamber walls. Examine the dome

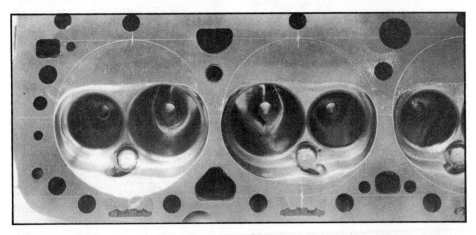

Scribe marks on deck surface show exact position of cylinders. Pistons must be able to fit inside these circles without interference.

Although you can center pistons in the chambers by eye when fitting domes, a more precise method is to mark exact piston centerline using a surface plate. With piston held on vertical pin, measure ring land diameter, divide by two, and then scribe piston skirt at center point.

Align scribe mark on skirt with reference point on cylinder head to center piston in combustion chamber.

Edges of combustion chamber frequently interfere with piston dome. Paint chamber and dome with machinists dye when trial fitting pistons; shiny spots highlight where additional clearance is needed.

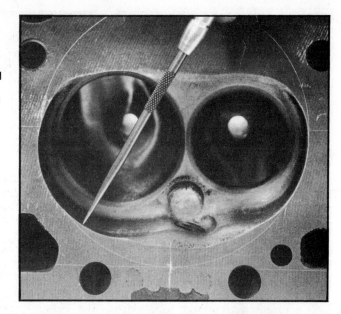

After relieving dome and chamberwalls, piston on left fits completely inside scribed circle on cylinder head; dome on unmodified piston (right) hits chamberwall before piston fits completely inside circle.

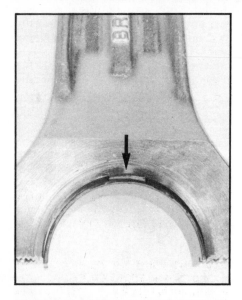

Rod stretch (at high rpm) is simulated by placing shim between bearing and connecting rod fork. If engine turns over with shim in place, then there is adequate piston-to-head clearance.

carefully for evidence of interference, especially in the areas where it meets the piston top.

If the dome and chamber walls are too close for comfort, the offending metal must be removed. You can either grind on the pistons or grind on the cylinder heads—or you may wish to remove a little material from both. A carbide burr or grinding stone works well on cast iron chambers; a high-speed steel cutter dipped in automatic transmission fluid or WD-40 will make quick work of aluminum piston domes and chambers. The simplest way to find and eliminate all the tight spots is by trial-and-error. After you trim a little off the dome or chamber walls, paint the piston dome with dye and try again to fit it inside the circle. Remember that every little bit of piston and chamber metal that you cut away will *reduce* the final compression ratio; if maximum compression is essential (racing), work slowly and carefully to remove

the *minimum* amount of metal needed to fit the dome to the combustion chamber.

This method works well with pistons that have large, flat deck surfaces, such as smallblock Chevrolets. Engines with smaller piston quench areas (smallblock Boss Fords and Hemis, for example) require a different technique. With these types of engines, the piston tops must be covered with clay, the heads installed, and the clay sectioned to reveal tight spots. Any areas where the clay is compressed thinner than the piston-to-head clearance dimension must be relieved.

Another way to check for dome interference is to use a special extra-long connecting rod. The center-to-center length of this rod should be increased by the total piston-to-head clearance dimension. For example, if your engine uses rods that measure 5.000 inches between centers and the total piston-to-head clearance is 0.050-inch, then you would need a checking rod that measures 5.050 inches center-to-center. This extra long rod simulates what happens at high rpm when the piston-to-head clearance is reduced to zero by rod stretch, pin flex, and piston rock. You can also make a checking rod by placing a shim between the rod fork and bearing. The thickness of this shim should equal the piston-to-head clearance dimension.

To check for dome interference with this method, install the piston on the long rod in the assigned cylinder. Bolt down the cylinder head *without* a gasket and then rotate the crankshaft. If the crank stops as the piston approaches TDC, there is interference somewhere between the piston and combustion chamber. Paint the dome with dye and remove material—where shiny spots indicate interference—until the crankshaft turns freely. When the engine is reassembled later with a head gasket in place, the gasket thickness will provide *running clearance* for the piston.

When the piston domes all fit their respective combustion chambers, they must be smoothed and contoured. Start with a 100-grit hardabrasive cartridge roll and polish away the tool marks left by the cutting burr. On pistons used in deep-wedge chambers, like smallblock and big-block Chevrolet V-8s, the edges of the dome should be rounded with a 0.250-inch radius. However, this generous radius is unnecessary on a piston designed for a shallow chamber (such as the Cleveland Ford family); all that is required is to break the sharp edges.

Some piston domes require grinding to clear spark plug electrodes. Mark location of relief by inserting scribe through plug hole with piston at TDC.

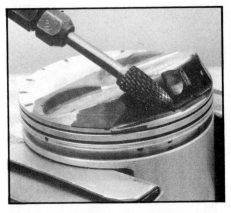

Edges of piston dome should be radiused to remove sharp edges and promote flame travel. Size of radius depends on chamber and piston design, desired compression ratio, plug location, and other factors. Lubricate high-speed cutter with WD-40 or auto trans fluid to prevent aluminum from clogging burr.

After radiusing dome, smooth and polish cutter marks with hard abrasive rolls.

Finish up with fine 220-grit rolls or a Scotchbrite wheel.

If the piston has an extremely large dome, it is important to unshroud the spark plug. A "fire slot" tunneling all the way across the piston is not usually necessary, but there must be enough clearance around the plug electrodes to prevent the dome from cutting off the flame front before it can spread evenly and completely across the chamber. An easy way to determine the location of the plug relief is to bring the piston up to TDC, set the cylinder head in place, and mark the piston dome with a scribe inserted through the spark plug hole. The type of plug you plan to use will dictate how much material must be removed for the plug relief. Extended-tip plugs, for example, will require much more metal removal than a regular gap design.

Another goal of piston dome contouring is to eliminate secondary pockets. These are formed when the dome blocks off portions of the combustion chamber. The fuel/air mixture trapped in these pockets may not burn completely, and heat energy is lost. Further, most automotive combustion chambers are designed to encourage turbulence as the pistons rise and fall. The swirling motion of the fuel/air mixture suppresses detonation and aids combustion efficiency. The carbon traces deposited on the piston tops of an engine that has been run only a short time provide a graphic illustration of the flame travel taking place inside the chamber. Areas that remain clean and shiny have probably been washed by the incoming fuel, or are the result of incomplete combustion in secondary pockets.

Carbon deposits on this well-rounded dome indicate that flame front is reaching all parts of the cylinder. Uncolored areas on piston domes often are signs of incomplete combustion or fuel separation in chamber.

After radiusing valve reliefs with high-speed cutter, finish with abrasive spiral roll.

Before you put away your hand grinder, the valve reliefs should also be radiused. This eliminates sharp edges that can cause preigniton, and helps the intake and exhaust gases move easily through the combustion chamber. The valves are very close to the

Valve notches should be lightly radiused to promote flow around the valve heads and to remove sharp edges which might cause preignition.

Custom piston is finally ready for installation after fitting dome to chamber, blending edges, cutting spark plug relief, radiusing valve pockets, and glass beading.

piston at times during the overlap stroke. Sharp edges on nearby valve reliefs can hinder flow across the valve heads. The intake pocket should have more generous radii than the exhaust, since the incoming fuel/air mixture is moving *away* from the valve.

This simple piston thickness checker is made by clamping steel rod in bench vise and then centering dial indicator plunger over tip.

Insert piston between rod and dial indicator to measure metal thickness. Watch for thin areas under corners of valve reliefs, beneath deck surface, and around plug notches.

CHECKING PISTON THICKNESS

Before any machine work is performed on a piston, the thickness of the deck and valve reliefs should be checked. Even under ideal conditions, the heat and pressure of combustion can burn holes through piston tops that are too thin. If the engine encounters *detonation*, it takes a thick deck to stand up to the hammering.

A fixture to check piston thickness can be assembled quickly on your workbench vise. Set up a dial indicator on a magnetic stand, as shown in the accompanying photos, then zero the indicator against a metal rod clamped in the vise. To measure the thickness of the piston top, insert the piston between the rod and indicator. Note the indicator reading as you move the piston around on the rod, paying particular attention to potential troublespots at the bottom edge of the valve reliefs and around spark plug notches. Mark the readings you take on the piston top to provide a "map" that will guide your machinist when he deepens the valve pockets or lightens the piston.

The metal thickness required for reliable piston operation depends on the intended use of the engine. Drag-racing engines, for example, can survive with piston tops as thin as 0.080-inch in very small areas; a circle-track or supercharged engine might not last 10 minutes with such thin piston sections. The piston material also makes a difference, since some aluminum piston alloys are stronger than others. The factor that influences piston life more than any other is *detonation*. Any

piston that encounters severe detonation is going to fail eventually, regardless of the deck thickness. Similarly, when combustion temperatures climb because of an extremely lean fuel mixture, the super-heated aluminum will soon fail, no matter how thick or thin it may be.

PISTON LIGHTENING

Lightening an automotive piston requires a delicate balance between weight reduction and durability. Lightweight pistons improve the throttle response of the engine, which is important in certain types of racing. Light

This is Patterson Racing's piston thickness checker; long-travel dial indicator makes it easy to insert a piston in the fixture, and sharpened point on the steel rod reaches into tight corners.

pistons reduce the loads on the connecting rods and piston pins, which in turn allows the weight of these components to be further reduced. The lighter reciprocating weight permits the crankshaft counterweights to be reduced, which further aids engine response. At some point, however, an engine builder reaches the point of diminishing returns. Usually he knows he's arrived there when the pistons start falling apart.

When reliability is more important than quick response, lightening the pistons offers no advantages. Street engines and high-speed oval-track motors operate at fairly constant en-

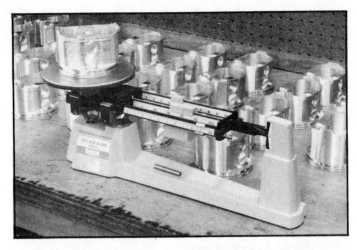

Piston skirts are lightened by sweeping inside of skirt with end mill. Nozzle sprays tool with water soluble oil to lubricate and cool cutter. All lightening work must be done with radiused cutters, since sharp edges invite cracks.

Piston lightening is never inexpensive because of the amount of machine work it involves. In some types of competition—notably drag racing—piston weight is a critical factor in engine performance. In endurance racing, though, it's more important to have a piston that will last than one that is ultra-light.

If you are lightening more than one batch of pistons, accurate records will cut your set-up time. Here's the "log book" that Patterson Racing keeps for each type of piston forging. Notations include depth and angle of all cuts.

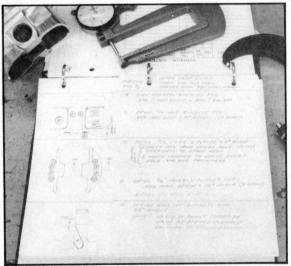

Digital position readout for vertical mill insures that every piston in a set is machined exactly alike.

gine speeds, so lightweight pistons are not essential. The situation changes drastically, however, when you are building a sprint-car engine or a state-of-the-art drag-racing motor. In these applications, engine acceleration is all-important, and every gram of piston weight counts!

One piston manufacturer has observed that when you are trying to take weight out of a piston, aluminum is more expensive than gold. If the dies in which the piston blank was forged are reasonably up-to-date, the only way to remove weight is to machine it away. This is tedious hand work that requires hours of set-up time and specialized tooling. Although an unknowing engine builder might attack the underside of a piston with an ordinary hand grinder in the hope of eliminating excess weight, the only way to really pare down a piston is with a mill and a wide variety of cutters. The accompanying photos illustrate the areas where a savvy machinist can safely cut down piston weight. It is essential that all lightening work be done with radiused cutters. Sharp corners are natural stress risers that can quickly lead to disastrous cracks.

Taking weight out of a piston is never easy. Piston forging design often determines where grams can be trimmed. Ball mill cutter is plunged under pin boss to remove weight without weakening forging.

Cuts on piston struts alongside pin boss remove weight and allow skirts to flex slightly, reducing cylinderwall distortion. Note large radius left by cutter. Lightened pistons must be checked carefully for cracks whenever the engine is disassembled.

Holes under ring land must be precisely angled to avoid breaking through to back of grooves. After lightening, all edges are carefully deburred to eliminate stress risers.

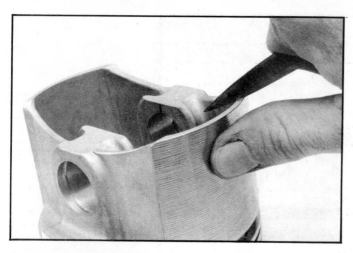

First step in skirt preparation is to deburr sharp edges left by piston machining.

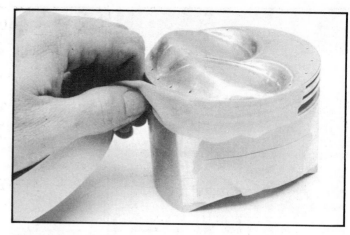

Protect ring grooves, ring lands, and pin holes from glass beads with several layers of masking tape. If grooves are glass beaded, ring seal will suffer.

PISTON SKIRT PREPARATION

Pistons don't just move up and down inside the cylinders. They also try to move sideways as they push against the connecting rod and crank pins. The skirts must stabilize the piston and absorb these *thrust loads* without distorting or damaging the cylinderwalls. The proper cam grind, the right surface finish, and the correct piston-to-wall clearance can all help the skirts do this job. Detailing the piston skirts will pay dividends in engine durability.

The first step is to thoroughly *deburr* the piston skirts. Using a sharp deburring tool, lightly go over all the piston edges and remove the ragged corners left by the factory tooling.

These burrs and nicks can score the cylinderwalls if they are not removed. Then carefully round the skirt edges with fine wet-or-dry sandpaper saturated with solvent. Then lightly sand the skirt surfaces with 600-grit paper.

Many engine builders glass bead the piston skirts, but this is still a controversial practice. Those who recommend glass beading claim that a slightly rough skirt texture traps oil and helps lubricate the skirt and cylinderwall. Doubters point out that the small glass particles can become embedded in the skirt material, leading to cylinder scratching. Certainly custom made-in-California pistons seem less susceptible to galling and scuffing after the skirts have been glass beaded, but you will have to decide for your-

Wash skirts with solvent, then buckets of hot, soapy water. Scour grooves with stiff bristle brush to remove glass beads and machining chips. Scotchbrite pads work well for scrubbing pistons.

This cutaway engine illustrates how little clearance there is between counterweights and skirts when piston is at BDC. If you have changed crankshaft stroke, rod length, or piston design, you must check for skirt interference.

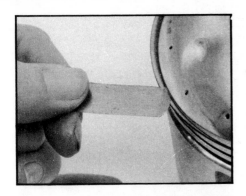

Cylinder pressure must be able to reach the rear of piston rings either through gas ports drilled from deck surface or via ring side clearance. Side clearance is measured by selecting feeler gauge strip which just slides between ring and groove.

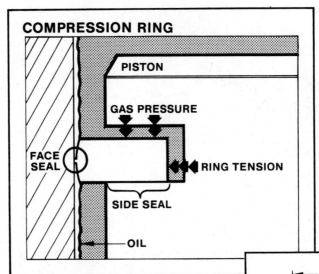

COMPRESSION RING

PISTON

GAS PRESSURE

FACE SEAL

RING TENSION

SIDE SEAL

OIL

Compression rings rely on cylinder pressure to seal the ring face against the cylinderwall. Clearance between the ring and the groove allows this pressure to reach the back of the ring.

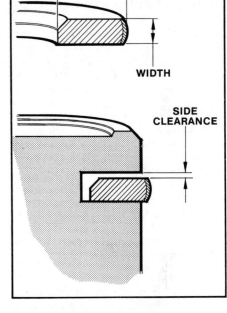

RADIAL THICKNESS

WIDTH

SIDE CLEARANCE

self whether the advantages outweigh the risks.

If you decide to glass bead the skirts, the ring grooves and piston pin holes must be protected with masking tape. Use only new, clean glass beads, and set the pressure regulator to 35 psi or less. The nozzle should be kept in constant motion across the skirts to prevent concentrating the stream of glass beads in a single spot. After the glass beading session, wash the pistons thoroughly in clean solvent, then scour the skirts with Scotchbrite. Finish up by scrubbing the skirts with a stiff brush and hot, soapy water.

SKIRT-TO-CRANKSHAFT CLEARANCE

If you are using specialty pistons, a stroker crankshaft, or non-stock connecting rods, you must check the clearance between the piston skirts and the crankshaft counterweights. The bottom of most piston skirts are scalloped to provide room for the counterweights to pass by when the piston approaches bottom-dead center. Occasionally, however, mistakes do happen—especially if the engine has a combination of non-original components. The skirt-to-crankshaft clearance should be checked visually when the short block is preassembled. As you slowly rotate the crankshaft, look for interference between the bottom of the skirts and the crank counterweights. If they collide, the skirts must be trimmed or remachined to prevent contact.

PISTON RINGS

Piston rings perform a number of vital functions. They seal the gap between the piston and the cylinderwall, preventing combustion gases from es-

caping into the crankcase. They stabilize the piston as it travels up and down. They cool the piston by transferring three-fourths of the piston heat to the block. They meter the film of oil left on the cylinderwalls. What is most remarkable is that they perform all these tasks automatically under the most severe conditions.

There are several ring designs to choose among. Ring materials range from cast iron to ductile iron to stainless steel. Ring facings run from uncoated iron to molybdenum, chrome, or even exotic ceramic coatings. There are rectangular rings in various thicknesses, L-shaped Dykes and headland (pressure-backed) rings, and spacers that allow an engine builder to install one type of ring in a groove machined for an altogether different ring. Yet, despite this wide array of choices, ring selection falls into rather rigid categories. For high-performance street machines and bracket racing engines, the overwhelming choice is a standard 5/64- or 1/16-inch wide moly ring. High-rpm drag-racing engines favor 0.043-inch moly rings, while 0.031-inch Dykes rings with either chrome or moly faces are almost universal in Super Stock engines (drag

racing). On the dirt, 1/16-inch chrome-plated rings are practically standard equipment.

All compression rings require combustion pressure to work properly, regardless of their material or design. Rings have a certain amount of radial tension—the resistance you feel as you squeeze a ring. This radial tension

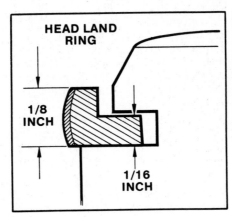

HEAD LAND RING

1/8 INCH

1/16 INCH

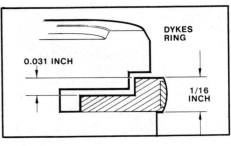

DYKES RING

0.031 INCH

1/16 INCH

A Dykes or pressure backed piston ring has an inside notch that reduces the weight of the ring and improves high-rpm performance.

Drilling gas ports is a delicate machining operation. Piston is set up in rotary table on vertical mill, then hole locations are marked with a center drill. Gas ports are then drilled with 0.040/0.060-inch diameter bit.

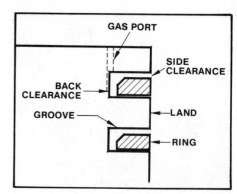

Gas ports eliminate the need for excessive side clearance by ducting cylinder pressure directly to the back of the top compression ring.

Rings must never stick out of grooves. To make sure ring has sufficient back clearance in groove, hold straight edge along skirt and top ring land; light should be visible between ring face and ruler.

keeps the ring in contact with the cylinderwall when the engine is lightly loaded. When the engine is really making power, though, it is combustion pressure that seals up the cylinders. The clearance between the rings and grooves allows the cylinder pressure to get *behind* the ring, forcing it

firmly against the cylinderwall.

This clearance between the ring and groove is called *side clearance*. In addition to sealing against the cylinderwall, the ring also seals against the groove. Almost all compression rings have a beveled edge or a tapered face. This non-uniform cross-section causes the ring to "dish," just like a dinner plate, when it is compressed. As the ring dishes, it seals against the top and bottom of the groove. To check side clearance, insert the ring in the groove and then find the feeler gauge that just fits between the two. Most compression rings require 0.002- to 0.004-inch side clearance to function properly.

The only time that less side clearance is acceptable is when the pistons have been drilled for *gas ports*. Gas ports are a means of applying combustion pressure directly to the back of the ring. When a piston is gas ported, a dozen or more small diameter holes (typically 0.040- to 0.060-inch in diameter) are drilled through the deck and dome to intersect the back of the ring groove. Since these holes supply the pressure that makes the top ring work, the side clearance can be reduced to almost nothing. By eliminating the side clearance, the ring has less opportunity to flutter at high rpm, since it is restrained by the groove itself. To take full advantage of the gas ports, a lightweight, narrow-faced 0.043-inch ring should be used. Disadvantages? Well, the gas ports will eventually fill with carbon, making

the top ring seal ineffective. This is why gas ports are used only on ultra-rpm drag-racing engines. These motors demand the highest quality ring seal, even at astronomical rpm levels, and are rebuilt frequently.

Another crucial dimension for piston rings is *back clearance*, the space behind the ring when the face is flush with the ring lands. For high-performance and racing applications, the back clearance should be as close to zero as possible. When the volume behind the ring is reduced, the gas pressure charges the ring more quickly, which improves the cylinder seal. Ring grooves in many production pistons are much deeper than they need to be. If your pistons have these extra-deep grooves, the back clearance can be reduced by using steel shim material, sold by Speed Pro and other sources. The rings must *never* protrude past the lands.

Providing the proper ring end gaps will pay big dividends in performance. A ring must be split to allow it to slip over the top of the piston; the space left where the ends of the ring meet is the *end gap*. This gap also allows the ring to expand as it is heated by the piston and the combustion gases. Ideally the ring should grow just enough to reduce the end gap to zero. The combustion pressure then has no way to escape, so more of the combustion energy is applied to pushing the piston down the cylinder bore. With perfectly round bores and the right end gaps, blowby—and the lost horsepower it represents—can be cut drastically.

When you buy a standard set of piston rings, the end gaps are invariably too large for best performance. The ring manufacturers recognize that production engine rebuilders don't take the time to tailor the ring end gaps. Consequently most ring sets will have about 0.030-inch of end gap—al-

This modified K-D rotary ring file is used to carefully trim the end of an oversize compression ring. File carefully to keep the ends of the ring absolutely parallel.

A fine-toothed file will also cut ring end gaps. Clamp file in vise and move ring along teeth. Remember to file from the outside of the ring toward the inside to prevent chipping delicate chrome or moly ring face.

One of the most important engine blueprinting operations is setting the correct piston ring end gaps. Standard rings have large gaps which allow combustion pressure to leak into crankcase; high-performance rings are available in 0.005-inch oversizes so you can tailor gaps to each cylinder. These rings often butt or overlap when first installed in the bores.

most twice as much as is necessary to accommodate normal thermal expansion. Fortunately, top quality ring makers—like TRW and Sealed Power—also realize that minimizing end gaps is an important part of engine blueprinting, so they offer ring sets that are 0.005-inch oversize. For example, you would order 4.035-inch rings for a 4.030-inch bore size. When these rings are first installed in the cylinder bore, their ends may butt or overlap. By carefully filing the ring ends, the engine builder can come up with the exact end gap he wants.

Ring end gap is measured by placing the ring squarely in the cylinder, then inserting a feeler gauge in the space left between the ends. Setting the ring end gaps is one of the last steps before the engine is assembled for the final time. The cylinder bores must be honed and cleaned; a change of only 0.00l-inch in bore diameter will increase the end gap by over 0.003-inch. When checking the end gaps, it is best to "sneak up" on the final gap dimension. This means that if you want a total end gap of 0.0l6-inch, you should start with the 0.0l3-inch feeler gauge. Then, progressively increase the gauge thickness, going from the 0.0l4- to the 0.0l5-inch thick gauge before finally inserting the 0.0l6-inch feeler. This technique ensures that the ring is in tight contact with the cylinderwall, and prevents the removal of too much material. If you cut the ring gaps too large, there's nothing to do but get another ring and start over!

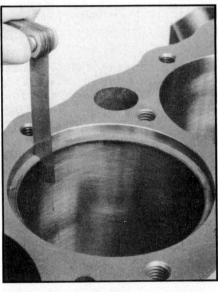

To measure end gap, insert ring into cylinder, then find feeler gauge that just fits. Start with a small gauge, then work your way up to larger ones to make sure that the ring is properly seated in the bore.

You can tailor the end gaps with a circular file made expressly for this purpose or with a standard metal file held firmly in a vise. Regardless of which tool you use, you must always cut from the outside of the ring toward the inside. This prevents chipping the molybdenum or chrome ring face. Check the straightness of your cuts frequently by squeezing the ends of the ring together and holding the ring up to a light. If you can see light seeping through the gap, because one of the ring ends is rounded or angled, carefully file the ends straight again—taking care not to let the total gap (when the ring is installed in the cylinder) become too large. When you are satisfied with all the ring gaps, use a fine whetstone to deburr the edges.

Ring should be square in the cylinder when end gap is measured. You can use a commercially available ring squaring tool like this one, or a flat-top piston inserted upside down into the bore.

After the end gaps are cut, break the sharp edges with a small whetstone or fine machinists file.

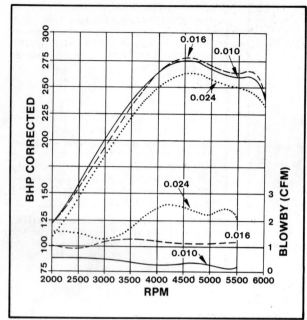

COURTESY OF SEALED POWER CORP.

This chart underlines the importance of proper piston ring end gaps to performance. Sealed Power Corporation found that reducing the end gaps from 0.024-inch to 0.016-inch added approximately 30 horsepower to a typical 350ci Chevrolet. Further reducing the end gaps to 0.010-inch hurt power because the ends of the rings were butting.

The size of the end gaps depends on the ring location and engine usage. As the rpm range and horsepower climb, the end gaps must be made larger to compensate for the greater heat they encounter. A general rule of thumb is to allow 0.004-inch of end gap for every inch of bore size for high-performance street engines. Using this formula, rings for a 4-inch bore cylinder should have 0.016-inch end gaps. Since second rings generally run much cooler than top rings, the end gaps can be closed up slightly, to 0.003-inch for every inch of cylinder diameter. The ring experts at Sealed Power Corporation have compiled the accompanying chart of recommended end gaps for typical applications.

You should resist the temptation to run ring gaps that are substantially tighter than these recommendations. If the gaps are too small, the ends of the rings will butt together. As the ring continues to expand, the ring face is forced against the cylinder wall, causing rapid wear. The ends of the rings should always be inspected when the engine is disassembled for overhaul; shiny spots are clear evidence that the ends have butted. If no shiny spots are apparent, the end gaps on the next set of rings can be reduced *slightly*—no more than 0.002-inch at a time.

End gaps for oil rings are much less critical. Most oil rings have three distinct components: two *rails* and an *expander*. The rails should be inserted in the cylinder bore to make sure that they have adequate end gaps. Since the oil ring does not seal the combustion pressure, even gaps as large as 0.030-inch are all right.

Many high-performance piston ring sets feature *low-tension* oil rings. These rings are intended to increase power output by minimizing frictional losses as the rings travel up and down the cylinders. Low-tension rings are created by deliberately mismatching the rails and expanders. For example, a standard tension oil ring for a 4.060-inch cylinder would have two rails and

You can fashion a dirt cheap piston ring holder from a scrap of lumber and a handful of nails. This will prevent mixing the rings after they have been assigned to a particular cylinder bore.

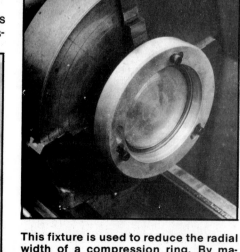

This fixture is used to reduce the radial width of a compression ring. By machining the back of a top or second ring, the tension—and thus the amount or ring "drag"—is reduced. This requires special shallow ring grooves, and should be considered a trick for serious racers only.

an expander specifically designed for a 4.060-inch bore. A so-called low-tension oil ring has the same rails, but the expander comes from a ring set designed for a 4.030-inch bore, a cylinder that is 0.030-inch smaller. To produce a "super low-tension" oil ring, an expander from a 4.000-inch bore ring set would be substituted.

These low-tension oil rings reduce internal friction, but at the cost of increasing oil consumption. Oil economy simply is not important to most owners of high-performance and racing engines. What is important, though, is keeping oil out of the combustion chambers, where it leaves deposits and fosters detonation. Engines equipped with low-tension oil rings usually require some kind of crankcase-evacuation system to help slow the migration of oil past the oil rings. The hoses often seen on racing engines that connect the valve covers, intake manifold, and header collectors are all part of an elaborate crankcase-evacuation system that is designed to improve oil control inside the motor.

You can measure the effects of ring tension with a common fish scale. To check ring drag, install the rings on a

A common fish scale measures oil ring tension as you pull the piston through the cylinder. Pull slowly so that the scale accurately records the ring drag, not the force needed to start the piston moving.

piston, then insert the piston into the cylinder bore, upside down. Push the piston to the bottom of the cylinder, then hook the fish scale to the piston pin. As you pull the piston upward, note the resistance on the scale. Don't be confused by the force needed to start the piston moving up the bore; instead, concentrate on the scale reading as the piston moves at a steady speed. By comparing the force required to pull the piston through the cylinder with different ring packages, you can quite graphically see differences in ring tension.

PINS

Even though pressed wrist pins have numerous advantages, floating pins have a racier image and are therefore more popular with performance engine builders. Floating pins simplify engine assembly and disassembly, a feature that appeals to backyard engine builders. The trick is making sure that floating pins stay in the pistons until you decide that it is time for them to come out.

Floating piston pins are held in place with either Tru-Arcs, Spiroloxs, or wire rings. Many performance pistons are machined for *double* Tru-Arcs

Double Tru-Arc or Spirolox pin retainers add an extra margin of safety for a high-rpm engine. Always install Tru-Arcs so that the sharp edge is against groove in piston and pin, with rounded edges facing each other.

A good pair of internal snap ring pliers are essential for installing and removing Tru-Arc pin retainers. Don't invite trouble by reusing Tru-Arcs; replace them at every overhaul! Spirolox are usually destroyed when you remove them, so there's no temptation to put them back into a motor.

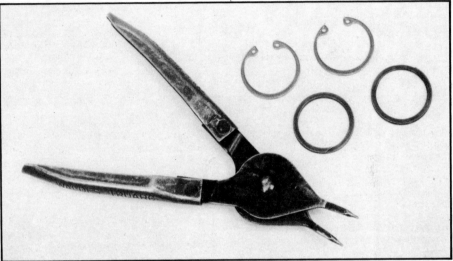

or Spiroloxs, based on the theory that a pair of retainers on each end of the pin are less likely to fall out than a single clip. With the aid of a good set of snap-ring pliers, Tru-Arcs are reasonably easy to remove and install. Spirolox, on the other hand, require a small, sharpened screwdriver and a great deal of patience to remove. Spirolox retainers are usually destroyed in the process of removing them, which at least removes the temptation to reuse them. Even though you can get a set of Tru-Arcs out of a piston without harming them, used Tru-Arcs should be discarded at every engine overhaul. These clips lose tension every time they are compressed, making them more likely to pop out on their own.

When you are preassembling the engine to check deck heights, valve clearance, and so forth, balls of masking tape will hold the wrist pins in place. Don't install the pin retainers until the engine is going together for the final time. If the pistons are machined for double Tru-Arcs, snap the two clips into the groove with their rounded edges facing each other. With a single Tru-Arc per side, the rounded edge should be against the pin, leaving the sharp edge to bite into the aluminum of the piston.

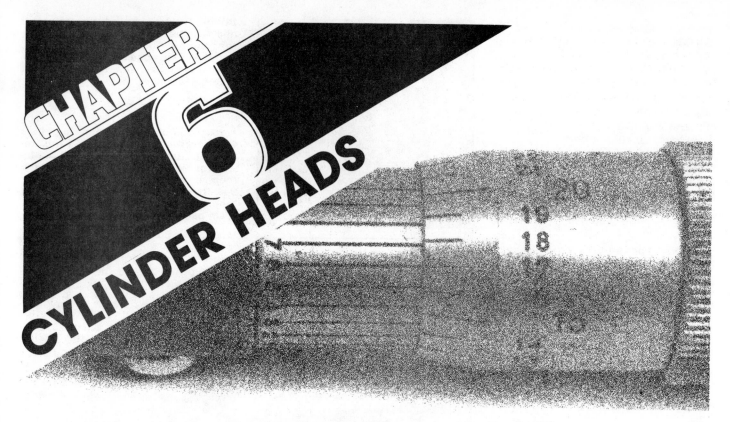

CYLINDER HEADS

An engine's cylinder head ports are the pathways to power! The air and fuel that pass through them are the sole source of energy. No matter what standard you apply to engine performance—horsepower, torque, fuel economy, or response—it is the valves, seats, and ports that are finally responsible for how well the motor works. Differences between high-performance short blocks are relatively minor; what makes one motor superior to another is likely to be the valve layout, chamber shape, and port volumes.

No book can thoroughly explain the mysteries of cylinder head porting. Porting techniques are as trendy as hair styles and musical tastes; yesterday's hot setup is today's old news. First of all, the design qualities of available head castings have a tremendous impact on what is possible and what is not. And with both the Detroit automakers and the specialty head manufacturers introducing radical new designs and revisions of old ones almost daily, the state of the art in head porting is constantly changing. For these reasons, we will concentrate on the basic blueprinting techniques that apply to *any* cylinder head: preparing the valves, seats, guides, and springs. And for those who have a compulsion to grind on cylinder heads, we will outline some simple port work that can make a substantial difference in airflow.

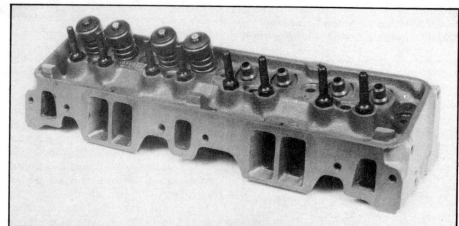

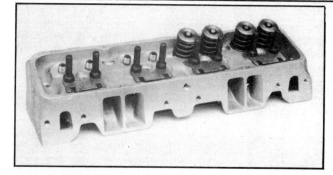

The range of cylinder head choices confronting performance enthusiasts has never been greater. Today an engine builder can select from a variety of factory and aftermarket castings in both aluminum and iron.

SELECTION & INSPECTION

Selecting and inspecting cylinder heads parallels very closely the steps involved in choosing a cylinder block. Many of the same procedures and cautions apply.

In general, late-model cylinder heads are inferior to older, Sixties-vintage iron. Current production castings have very thin metal sections, and the ports are likely to be extremely restrictive. These small runners promote high mixture velocities, even at low engine speeds, so they are favored by mileage-conscious automakers. Power, though, comes with an increase in port volume—which is why you must go back to the ample passages found in older cylinder heads if you are building a serious street performance or bracket racing engine.

For an all-out racer, however, nothing less than the very latest factory or specialty castings will do. The series of "Bow Tie" cylinder heads developed by Chevrolet, the SVO offerings from Ford, and even the so-called "corporate" smallblock heads (for the Chevrolet cylinder block) available from Pontiac all represent the latest thinking in the science of engine airflow. And when both your budget and the rulebook allow specialty castings, the racing-only designs from Dart, Brodix, Brownfield and other non-Detroit sources are vastly superior to anything you can find in a salvage yard.

If your head choices are confined to used parts, then you must look carefully before exchanging cold cash for cast iron. Cylinder heads, like blocks, are prone to cracking if they have been overheated or frozen during their lifetime. The advent of unleaded gasoline in the early Seventies prompted many automakers to induction-harden the valve seats in cylinder heads. This allows the seats to survive without the lubrication provided by small amounts of lead—but this process also made the seats much more susceptible to cracks, especially on the hot exhaust side. This is another point in favor of early, "pre-smog" head castings. Cylinder heads can be checked for cracks with Magnaflux inspection or by pressure testing the water jackets, as discussed in the chapter on cylinder blocks.

A thorough head inspection should also include a close look at the valve seats and guides. If you have a choice, avoid heads that have already had a valve job performed on them. During a typical quick-and-dirty valve job, the seats are ground with little concern for airflow characteristics. The usual result is that the valves are "sunk" in the chambers. This reduces compression, by increasing the combustion chamber volume. In addition, the bumps and ridges left around the seat by a careless machinist can disrupt the flow of air around the valve head. It may be difficult to find this telltale evidence of a previous valve job in a cylinder head that is coated with baked-on carbon. When you go head hunting, take along a valvespring compressor and remove several valves. If you find distinct ridges surrounding the seats, chances are good that someone has already worked over—and perhaps ruined—the castings.

A sharp parting line around a seat

Casting numbers are the key to spotting desirable cylinder heads. Heads with the same casting numbers may have different valve diameters, however.

indicates that at some time in the past it has been repaired with an *insert*. An insert is a metal ring that is pressed into the head to repair a damaged or cracked seat. There is nothing intrinsically bad about a seat insert; after all, most aluminum heads are outfitted with seat inserts at the factory. However, you have no way of knowing if the insert was installed properly or what type of damage it conceals. Unless the casting in question is extremely rare or valuable, it is probably better to continue your hunt than to buy someone else's problems.

A little preliminary research can make your head shopping more successful. Every brand of performance engine has some prized head castings. For example, smallblock Chevrolet enthusiasts seek out "fuel-injection" heads and "turbo" castings; Mopar fans covet various W-2 and Stage heads, while the Ford contingent stalk Boss and Cleveland components. Unfortunately, a reputation for high performance is likely to add a premium to the price of a set of cylinder heads. You can, however, cut the high cost of hot rodding by recognizing that the real distinction between a set of high-priced heads and cheaper castings may be only an insignificant difference in valve sizes or combustion chamber volume.

Among smallblock Chevy head castings, for example, the early large-port heads with 2.02-inch intake valves—usually identified as "fuel-injection" heads—can fetch twice the price of a pair of similar castings with I.94-inch intakes. In truth, the heads with smaller valves are really the better buy. They have the same ports and chambers as the big-valve castings. And if you upgrade them by installing larger valves, your machinist will have virgin metal to work with when he grinds the critical valve seats. This is just one instance of smaller being better—and a bargain, too.

Before starting work on your chosen cylinder heads, a thorough cleaning is in order. An overnight stay in a hot tank (cast iron heads only!) or some time on a jet-cleaner turntable will remove most of the grease and grime. Carbon deposits in the chambers and ports can be dislodged with a wire brush mounted in a drill. A glass beader will blast the runners clean while simultaneously deburring and smoothing the passages. Use caution, though, if your heads are destined for a racing engine that requires stock cylinder heads; the tech inspectors will be looking for ports that are suspiciously smooth. If you glass bead the heads, take extra care to get all the grit out of the bolt holes and valve

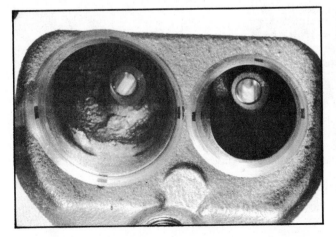

Three-angle valve seats have become standard for most high-performance and competition engines. Although the preferred angles and widths may vary—depending on the type of cylinder head and the intended use—all three-angle seats have a bottom cut, a seat cut (which seals the valve face), and a top cut.

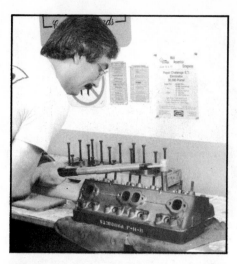

The search for precision has led some cylinder head specialists to use torque plates when grinding the valve seats. Here Darell Wikle bolts a head to a thick steel plate. This recreates the stresses in the casting which occur when the head is installed on the block.

Machined reliefs in the torque plate provide clearance for the grinding stones. A head gasket is sandwiched between the plate and the deck surface.

guides before proceeding.

VALVES & SEATS

The seats are where the valves meet the cylinder heads. Whether the head castings came out of a factory parts box or a station wagon with l00,000 miles on it, the time and effort lavished on preparing the seats properly will be well spent. The seats are the most critical area in the engine in terms of airflow. Every molecule of fuel and oxygen the engine burns must pass through these critical points.

Since air is invisible, it is some-times difficult for beginning engine builders (and even some experienced ones) to imagine how it moves through a motor. It may be helpful, therefore, to visualize the air as if it were a liquid. If you can picture a wild river brimming with rocks and boulders, you will have a good idea of the obstacles in the pathway of the air/fuel mixture as it winds through the head ports. As the water in this imaginary river rushes downstream, it forms turbulent whirl-pools and eddies, as well as stagnant pools where there is little movement. These white water rapids may be spectacular, but they make river travel difficult. A smoothly flowing river channel seems tame in comparison, but it does a better job of moving large volumes of water. Like the water in a river, the air/fuel mixture that flows through an engine has mass. Obstacles in the path and quick changes in direction cause it to become turbulent; it forms invisible swirls and whirlpools. As a result, fuel droplets, which are heavier than the air molecules that surround them, separate from the main flow and collect in pockets, like driftwood along the banks of a river. Since this upsets the delicate balance of fuel and air that is needed for optimum power, engine performance suffers. So the goal of most cylinder head work is to create the conditions that allow the "river" of fuel and air to move through the ports as smoothly as possible.

Valve seats in factory-installed heads are designed for durability, not maximum airflow. Factory valve seats are ground at only one angle—usually 45°, although some automakers use 30 or 37° seats. This single angle causes the air and fuel (or exhaust gases) to make an abrupt change in direction as they flow past the valve head. And, as you might expect, this sharp turn causes problems. The flow becomes turbulent, restricting the

Steel cutters remove material quickly when installing oversize valves or opening up the "throat" just below the valve seat.

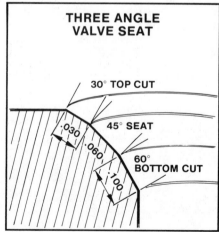

THREE ANGLE VALVE SEAT

30° TOP CUT

45° SEAT

60° BOTTOM CUT

.030

.060

.100

A typical three-angle valve job consists of a series of cuts which will promote a smooth flow of gases between the ports and combustion chambers.

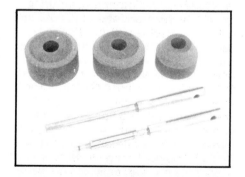

Grinding high-performance valve seats requires a selection of stones and pilots. Each stones is cut to produce one distinct angle of the valve job (from left to right: 30-degree top cut, 45-degree seat, 60-degree bottom cut). Pilots for grinding stones must fit guides tightly to ensure that seats are concentric with valve stems; expandable and oversize pilots are available.

Stones are dressed to the desired angle with a diamond-tipped cutter.

First step in performing high-performance valve job is to clean guides and insert pilot. Pilot remains in place until all three angles have been ground.

Stone is mounted on holder and installed over pilot.

amount of air that can enter or leave the combustion chamber. Fuel droplets fall out of the airstream and collect on the port walls and valve heads, which causes the air/fuel mixture to fluctuate. Surely, you say, there must be a better way to grind a valve seat. And indeed there is. The *three-angle* valve job has become nearly universal among builders of high-performance engines.

Each of the three angles has a distinct function. The *bottom cut* is typically ground at a 60° angle; it marks the beginning of the transition from the valve bowl to the combustion chamber. The width of this bottom cut depends on how much metal the machinist has to work with beneath the seat, although a figure of around 0.100-inch is typical.

The actual *valve seat*, which seals against the valve face, is ground at a 45° angle. The width of this seat will vary according to the machinist's preferences and the intended usage. Darrell Wilke, the proprietor of Wilke Performance Specialties in Wichita, KS, performed the cylinder head and valve work pictured here. His years of experience have shown that 0.040-inch wide intake seats and 0.055-inch wide exhaust seats work well with the limited valvespring pressure of a street or bracket racing engine equipped with a flat-tappet camshaft. With the higher spring pressures that accompany a roller cam, wider 0.060- and 0.080-inch seats are more resistant to "pounding out."

In general, it is good to remember that a narrow seat usually flows somewhat better than a wide seat, but it is not as durable. Also, heat in the valve head transfers to the cylinder head through the seat, so a wide seat helps to cool the valve. This is why exhaust

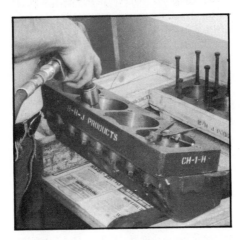

Grinding stone is spun with high-speed pneumatic or electric driver.

Valve seat indicator confirms accuracy and concentricity of finished valve job.

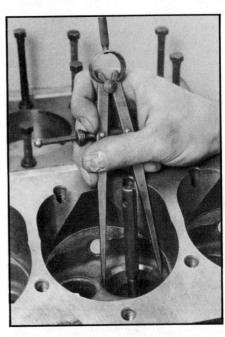

Machinist constantly checks his progress by measuring seat diameter with dividers. Seats in used heads are ground until all pits and grooves are removed, then narrowed with top and bottom cuts. Seats should be as high as possible for best airflow.

Moroso valve depth checker allows engine builder to equalize valve seat heights. This produces consistent valve-to-piston clearances and uniform combustion chamber volumes.

Valve facing machine grinds new seats on valve heads. Valve rotates against abrasive wheel while cutting fluid carries away grit and metal particles. Valve facer can also regrind seat angles and back cut valve heads.

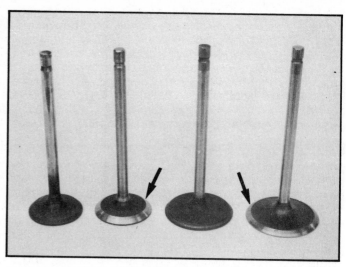

Intake and exhaust valves are back cut to eliminate sharp edges under heads which disrupt airflow.

seats are usually ground slightly wider than intake seats.

A *top cut* is the finishing touch for a three-angle valve seat. The angle of this cut can run from a shallow l5° to a relatively steep 37°, depending on the condition of the cylinder heads and the depth of the valve seats. This top cut narrows the seat to match the diameter of the face of the valve head, and eliminates the sharp edge where the seat meets the combustion chamber. If the cylinder head is new, or if oversize valves are being installed, this top cut may be omitted to keep the seat as high as possible.

A *radiused valve seat* is a refinement of the three-angle seat. This type of seat is sometimes used in racing cylinder heads. Actually, the seat itself is not radiused—although it may be narrowed considerably. Instead, the angles above and below it are carefully rounded. The valve seat remains at a 45° angle, but the top and bottom cuts are blended by hand, using a hard abrasive roll in a high-speed grinder. Some head porters also use specially prepared grinding stones to radius the approaches to the seat. A radiused valve seat has no sharp edges to disrupt the airflow; instead, there is just a gradual transition from the combustion chamber to the port. The cost of preparing radiused seats is usually higher than a simple three-angle valve job because of the skillful handwork required to blend the approaches without disturbing the seat itself. For any street or moderate competition engine, radiused seats are probably an unnecessary luxury.

New valves require very little preparation. The faces are normally pre-machined to the engine manufacturer's specified angle. If, however, the angle of the valve seats in the cylinder head has been changed, then the valves must be reground. This is required when an unusual seat angle (30° or 37°, for example) is replaced by a conventional three-angle valve job with 45° valve seats. Used valves must be refaced in a valve grinding machine to remove pits and wear marks. Regrinding a valve narrows the *margin*—the straight portion of the valve head. As much of the margin as possible should be preserved when refacing valves; if the margin is ground away when refacing a valve, then the valve should be discarded and replaced with a new piece. A knife-edged valve head is weak, and the sharp outer edge hurts flow.

Stock valves can usually benefit from a practice called *back cutting*. Production valves often have excessively wide faces and sharp edges behind the valve heads. Both features restrict airflow. A valve grinding machine is used to cut down the underside of the valve head, usually at a 30° angle. This both removes the sharp edge and narrows the valve face. The amount of material that can be safely removed depends on the shape of the valve head. The width of the remaining valve face should always be slightly larger than the seat width in the cylinder head. Valves that are designed for racing or high-performance applications generally have much narrower faces than stock valves, and usually require only a slight back cut to narrow their faces to match the width of the valve seats.

VALVE LAPPING

The operations described up to this point—seat grinding, valve facing, and back cutting—all require expensive machinery and considerable knowhow. There is one head preparation chore, however, that demands no exotic equipment. *Valve lapping* is a task you can do on a garage workbench. It will provide the best possible valve seal, and allow you to check the workmanship of your machinist.

To lap the valves in a cylinder head, you will need some extra fine *lapping compound* (Clover 3A to 6A is recommended by many experts) and a valve lapping stick, which is nothing but a wooden dowel with a suction cup on the end. (Most auto parts stores stock these items.) Add a little water to the lapping compound to make a thick paste, then smear the compound around the circumference of the valve face. Squirt a few drops of oil into the valve guide, then insert the valve into

Lapping valves is an easy way to check condition of valve seats. Mix water with fine lapping compound to form paste, then apply compound to valve head.

the head. Wet the suction cup on the lapping stick and apply it to the valve head. Twirl the stick between your palms while lightly pressing the valve against the seat. After a few seconds of lapping, lift the valve and rotate it 90°, then continue lapping.

When you feel the abrasive lapping compound no longer cutting, pull the valve out of the head, wipe off the compound, and examine the face. You will see a light gray ring on the valve face where it was rubbing against the seat. This ring indicates the point of contact between the valve face and the seat. It should be of uniform width all the way around the valve, and it should be located near the outer edge of the valve face. If the gray ring is inconsistent or disappears entirely on one side of the face, the valve has been faced improperly or the valve stem is bent.

You can also check the valve seat after lapping. The lapping compound will mark the seat with a light gray line where it contacts the valve head. Again, this gray area should be consistent in width, and it should completely encircle the seat. If the ring is narrow or faint in spots, repeat the lapping procedure; then re-examine the seat. If the lap marks still show spotty contact between the valve and seat, then it is almost certain that the valve will not seal properly when the engine is running. The pressure of the valve spring *might* distort the valve head enough to seal the seat, but then again it might not. If lapping the valves reveals a problem, it is time to have a heart-to-heart talk with your machinist about the situation.

Lapping the valves is an excellent way to freshen up the valve seal in a racing engine. Lapping allows you to visually check the contact between the valve faces and seats, and will quickly indicate a valve that has bent or a seat that has pounded out. Lapping the valves every time the engine is overhauled will prevent unnecessary valve jobs by allowing you to constantly monitor the condition of the valves and seats. Regrinding the seats should be a last resort, since every valve job sinks the valves a little farther down into the ports, and this will generally hurt flow and engine output.

VALVE GUIDES

If valves moved only up and down, the *valve guides* would last forever. Unfortunately, a valve also moves sideways a tiny bit as it opens and closes, thanks to the force exerted by the rockerarm as it sweeps across the valve stem tip. Even overhead cam systems, which eliminate the rockerarm altogether, are hard on valve guides; in these engines, it is the rotating cam lobe that gives the valve stem a sideways shove.

Cast iron is a reasonably good valve guide material, which is why most automakers simply drill holes in the head casting for the valve stems. Aluminum, on the other hand, is a terrible valve guide material, so aluminum heads always need some type of *valve guide inserts* to support the valve stems. Cast iron, brass, bronze, and aluminum-bronze inserts can all be found in various aluminum cylinder heads. These valve guide inserts are pressed into the head with an interference fit. The guides in some aluminum cylinder heads—notably late model big-block Chevrolet castings—are notorious for working loose, and the only solution is to pin the guides in place to prevent them from falling out.

High-lift camshafts increase the loads on the valve guides. As the cam profile becomes more radical, the arc of the rockerarm grows larger. (At the valve lifts that are common in current racing and high-performance engines, the end of the rockerarm can come very close to the edge of the valve stem tip.) And, unfortunately, adding a roller to the end of the rocker—as is commmon on high-performance rockerarms—does little to reduce the side loads that wear out the valve guides. This is why many experts recommend that the valve guides in brand new cast iron cylinder heads should be lined with some type of bronze insert.

Two types of inserts are commonly used by cylinder head specialists. The Winona brand *bronzewall guides* are similar to Helicoil thread inserts; the original valve guide is threaded with a self-piloting tool, and the spiral-like Winona insert is screwed into the guide. The insert is then swedged to lock it in place, and finally reamed and honed to produce the proper valve stem clearance. The popular K-line *bronze inserts* resemble thin bronze tubes. This type of insert does not require threading the inside of the existing valve guide, but the installation

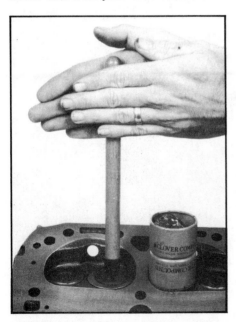

Lap valves by spinning stick between palms. Lift and turn valve occasionally to distribute compound over seat and valve head mating surfaces.

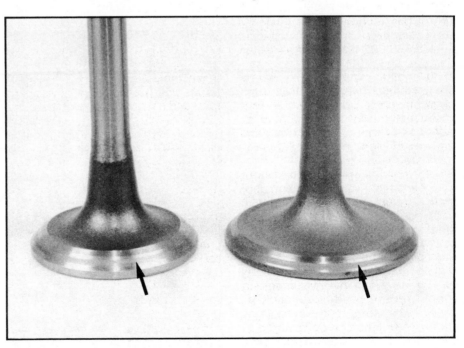

Dull gray line indicates contact area between valves and seats. If contact is spotty or inconsistent, valve may be bent or seat not concentric with valve guide.

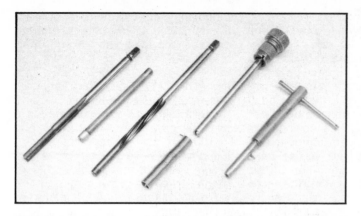

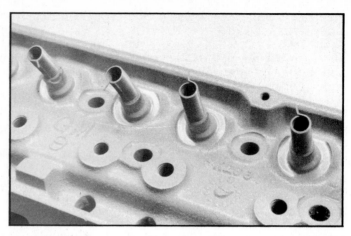

Winona bronze valve guide liners are similar to spiral Helicoil thread inserts. Valve guide is threaded with self-piloting cutter, then liner is installed and swedged in place. Guides are then reamed or honed to final size.

Extra-long spiral inserts are trimmed and then pinned to top of valve guide.

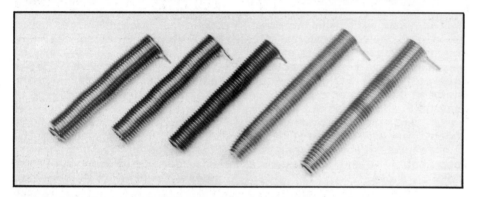

Bronze wall guides are available in a variety of diameters. Three inserts on left are for standard 3/8-, 11/32-, and 5/16-inch guides. Thick-wall guides (right) adapt valves with small diameter stems to standard guides.

procedure is quite similar to outfitting a cylinder head with Winona guides.

These specialty valve guide inserts offer several advantages. First, they are very kind to valve stems; scuffing and galling is almost nonexistent. Darrel has found that the guide-to-stem clearance can be reduced to as little as 0.0006-inch for drag-racing engines and 0.0008-inch for endurance engines when Winona inserts are installed. These relatively tight stem clearances prolong valve seat life by restricting the movement of the valve head. He also feels that the spiral grooves of the Winona guide inserts lubricate the valve stem.

Bronzewall stem liners also make it possible to use valves with standard stem diameters even in heads with badly worn guides. Since stainless steel and titanium high-performance valves are not available with oversize stems, this is an important feature to consider (especially if a lot of money has already been invested in porting the cylinder head). In addition, bronzewall inserts are replaceable, so the valve guides can be restored to like-new condition after a long season of racing.

Finally, a special *thick-wall insert* makes it practical to reduce the diameter of the valve stem. This lightens the valve, and, in some cylinder heads, improves flow. Thick-wall inserts are available from Manley to adapt valves with 0.3125-inch (5/16) stems to 0.34375-inch (11/32) and 0.375-inch (3/8) diameter valve guides.

PORTING FOR STREET PERFORMANCE

Modifying cylinder heads for all-out racing has become such a specialized talent that it is best left to professional head porters. Without an expensive *flow bench* to monitor the effects of changes in port design and without constant feedback from successful racers, it is extremely difficult to determine whether your grinding and shaping is really making an improvement. Prices for professionally ported cylinder heads range from $1,000 to over $10,000, depending on the extent and difficulty of the work that is performed. At the high end of this scale, the entire cylinder head may be remanufac-

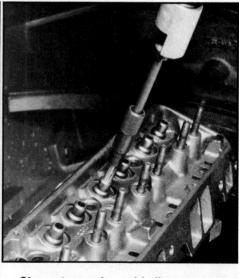

Sleeve-type valve guide liners are used by many engine builders. These are installed by first reaming the guide oversize, then driving the split liner into the head.

Silicon/bronze guides are often installed in aluminum cylinder heads. They are also used to recondition cast iron heads when the original guides are in such poor condition that Winona or K-line inserts cannot be used.

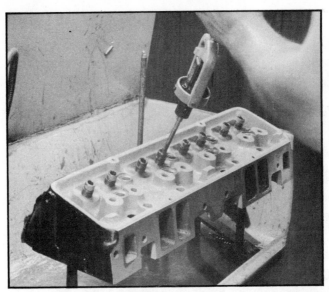

Valve guides should be honed to provide correct stem-to-guide clearance. Proper clearance depends on valve guide material and the engine's intended use.

Sunnen valve guide bore gauge is calibrated by inserting two valve stems in setting fixture.

tured by welding and relocating the ports. But for a street performance, bracket-racing, marine, or limited oval-track engine, such radical measures are unnecessary. In fact, even if you have never tried your hand at porting before, you can achieve measurable improvements in port flow with an afternoon's work.

The most important area in any cylinder head port is the *valve bowl* directly behind the seats. In most cylinder heads, the valve bowls are machined at the same time that the seats are cut. The factory tooling almost invariably leaves sharp edges that are very disruptive to airflow on both the intake and exhaust sides of the head. By simply blending and smoothing these sharp edges with a small grinding stone or a carbide burr, the runners will be able to move more air with less turbulence. The trick is to remove as little metal as possible while smoothing the flow path; it's important not to disturb the "venturi" beneath the valve seats where the valve bowl narrows. It is best to do this work *before* the valve seats are ground to eliminate the risk of ruining a seat with a slip of the grinder.

The second area to concentrate on is the *short-side radius*—the bump in the runner floor where the gases "turn the corner" as they enter or leave the combustion chamber. This radius is the shortest distance between the valve and the port entry, and it is where the airflow is concentrated at low valve lifts. Again, by simply rounding and blending this radius as shown in the accompanying photos, a startling improvement in port flow can be achieved.

The final step in do-it-yourself head

Dial indicator measures stem clearance and checks taper in valve guide.

porting is to match the intake runners to a manifold gasket. This operation will not dramatically increase the airflow capacity, but it will make it much easier to match the cylinder head ports to the intake manifold passages later. Using an intake manifold gasket as a template, scribe around the port entries, taking care to keep the gasket aligned with the cylinder head bolt holes. As you square up and straighten the entries with a stone or burr, you should grind no more than 0.500-inch into the port.

Do *not* match the exhaust ports to a header gasket. An intentional mismatch between the exhaust port exits and the primary header pipes (or exhaust manifolds), creates a "reversion dam." This sharp edge around the exhaust port opening helps prevent burned gases from re-entering the combustion chamber as pulses travel back and forth through the exhaust system. Since exhaust gases will not burn again, the steps taken to reduce exhaust-gas contamination of the fresh charge in the cylinder will increase power!

91

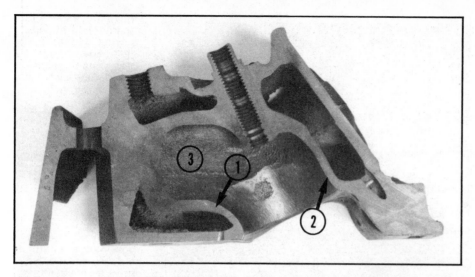

High-performance engines can benefit from simple port work in the bowl just beneath valve seats. Cylinder head section illustrates effective porting technique for street performance. Critical "short-side radius" (l) is carefully rounded to provide smooth turn from port to valve head. Sharp edges in valve bowl (2) are removed to prevent disruption of incoming air/fuel mixture. Intake runners (3) are not modified; rough surface helps atomize fuel droplets, while small cross-section keeps air velocity high.

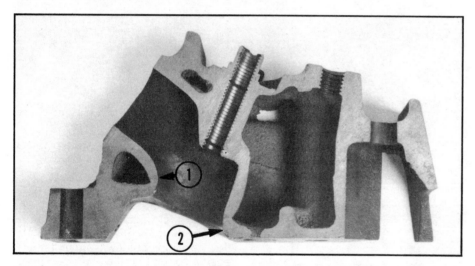

Similar treatment on exhaust side improves cylinder scavenging. Rounded short side radius (1) reduces turbulence in port, while small venturi under seat (2) improves flow around valve head.

Intake ports are matched to manifold by squaring runner entry. Remove minimum amount of metal necessary to smooth transition between head and manifold.

MILLING

There are two reasons to *mill* a cylinder head. The first is to straighten and true the deck surface. Like engine blocks, cylinder heads "season" with use. After the fresh casting is machined on the factory production line the metal tends to "relax," causing the deck surface to curve and bend. Also, a head that has been severely overheated may be warped or distorted. Since a perfectly flat deck is essential for long head gasket life, a modest clean-up cut on the cylinder heads should be a part of your engine blueprinting regimen. Unless the head is badly warped, a 0.005-inch cut will usually straighten the deck surface.

Milling a head also reduces the

volume of the combustion chambers, which in turn raises the compression ratio. As the section on computing compression points out, combustion chamber volume is a major factor in the compression equation. The exact amount of metal that must be removed from the deck surface to bring the chamber volumes down to a specified volume depends on the size and shape of the combustion chambers. The rule of thumb for a wedge-type smallblock Chevrolet head is that cutting the head 0.004-inch reduces the chamber volume by approximately one cubic centimeter. Thus if you wanted to bring down the chamber volume by 5.0, you would ask your machinist to cut 0.020-inch off the head deck surface (5.0 x 0.004 = 0.020).

When the heads on a V-type engine are milled, the horizontal distance between the heads, sometimes called the "valley," becomes smaller. To compensate for this change, and to maintain correct alignment with the intake manifold bolt holes and runners, the intake side of the cylinder head or the manifold itself should also be milled. Cutting 0.010-inch from the deck surface of a smallblock Chevy head, for example, requires milling 0.012-inch off the sides and 0.017-inch off the bottom of the intake manifold. Some manufacturers provide information on how much to cut the intake manifold to match milled heads; however, if you are using a specialty intake manifold or ported cylinder heads, this step is probably unnecessary. In these instances, you can simply grind the intake runners to match the cylinder head ports. Bolt-hole misalignment problems can be solved by enlarging the manifold bolt holes and using large, flat washers under the manifold fasteners.

There are limits to how much a head can be milled. Whenever metal is removed from the deck surface of a cylinder head, the head casting is weakened to some extent. Since many late-model cylinder heads have particularly thin decks, removing a substantial amount of iron can invite cracks. Also, the intake valve seat is located very close to the deck surface in a typical wedge-type combustion chamber. So if the head is milled severely, the edge of the intake seat may be cut away. This can be remedied by regrinding and lowering the seat, but this has the undesirable side effect of sinking and shrouding the intake valve.

An ingenious solution to these problems was developed in the mid-Seventies with a technique called *angle milling*. When a cylinder head is milled conventionally, it is set up in the grinder or surfacer so that metal is removed evenly across its deck. When a head is angle milled, however, it is intentionally cocked in the milling machine so that more metal is cut off one side of the head than the other.

In a typical angle milling setup, the exhaust side of the head might be cut as much as 0.125-inch, while the side closest to the intake manifold is left untouched. This would be called a "zero-to-125 cut" and would reduce the volume of an average combustion chamber by approximately 10cc. Of course, other angle cuts are also possible—some aluminum big-block Chevy heads withstand a radical "zero-to-250" cut, in which 0.250-inch of metal is trimmed off the exhaust side of the head!

Angle milling eliminates two of the drawbacks of straight milling. Since the majority of the metal is removed from the exhaust side of the head, the deck surface is not dangerously weakened. Also, the intake valve seat is less likely to be disturbed when a head is angle milled.

After a head has been angle milled, the bosses around the head bolt holes must be *spotfaced*. This prevents the head bolts (or studs) from cocking to one side as they are tightened down. Also, the intake manifold surface of the head must be milled to restore it to the correct angle, since angle milling a head "tilts" the manifold surface. If the intake side of the head is not resurfaced, the manifold will never seal properly.

Although most cylinder heads have a 90° angle between the deck and intake manifold flange, there are some notable exceptions. Smallblock Chevrolet heads, for example, have an 80° included angle. The extra set-up time required to angle mill a cylinder head, along with the extra labor involved in spotfacing the bolt holes and correcting the angle of the intake manifold surface, means that the cost of angle milling will often be two or three times the price of conventional milling. But when you are trying to coax the last bit of compression from a wedge-type cylinder casting, angle milling is a performance bargain.

MEASURING PORT VOLUME

One of the real advances in engine building in the past decade is the growing appreciation of *port volume* as a major performance factor. Racers and hot rodders have long had an understanding that "big ports" were better

Milling a cylinder head straightens the deck surface and reduces the volume of the combustion chambers. When a head is angle milled, it is intentionally cocked so the cutters will remove more material from one side. The intake manifold surface must also be milled to restore the original angle.

After a head has been angle milled, the head bolt holes must be spotfaced so they will be parallel to the deck surface. In extreme cases, the bolt holes may have to be enlarged as well.

for high-rpm horsepower and that "little ports" boosted low-rpm torque. By measuring the exact volume of the intake runners in question, these size differences can be stated with accuracy.

Measuring port volume is simple. You will need a basic chamber cc'ing kit: a burette or graduated cylinder, solvent, and a plexiglass plate. Install a valve in the port to be measured and seal the seat with a light coat of grease. Prop the head on a bench so that the port entry is level. Fill the port to the brim with solvent, checking for leaks around the valve stem and seat. Note how many cc's of solvent were needed to fill the runner—the answer is the true port volume.

If you measure a selection of cylinder heads, you are likely to find a wide variation in port volumes between even supposedly identical castings. Selecting heads on the basis of port size has been one of the closely

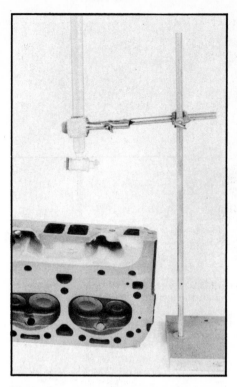

The volume of a cylinder head port can be quickly measured by filling it with liquid from a burette or graduated cylinder.

guarded secrets of winning racers in the Stock and Super Stock drag-racing classes, where the rulebook insists on unmodified heads. The same technology works well for a low-budget street performance or bracket-racing motor; you might as well use the heads with the largest runners you can find. Size differences that are difficult to see become quite clear when you read the numbers off the burette scale.

Comparing ports on the basis of volume is not a foolproof standard, be-

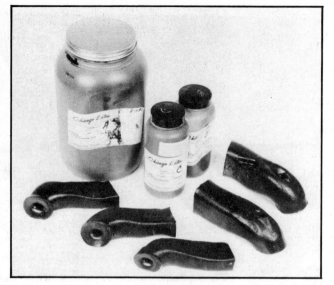

Port molds are made by filling the runners with flexible latex rubber. These molds make differences in port shapes quite apparent. They can also be sliced for quick comparisons of cross-sectional area at various points in the runner.

cause the *shape* of the runner may be more important than the size! This is especially true of cylinder heads with ported or modified passages. If you visit the shop of a successful Pro Stock or NASCAR racing team, chances are you will find a workbench littered with *port molds*. These soft-rubber castings offer a graphic representation of port curves and contours. When you are peering down a port, it may be difficult to see what makes one port different—or better—than another. But with two molds sitting side-by-side on the workbench, the variations are easy to spot.

Port molds are easy to make. You will need a latex rubber kit (available by mail from Chicago Latex Products). Mix the ingredients according to the instructions, then pour the liquid rubber into a port that has been coated with WD-40 (the WD-40 prevents the

rubber from sticking to the runner walls). In several hours, the latex will harden to the consistency of a rubber eraser. The best way to remove the latex is to pull it out through the valve opening. It may take some effort to work it past the valve guide, but once it is loose it will come out easily. By taking molds of various port contours and comparing the on-track performance produced by the ported heads, you can eventually sort out and understand what kind of port characteristics a particular engine prefers. And this information just might provide the winning edge!

SPRING SEATS

Stock valvesprings work well on a low-rpm engine, but a racing or high-performance motor needs something stronger. The valvesprings are responsible for keeping the valvetrain under control. A performance cam profile opens the valves faster, holds them open longer, and closes them quicker than a standard cam grind. You don't have to be a camshaft engineer to understand that this dramatically increases the spring requirements. If the springs do not have enough tension to ensure that the valvetrain precisely follows the cam lobes, then the valves will float—usually with dire results.

Making a spring stiffer usually means making it bigger. There are only three alternatives for a manufacturer when designing a stronger spring: make it out of better material, increase the size of the coils, or increase the number of coils. When a spring is intended to withstand the stress of racing, usually all three tactics are used. This is why exotic *Vasco Jet* and *Carpenter steel* alloys are the preferred materials for racing val-

The spring seats on many cylinder heads must be machined to accommodate large diameter valvesprings. Many cam companies rent or sell cutters to enlarge the seats.

vesprings. It also explains why large diameter two- and three-coil springs are standard equipment on high-rpm engines.

Obviously there are some potential problems when you increase both the valvespring outer diameter and overall length. Smallblock Chevrolets, for example, are equipped at the factory with 1.250-inch diameter valvesprings that exert less than 200 pounds of pressure. But on a smallblock racing engine, the springs may measure 1.625 inches in diameter and apply over 600 pounds of force! Fitting these oversize springs requires modifying the cylinder heads and beefing up the entire valvetrain to withstand the additional high-rpm forces. Of course, not every engine needs monster valvesprings: a hot street, bracket, marine or limited-oval-track engine will be content with an inexpensive dual-spring setup. But even a moderate increase in spring size usually requires some additional machining of the cylinder heads before the over-size springs can be mounted to the heads!

Nearly every camshaft company sells—and in some cases, rents—spring seat cutters. These cutters have a pilot that centers the tool on the valve guide and tough carbide tips that will readily plunge mill the spring seats in either aluminum or cast iron heads. Combination cutters are also available that will machine the top of the valve guide for Teflon valve seals at the same time they enlarge the diameter of the spring seat. All that's necessary to accomplish this job is the proper cutter (several sizes are available), a 1/2-inch drill motor, and a steady hand.

There are some pitfalls to avoid when enlarging the spring pockets. The most common problem is "striking water"—cutting through to the internal coolant passages. This is a serious problem with early cylinder head castings. However, in recent years Detroit designers have finally acknowledged this problem—of course, this is only a "problem" with heads that are being modified for racing and high-performance use—and many of the late-model "off-road" or "racing-only" cylinder heads have unique water jackets that eliminate or greatly reduce this problem.

Early Chevrolet heads, like the desirable fuel-injection castings, are notorious for breaking through—especially the spring seats at the very ends of the cylinder heads—and cutting the seats on these heads is very risky. Nonetheless, there are two workable solutions to this limitation.

Spring seats can be cut with a large hand drill, but a vertical mill generally does a neater job. Verify that the springs and shims sit flat on their new seats.

The first is to *step cut* the spring seats by inserting a spring shim under the cutter. The tool enlarges the seat diameter, but the shim limits how deeply it can cut into the seat. The second way to prevent hitting water on these heads is to radius the edge of the cutter blade. This trick allows you (or your machinist) to machine the spring seats to the full depth required for most valvesprings, while still avoiding the water passages lurking behind the corners of the spring pockets. The bottom coil of the valvesprings should then be rounded with a grinding wheel to match the radius of the modified seat.

If you are deepening the spring seats as well as enlarging them, then a mill should be used for this machine work. Cutting the spring seats with a vertical mill allows the machinist to equalize the depth of the pockets so that all the springs will have the same installed height. When deepening the valve pockets with a hand drill, there is a danger of the tool chattering and leaving an uneven spring seat. With a mill, it is much easier to control the rate at which the spring cutter removes material, so chattering is eliminated.

This job is really pretty straightforward and it can be completed in a home workshop. However, most cylinder head shops don't charge very much to do this type of work. A topnotch shop will probably use a mill to do the job, ensuring that all the pockets are finished smoothly and identically. In the long run, it may be easier to just let a professional do this job.

SPRING PRESSURE

Taking the time to set up and check the valvesprings is an essential step in

Most shops use a Rimac machine to measure valvespring pressure. The spring is compressed to the installed height and the resultant seat pressure (closed) is indicated. If the pressure is below specifications, hardened steel shims are inserted under the spring.

engine blueprinting. Despite the spring manufacturers' best efforts, there is a great deal of variation between different batches of springs—and even between springs that are part of the same set. Springs that have less tension than the design standards will contribute to valve float, while springs that are stiffer than the recommended specifications can cause a flat-tappet cam to wear rapidly.

Spring tension is measured at two points. *Seat pressure* is the static pressure when the valve is closed; *valve-open pressure* is the force exerted by the spring when the valve is at maximum lift. A spring can meet the specified tension for seat pressure, yet it may not have enough open pressure—and vice versa. Before a spring is installed, the tension should be checked at both points.

The most common device for measuring spring pressure is a *Rimac machine*. This tool resembles an arbor press, with a lever that compresses the spring and a scale that indicates the pressure. Any well-equipped cylinder head shop should have a Rimac machine, but it is a rather expensive tool for most part-time engine builders. Inexpensive hydraulic testers are available from specialty tool supplies. These hydraulic testers are not as convenient to use, since the spring must be compressed with a bench vise—but they are quite a bit cheaper. As a last resort, you can improvise a spring tester with a bathroom scale and a drill press, as shown in the accompanying photos.

To check seat pressure, you must first measure the *installed height* of the spring when the valve is closed. This is the distance between the spring seat and the bottom of the retainer. Insert the valve in the guide, then place the retainer and locks over the stem without the spring in place. Pull up on the retainer firmly, then measure from the retainer to the spring seat with a dial caliper or small steel ruler. Note the distance to the *top* of the retainer, which is the installed height plus the retainer thickness. Then remove the retainer, place it on top of the assigned spring, and insert the pair in the testing machine. Compress the spring and retainer assembly until the overall length equals the dimension you just noted on the cylinder head. The reading on the tester scale is the seat pressure of the spring.

Before measuring the open pressure, you must compute the spring height when the valve is fully opened. Subtract the *net valve lift* from the *seat-to-retainer dimension*. For example, if the distance from the spring seat to the top of the retainer with the valve closed is 2.000 inches, and the total valve lift is 0.500-inch, then the open pressure should be measured with the spring compressed to 1.500 inches. Compress the spring in the tester to this dimension and note the reading.

If either the seat or open pressure is below specs, the spring must be shimmed. Spring shims are commonly available in 0.015-, 0.030-, and 0.060-inch thicknesses. Add shims under the spring until both the seat and open pressure meet the recommended specifications.

Always use *hardened* shims under high-performance valvesprings; the sharp coil ends and flat steel dampers will quickly chew up unhardened shims. Also remember, valvesprings and dampers will quickly gouge unprotected aluminum cylinder heads; always use at least one hardened shim, or a hardened steel spring cup, under springs installed on aluminum heads.

The final step is to check for *coil bind*. Coil bind occurs when the wire coils of the spring stackup solid because the valve lift is greater than the spring design can accommodate. Adding a number of shims under a spring to increase the tension can also invite coil bind, since the installed height is reduced by the thickness of the shims. Coil bind is, of course, hazardous to engine health because it means that something in the valvetrain has to give. In most cases, when the valvesprings bind, one or all of the following will occur: the pushrods bend, the rockerarms and rocker mounts bend or break apart, and/or the lifters wedge against the cam lobes.

To check for coil bind, compress the spring in the tester until the coils stack solid. Note the spring height. There should be at least a 0.060-inch safety margin between the *maximum valve lift* and the point at which the spring binds. Consider this 0.060-inch figure the minimum allowable clearance; the farther from coil bind you keep the springs, the longer they will last! In a street or oval-track engine that will see long service between overhauls, an extra 0.100-inch of travel (before coil bind) will prevent the springs from fatiguing and prematurely losing pressure.

There is a second way to check the springs for coil bind, although it is not as convenient as using a spring testing machine. When the engine is preassembled and the springs are installed and shimmed, rotate the crank until one of the intake valves is at full lift. You should then be able to insert a 0.060-inch feeler gauge between the coils. After the intake spring is checked, the crank must be rotated until the exhaust valve reaches full lift; once again the feeler gauge should fit comfortably between the coils.

If the valvespring has two or three

Valvespring open pressure is measured by compressing the spring to the length at maximum valve lift. To check coil bind, continue to compress the spring until the coils stack solid. If the springs coil bind within 0.100-inch of maximum lift, then spring life is likely to be short.

If you do not have access to a Rimac machine, you can improvise a substitute using a drill press and a bathroom scale. Use the drill press spindle to compress the spring to the installed height and read the pressure on the scale. This setup works well for checking seat pressure, but don't expect it to measure open pressure with stiff racing springs.

Telescoping gauges are ideal for measuring installed height. Pull up on the retainer firmly to seat the valve and the split locks before expanding the snap gauge.

There are several ways to measure valvespring installed height. The least expensive (and least accurate) method is to use a steel rule to measure the distance from the spring seat to the bottom edge of the retainer.

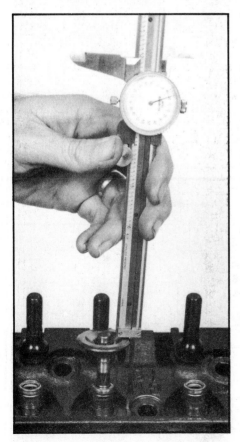

A more accurate technique is to use dial calipers to make the measurement from the spring seat to retainer.

coils, it may be difficult to check the innermost spring using this method. If you cannot reach the inner coils, then you must disassemble the heads, remove the outer springs, reinstall the heads, and then check for coil bind on the inside spring at maximum valve lift. Don't assume that the inner spring is all right simply because the outer springs passed inspection. Most spring retainers for dual and triple springs are stepped, which decreases the installed height of the inside coils. An inside spring that is binding can be just as destructive as an outer spring!

There are several potential cures for coil bind problems. In most instances, substituting another spring is the simplest solution. There is a staggering variety of springs available from the camshaft companies. Selecting a spring with fewer coils or with smaller diameter wire will allow the spring to compress farther before the coils touch. The second tactic is to increase the installed height of the spring, by either substituting a retainer with more "dish," remachining the spring seats deeper in the cylinder head, or installing valves with longer stems.

Be aware, though, that these alternatives can create more problems than they solve. Whenever the installed height is increased, the seat and open pressure is reduced. If you remachine the spring seats, you run the risk of cutting into the water jacket. And if you switch to different spring retainers, you may have interference problems between the rockerarm and spring retainer. All things considered, finding a suitable valvespring that will accommodate the valve lift generated by the camshaft is the easiest, cheapest, and best mechanical solution to coil bind problems.

RETAINER-TO-GUIDE CLEARANCE

If you have changed the camshaft, valves, rockerarms, or retainers from stock components, then you must check for interference between the

If you assemble cylinder heads frequently, then you might consider a tool designed specifically for the job. The BHJ Products special dial caliper is designed to measure valvespring installed height quickly and accurately.

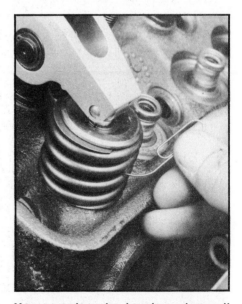

You can also check valvespring coil bind by inserting a paper clip or feeler gauge between the coils when the valve is at maximum lift. Be sure to check the inner coils carefully for coil bind when using two or three-piece valvesprings.

valvespring retainers and the tops of the valve guides (or valve stem seals, if your engine is equipped with them). Checking retainer-to-guide clearance is easy if you install light tension springs on the valves when preassembling the engine. After installing the valvetrain and rockerarms, set the lash for each valve and check the clearance at the retainers as you bring each valve to maximum lift. (If you are using a hydraulic camshaft in your engine, substitute solid lifters while performing this check. Otherwise the plunger in the hydraulic lifter will compress, and the valve will not reach true maximum lift). You should be able to insert a 0.060-inch feeler gauge between the

There should be at least 0.060-inch clearance between the bottom of the spring retainer and the top of the valve guide (or seal) when the valve is at maximum lift.

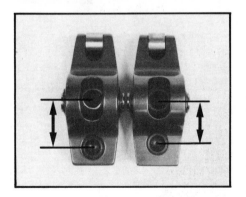

Rockerarm ratio is increased by moving the pushrod cup closer to the fulcrum. High-ratio rockers increase valve lift and effective duration without affecting seat timing.

This chart illustrates the effect of increasing rockerarm ratio. The shaded area represents the higher valve lift produced by substituting a 1.65:1 rocker in place of a standard 1.5:1 rocker on a smallblock Chevrolet. Although seat timing is unchanged, there is a considerable increase in effective duration at 0.500-inch valve lift with the high-ratio rockers.

bottom of the retainer and the top of the valve guide or seal.

If your engine is short on clearance, there are several ways to increase it. When the interference is caused by the height of the valve stem seal, you may be able to gain the clearance you need by substituting a different type of seal. For example, Raymond brand metal seals and Speed Pro brand rubber seals are generally shorter than the Perfect Circle one-piece Teflon seals. Sometimes, in extreme cases, you can shorten the valve guides without causing any serious side effects. As a last resort, you can substitute valves with longer stems, but this fix may upset the valvetrain geometry. At the very least, you will have to re-shim the springs to maintain the correct seat and open pressure.

ROCKERARMS

Unless the engine has an overhead-cam arrangement that operates the valves directly, rockerarms are an essential element of the valvetrain. The rockers are part of a complex linkage that both transfers and magnifies, through the *rockerarm ratio*, the motion of the lifters riding on the cam lobes. The rockerarm ratio is determined by the distances between the pushrod cup, the rocker pivot, and the tip that pushes against the valve stem.

The rockerarm ratio is usually different for each engine design. A small-block Chevy, for example, has a *theoretical* rockerarm ratio of 1.5:1, while a big-block Chevy or Boss Ford has a theoretical rocker arm ratio of 1.7:1. These are "theoretical" ratios because under actual operating conditions, the true ratio rarely equals the ideal figures. A rockerarm with a 1.5:1 ratio should produce a *net valve lift* that is exactly 1.5 times greater than

the *cam lobe lift*. For instance, a cam with a 0.300-inch lobe lift should produce a maximum valve lift of 0.450-inch (1.500 x 0.300 = 0.450). However, due to manufacturing tolerances, deflections in the valvetrain, and the complex motion of the rocker as it sweeps across the valve stem tip, the *actual valve lift* seldom equals the theoretical value.

Increasing the rockerarm ratio is a horsepower-producing trick that has been widely adopted by hot rodders and racers. (High-output smallblock Chevrolets are routinely outfitted with 1.6:1 rockers in place of the standard 1.5:1 rockers.) To get these higher-than-stock ratios, it is necessary to use non-stock, specialty rockerarms. Increasing the rockerarm ratio offers several advantages. It makes the cam "bigger" without increasing the duration. As the accompanying chart illustrates, high-ratio rockers open the valves quicker, lift them higher, and

To check the ratios of a set of rockerarms, measure the maximum valve lift that each rocker produces on the same camshaft lobe. To ensure consistent readings, adjust the rockers for zero lash, and leave the dial indicator in the same position throughout the test.

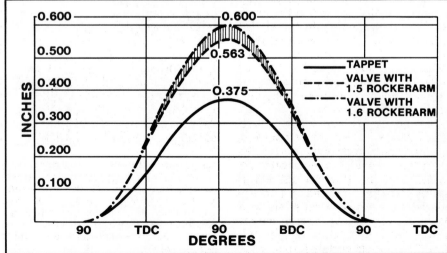

close them later—all without affecting seat timing. Of course, there are trade-offs. The faster valve accelerations and decelerations produced by higher rockerarm ratios reduce valvetrain stability, inviting early valve float. Valvespring coil bind clearance becomes more critical, and the valve notches in the piston may have to be deepened to accommodate the increased net valve lift.

Whether you are using stock or specialty rockerarms, it is important to check the true (actual) ratio. This is easily done by installing each rocker in turn on the same cam lobe, adjusting the lash, and noting the maximum valve lift it produces. An assortment of stamped steel rockerarms is likely to have significant differences in ratio between the highest and lowest. In classes of competition where factory valve lift specifications must be maintained (Stock eliminator drag racing, for example), rockers that produce the maximum allowable valve lift should be chosen. If you are not concerned with meeting the standards laid down by a rulebook, then it is a good practice to divide your rockers into high-ratio and low-ratio groups (while discarding or replacing any rockers that vary more than 0.030-inch from the average valve lift figure). Since intake flow is generally more important to engine performance than exhaust flow, the high-ratio rockers should be assigned to the intake valves and the low-ratio rockers reserved for the exhausts. Use a dab of machinist's dye or a punch mark to identify the rockers you have selected for the intake valves.

Stud-mounted rockers must also be checked for adequate *stud clearance*. Many stock rockers cannot be used with high-lift cams because the slotted holes bottom out against the rocker studs as the rocker approaches maximum valve lift. "Long slot" rockers are available to correct this problem, or you can elongate the slotted holes in the stock rockers with a grinding tool. If there is adequate clearance, you should be able to insert a piece of paper-clip wire between the stud and the rockerarm slot when the valve is at maximum lift.

If you have installed specialty rocker studs, you must also check for adequate clearance at the sides of the rockers. Most high-performance screw-in studs have an extra-large radius between the shank and hex head. This increases the strength of the stud, but this extra material may interfere with the bottom of the rockerarm. Aluminum and steel roller rock-

The slot in a stamped steel rockerarm may bottom out against the stud at maximum valve lift when a high-lift cam is installed. The clearance is adequate if you can insert a paper clip between the stud and rockerarm slot when the valve is wide open.

ers can be relieved with a high-speed cutter to eliminate this interference.

Finally, if you plan to use "poly lock" valve-adjusting nuts or a stud girdle to stabilize the valvetrain, you must check the clearance between the adjusting nut and the rocker. If the nut hits the rocker, it will be impossible to obtain an accurate valve lash setting. Again, a piece of paper clip wire makes a good checking gauge. If the paper-clip will not fit between the rocker and the adjusting nut, you must relieve the rocker to provide clearance.

Special *grooved pivot balls* are an excellent addition to any valvetrain

Large diameter valvesprings and deeply dished retainers can hit the underside of the rockerarm. If the rockerarm pushes against the spring or retainer, the split locks can pop out, causing a dropped valve. Avoid this disaster by checking the clearance during preassembly.

that utilizes ball-pivot rockerarms. The grooves help lubricate the rocker fulcrums, which minimizes the likelihood of "burning" a rockerarm. High valvespring pressures and radical cam profiles increase the stress on these pivot balls. If a rockerarm or pivot ball on an exhaust valve should fail, replace it with a rocker that has already been broken in on an intake stud. The exhaust rockers usually run hotter than the intakes, and putting a well broken-in rocker on the exhaust will ensure against premature failure. Also, when assembling the engine for the final time, remember to coat the rocker balls with moly lube and plenty of oil!

A *roller-bearing rockerarm* design eliminates these troublesome pivot balls, and "roller rockers" are considered almost mandatory on racing engines (where the rules allow). Roller rockers have their own special shortcomings, however. Occasionally the roller tips are bored off-center. This causes the tip to run eccentrically and makes it impossible to adjust the valve lash consistently. You can check a roller tip for excessive run-out by setting up a dial indicator on the roller and turning it with your fingertip. And, before a rocker passes your final inspection, you should make certain that the pushrod cup is fully seated, that the oiling hole from the cup is unobstructed, and that the C-clip retainers for the pivot-bearings are seated fully in their grooves.

GUIDEPLATES

Stud-mounted rockerarms, unlike *shaft-mounted* rockers, require some type of aligning device to keep the

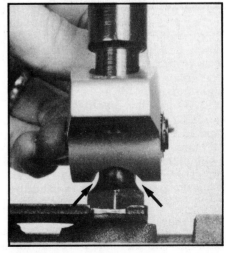

Check the clearance between the bottom of the rockerarm and the rocker stud. Many heavy-duty studs have extra-large fillets between the nut and shank.

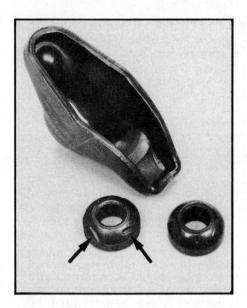

Grooved pivot balls are an excellent addition to any high-performance engine using stamped rockerarms.

Occasionally a rockerarm roller is bored off-center. Check the roller run-out with a dial indicator.

Bridgeport with an end mill; simply drilling the holes oversize is usually not recommended.

The pushrod clearance holes must also be enlarged whenever the diameter of the pushrods is increased. Large diameter pushrods are generally stiffer, making them less likely to bend and deflect due to the heavy valvetrain loads created by high-pressure racing valvesprings. High-output smallblock Chevrolets, for instance, are often upgraded by replacing the stock 0.3125-inch (5/l6) diameter pushrods with larger 0.375-inch (3/8) diameter pieces. These oversize pushrods need extra room where they pass through the cylinder heads, so the pushrod holes must be carefully opened up with a hand grinder to accommodate them (and, of course, when non-standard pushrods are used, the pushrod guideplates will also have to be replaced with plates that will accept the larger pushrods.)

PUSHRODS

There is very little that can go wrong with pushrods. If your pushrods have *hardened tips*, make certain that the tip inserts are seated fully in the pushrod tubes. Check for cracks around the oil holes, and if your engine has guideplates or slots in the cylinder head to maintain alignment between the rockers and valve stems, check for signs of excessive wear in the area where the pushrod passes through the head and guideplate.

Before slipping the pushrods in place, it is a good idea to check that they are all straight. There are two easy ways to check pushrod straightness. You can roll them across a flat piece of thick glass, or spin them in a drill press

rocker tip centered on the valve stem. *Close-tolerance slots* in the cylinder head and *pushrod guideplates* are the most common means of maintaining correct rockerarm alignment. If your cylinder heads are outfitted with guideplates, you must use *hardened pushrods*; otherwise the steel-to-steel contact between the guideplates and the soft pushrod material will quickly gall the pushrod tubing. Most guideplates are punched out of sheet steel, which can leave rough edges along the pushrod slots. To deburr and dress these slots, wrap a piece of fine emery paper around a bolt, then polish the inside edges of the guideplate slots with this homemade tool.

And remember, if you are using a high-ratio rockerarm, the pushrod cup is located closer to the fulcrum than the pushrod cup in a standard ratio rocker. This can cause the pushrod to "bottom-out" in the guideplate slot. When you are checking the rockerarm ratios, also make certain that the guideplate slots are deep enough to clear the pushrods at maximum valve lift. TRW and other manufacturers offer guideplates with extra-long slots to correct these interference problems.

Many of the non-stock specialty guideplates also feature elongated holes for the rockerarm studs. This allows the engine builder to slide the guideplate from side-to-side before torquing down the rockerarm stud, thereby ensuring the best possible alignment between the valvestem and rockerarm tip. Ideally, the rockerarm should be precisely centered over the tip of the valve stem. However, this may not always be possible when an in-

take and exhaust pushrod share the same guideplate. In extreme cases, such as when the valve guides have been relocated to provide room in the combustion chamber for oversize valves, the pushrod guideplates will have to be cut in half, the rockers and valves lined up, and the guideplates welded back together to maintain the proper alignment.

The pushrods must also have adequate clearance where they pass through the cylinder heads. Again, when high-ratio rockerarms are used, remember that the pushrod will be closer to the rockerarm pivot, which can cause the pushrod to rub against the side of the pushrod clearance holes in the heads. These holes can be carefully elongated with a hand-held grinding tool or opened up on a

Slots in the pushrod guideplates must be long enough to prevent binding the pushrods as the valves open and close.

Deburr slots in guideplates by polishing them with emery paper wrapped around bolt.

chuck. If a pushrod does not roll smoothly across the glass or if it wobbles in the drill chuck, discard it. Once a pushrod becomes bent, there is no saving it!

Determining the correct pushrod length is not so simple. Pushrod length is a major factor in determining *valvetrain geometry.* "Geometry," in this case, refers to the dynamic relationship between the rockerarm and valve stem during the time when the valve is opening and closing. Ideally, the rocker should always push against the exact center of the valve stem. This reduces the side loads on the stem, which cause the valve guides to wear. This rarely happens, however, since the rocker travels in an *arc* as it moves up and down. Therefore, one of the goals of engine blueprinting is to keep the rockerarm as close to the center of the valve stem as possible throughout the entire valve-lift cycle. Many factors can affect this relationship, but in a nutshell, the easiest way to accomplish this is to find the pushrod length that produces the best geometry.

Many engine modifications can upset the original valvetrain geometry. A high-lift camshaft, for example, has a smaller *base circle* than a stock cam. This causes the lifters to drop lower in the lifter bores when the valves are closed, which, in turn, causes the ends of the rockerarms to rise higher at the valve-closed position. Milling the cylinder heads and engine block, installing oversize valves, increasing the valve stem length (to accommodate larger valvesprings), and even grinding three-angle valve seats can all cause

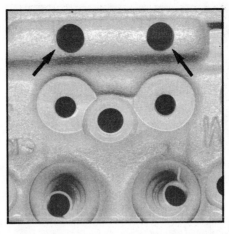

High-ratio rockerarms and large diameter pushrods often require enlarging pushrod holes in smallblock Chevy cylinder heads. Guideplates must be used to maintain alignment between rockerarms and valve stems.

the relationship between the rockerarms and valve stems to go out of kilter.

Fortunately, the specialty cam companies are very familiar with this problem and offer special-length pushrods to compensate for these changes. These custom pushrods are typically available in lengths that are 0.050-, 0.100-, 0.250-, and 0.300-inch shorter than stock. For those rare instances when an engine needs a slightly *longer* pushrod, custom pushrods are offered in 0.050-and 0.100-inch longer versions. Unfinished pushrods are also offered; these can be tailored to any engine by trimming the pushrod tubing to length and pressing in a hardened tip.

Early-model Chevy smallblock heads were equipped with pressed rockerarms. These should be replaced with screw-in studs for serious performance applications. Stud bosses must be tapped and spot faced.

You can determine the correct pushrod length by carefully watching the rockerarm (from the side) as it opens and closes the valve. With the engine preassembled and the valve lash set, look at the end of the rockerarm as it sweeps across the valve stem. The rocker contact point should be slightly off-center toward the inside edge (the edge nearest the rockerarm fulcrum) when the valve is closed. As the valve opens to about mid-lift (one-half of total valve lift), the contact point should pass across the valve centerline and move slightly toward the outside edge. Then during the last half of the lift cycle, the contact point should swing back across the centerline and return to about the original position—slightly inboard of the centerline—just as the valve reaches full lift. If the contact point starts at the center of the stem and then moves toward one edge as the valve lift increases, the pushrod is too long or too short.

Finding the best pushrod length is a trial-and-error process that requires you to try various pushrods until one produces satisfactory valvetrain geometry. An adjustable length pushrod will simplify this procedure. These pushrods have a threaded insert that can be adjusted to lengthen or shorten the pushrod. Once you have found a length that produces the desired results, measure the overall length of the adjustable pushrod and use this dimension to order a suitable set of specialty pushrods. Checking and, if necessary, correcting the rockerarm geometry is a detail often overlooked by neophyte engine builders, but it is crucial to extending valve guide life and reducing valvetrain failure.

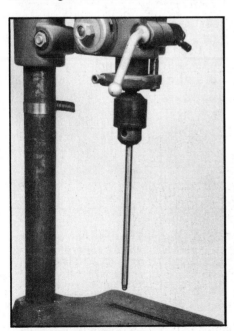

Spin pushrod in drill chuck to check straightness.

Manley Performance pushrod fixture quickly checks pushrod length. Gauge should touch end of pushrod and valve stem tip if length is correct.

CAMSHAFT

The camshaft has often been described as the "brain" of the engine. In effect, the cam regulates engine "breathing" by opening and closing the valves. But unlike a living brain that controls heart rate and respiration, a camshaft cannot speed up or slow down the valve events. Without this ability, cam profiles are always a *compromise*. At low engine speeds and during part-throttle operation, an engine needs a camshaft design with short duration and relatively little valve lift to produce sharp throttle response and good fuel economy. At high rpm, however, there is very little time to fill the cylinders, so a long-duration cam with high valve lift is the answer. So when a builder selects a cam grind that's right for one end of the operating range, it will without question hurt performance at the other extreme.

There is a staggering variety of cam designs available for modern performance engines. Choices range from sedate hydraulic grinds that emphasize fuel economy to roller cams designed expressly for all-out racing. The ends of the camshaft spectrum are easy to understand; it's the subtle shades in the middle that are difficult to distinguish. A current maximum-effort street machine may rely on a profile that was considered a racing-only camshaft just a short time ago. The cam companies have shaved the distinctions between performance and economy grinds very fine.

Expert engine builders continually test new cams in the constant search for the "perfect combination," but the average guy doesn't often have the time or money to perform extensive dyno testing. Only by studying the catalogs, talking with other car enthusiasts, and consulting with the technical experts at the cam companies can you be certain of finding a profile that is right for your particular needs. And this is one area where every engine builder should think long and hard before making a decision. The cam you select will determine, to a great degree, the overall performance and "driveability" of the engine. And if you select the wrong grind, the engine will be disappointing, despite all of the time and effort you have spent

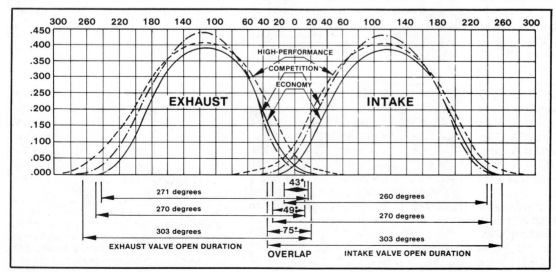

The camshaft controls airflow through the engine, and is an important factor in performance. These graphs illustrate differences in valve lift and duration between economy, performance, and competition profiles.

blueprinting it.

Before your new camshaft can make good on all its performance promises, it must be installed *properly*. This requires a bit more work than just inserting it in the cam bearings, lining up the timing marks, and tightening down the cam drive. The cam must be properly *phased* with the pistons if it is to perform up to its full potential. This is called "degreeing the cam," and it is a procedure that is much easier to do than to describe. Don't despair; nearly everyone who builds high-performance engines has learned to degree a camshaft by reading a book or magazine article. The first time you attempt the task, the entire process may seem hopelessly complex. But by the second or third time around, degreeing a cam will be a snap. Follow the steps outlined below, and your cam will soon be degreed to perfection.

FINDING TOP-DEAD CENTER

The first step in degreeing a cam is to preassemble the short block. Bolt the crankshaft in place and install the number-one piston and rod. Install the cam and timing chain, taking care to align the marks on the camshaft and crank gears. Bolt a degree wheel to the crankshaft snout; if the snout is not drilled and tapped, attach the degree wheel to the harmonic balancer and press the balancer into place. Fabricate a pointer from a piece of coat hangar wire or welding rod and fasten it to the front of the engine; the bolt holes for the water pump and timing chain cover are good places to mount this temporary pointer. Turn the crank until your eyeball tells you that the number-one piston is at *top-dead center* (TDC). Then, without rotating the crank, line up the pointer with the TDC mark on the degree wheel. Now turn the crank until the piston is halfway down the cylinder bore.

Before you can zero in on top-dead center, you will need a *piston stop*. A short length of bar stock or angle iron, like the one shown here, works well. If your engine has domed pistons, the stop merely has to straddle the cylinder bore so that the piston dome will contact it. With flat-top pistons, however, you must drill and tap the stop, then screw in a bolt to contact the piston before it reaches TDC. Tighten down the piston stop, and get ready to pinpoint top-dead center.

Turn the crankshaft *clockwise* until the piston contacts the stop and note the reading on the degree wheel. Now rotate the crank *counter clockwise* until the piston again hits the stop, and

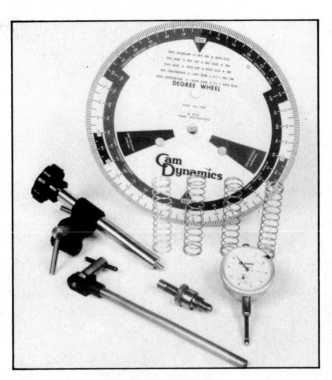

A long bolt screwed into the end of the camshaft makes a convenient installation tool.

note this second reading on the degree wheel. If the crank stopped turning at exactly the same point both *before* and *after* the TDC mark on the degree wheel, you have lucked out and hit top-dead center on the first try.

Usually, though, the two readings on the degree wheel are not identical. For example, the piston may stop at a reading of 28° after TDC when you turn the crank clockwise, and 32° before TDC when you turn it counter clockwise. True top-dead center lies halfway between these two readings. To pinpoint TDC you must take the *average* of these two readings, and then adjust the pointer to line up with this number on the degree wheel. In our example, the average of 28 and 32 is 30 degrees. With the piston still

The bigger the degree wheel, the more accurate the readings. This anodized aluminum wheel can be rotated on the crankshaft snout by loosening the center hub, a feature which simplifies the chore of locating top-dead center.

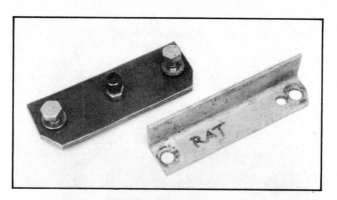

A piston stop can be elaborate or simple. A length of angle iron works well with high-dome pistons. For flat-top or dished pistons, you'll need a stop with a bolt that extends down into the bore to contact the piston before it reaches TDC.

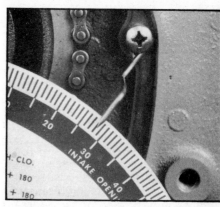

Rotate the crankshaft clockwise until the piston contacts the stop and note the reading on the degree wheel. Here the crank has stopped turning at 28 degrees before TDC.

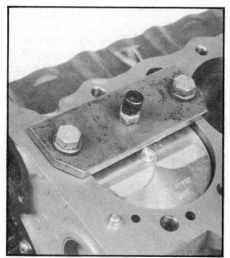

The stop must be rigid enough to resist flexing when the piston pushes against it.

A spark plug stop can only be used when the plug hole intersects the piston top. A small hole in the center of the stop bleeds off pressure in the cylinder as the piston rises.

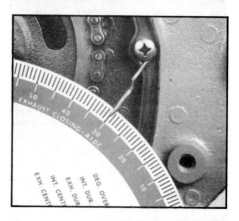

Now turn the crank counter-clockwise until it stops again. In this example, the crank has stopped at 30 degrees after TDC. This means that the degree wheel must be turned on the crank snout one degree, or the pointer bent slightly so that the crank stops at an indicated 29 degrees before and after TDC.

This piston stop screws into the spark plug hole. It is used to degree a cam after the heads have been installed.

work up to this point, set up a dial indicator on the piston top. Turn the crank clockwise until the dial indicator shows that the piston has risen to 0.100-inch below the deck surface, and note the reading on the degree wheel before TDC. Now continue to turn the crank clockwise; the piston will reach TDC, and then begin moving back down the cylinder bore. Stop when the piston is again 0.100-inch below the deck surface. The reading should be the same number of degrees after TDC as the earlier reading.

Once you have found TDC, you must be careful not to disturb the degree wheel or pointer until you have finished degreeing the camshaft—otherwise you will have to start over from the beginning. Although we have described how to find TDC with the heads off the engine, this procedure can also be done with the heads in place. You will need to buy or fabricate a piston stop that can be inserted through the spark plug hole. Remove the remaining spark plugs and rockers so the engine can be turned over easily with a long breaker bar.

CHECKING INTAKE CENTERLINE

Although there are several ways to

firmly against the stop, the pointer is bent so that it indicates 30 degrees before TDC. Now rotate the crank in the opposite direction until the piston again hits the stop. The crank will stop turning at precisely 30 degrees after TDC if you have correctly split the difference between your original readings.

You can now remove the piston stop. If you want to double-check your

Double-check the TDC location by removing the piston stop and setting up a dial indicator as shown. Note the degree wheel readings when the piston is 0.100-inch from TDC as you slowly rotate the crankshaft. The reading before TDC should be the same as the reading after TDC.

The dial indicator plunger should contact the edge of the lifter. Note the degree wheel readings before and after the point of maximum lobe lift (using the intake centerline method) or at 0.050-inch lobe lift (for asymmetrical cam grinds).

Use a pushrod as an extension of the dial indicator plunger when degreeing the cam with the cylinder head in place.

degree a cam, the intake centerline method is the most common and reliable procedure. The *intake centerline* is the point at which the intake valve reaches maximum lift. In the vast majority of engines, this takes place between 100 and 120° after top-dead center. Unless the cam grinder recommends otherwise, it is usually best to install a new cam in the "straight up" position—that is, neither *advanced* nor *retarded*. This means that a cam ground with 110° *lobe centers* (the angle between the intake and exhaust lobes) should be installed with a 110° *intake centerline*. The timing cards that accompany most cams usually specify both these lobe centers and the recommended intake centerline.

To find the point of maximum intake valve lift, install a lightly oiled lifter on the intake lobe for the number-one cylinder. Watch the lifter as you rotate the crank assembly. Stop when the lifter is at the lowest point in the bore; it is then on the *base circle* of the cam. Now set up a dial indicator so that the plunger contacts the edge of the lifter and is parallel to the lifter travel. (Don't set up the dial indicator in the pushrod cup; the curved surface can cause inaccurate readings.) Slowly turn the crankshaft in the normal direction of rotation until the lifter reaches maximum lift. Then turn the crank backward until the dial indicator reads 0.100-inch below this maximum figure. Now turn the crank forward again as smoothly as possible until the dial indicator reads 0.050-inch below the maximum lift point. Note the reading on the degree wheel. Continue turning the crank past maximum lift until the needle on the dial indicator is again 0.050-inch below the maximum; note this second reading on the degree wheel.

It is important to avoid jerking the crankshaft while taking these readings. If you inadvertently miss the points 0.050-inch below maximum tappet lift, turn the crank backwards a quarter turn and then slowly "sneak up" on them again. Always take the degree wheel readings while turning the crank in the normal direction of rotation; this prevents slack in the timing chain or cam drive from causing erroneous readings.

The point of maximum intake valve lift—the intake centerline—is exactly halfway between these two readings. To find the intake centerline, add the two readings and divide by two. For example, if the tappet is 0.050-inch below maximum lift at 80° after TDC, and again at 140° ATDC, then the intake centerline is 110° (80 + 140 divided

by 2 = 110). The exact numbers are not important; you could have measured tappet lift at 0.020-inch or 0.100-inch on both sides of the maximum lift point without affecting the accuracy of the readings. What is important is the *relationship* between the maximum lift point and top-dead center.

CHANGING CAM PHASING

Once you have found the intake centerline point, you can determine whether the cam is advanced, straight up, or retarded. If the intake centerline is *less* than the lobe center angle, the cam is advanced. For example, if you find that the intake centerline is 108° after TDC, and your cam has 110° lobe centers, then the cam is 2° advanced. Similarly, if the intake centerline is

Cam Dynamics	3926 RUNWAY ROAD MEMPHIS, TENNESSEE 38118 (901) 794-2870

ENGINE	CHEVY 396/454		
CAM GRIND NO.	CHB-R 318/320/110		
CAMSHAFT SERIAL NO.	Q 724		
		INTAKE	EXHAUST
VALVE ADJUSTMENT (HOT)		.030	.030
GROSS VALVE LIFT		.765	.680
DURATION AT A TAPPET LIFT OF	.020	318°	320°

VALVE TIMING AT .020 TAPPET		OPEN		CLOSE	
LIFT	INT	49 °BTDC		89 °ABDC
	EXH	91 °BBDC		51 °ATDC

CAM IS GROUND WITH LOBE CENTER SEPARATION OF 110 °

RECOMMENDED VALVE SPRING INFORMATION
OUTER SPRING PART NO. 991
INNER SPRING PART NO.

INSTALLED HT.	1.880	INS =	180 LBS.
OPEN HT.	1.150	INS =	600 LBS.

The timing tag reveals essential information about a camshaft. In addition to lift and duration figures, it provides the numbers you need to accurately degree in the cam.

Offset cam bushings are used to change camshaft phasing. Each 0.005-inch offset in the bushing hole changes cam timing approximately one degree.

greater than the lobe centers, then the cam is retarded. To cite another example, if you find that a cam with 110° lobe centers has the intake centerline at 112° ATDC, then it is retarded 2°.

Camshaft phasing has a definite effect on engine performance. A cam that is advanced both opens and closes the valves *sooner* in relation to the piston position than a cam that is retarded. As a general rule, advancing the cam increases low-speed torque, while retarding it boosts high-speed horsepower. Tuning a cam by changing the phasing can pay enormous dividends in performance, as many racers will attest. The thousands of variables between engines make it impossible to predict the precise cam phasing that will produce the best performance. Trial-and-error testing is the only way to discover which cam phasing the engine prefers.

Fortunately, it is quite easy to advance or retard a cam. You will need a selection of *offset cam bushings*, which can be obtained from any cam company or speed shop. The holes in these bushings are intentionally drilled off-center. When installed in the timing gear, these bushings move the camshaft dowel pin forward (to advance the cam) or backward (to retard it). The dowel pin hole in the cam gear must be drilled oversize to accept these bushings. Drill from the back side of the gear, but don't drill all the way through. A small lip around the bushing hole will prevent the bushing

from falling out and changing the cam phasing. Make sure, however, that the bushing does not protrude above the surface of the cam gear where it rubs against the front of the block. You should also elongate the cam bolt holes with a rat-tail file.

The offset of the dowel pin hole in the bushing determines how much the bushing will change the cam phasing. Some of these bushings are color coded or stamped to indicate their offset; don't trust these markings. Moving the cam dowel 0.005-inch changes the cam timing approximately 1°, so you can get a good idea of how far a particular bushing will advance or retard the cam by measuring the offset of the dowel hole with a dial caliper. However, *the only way to determine the true effect on cam timing is to recheck the intake centerline after the bushing is installed in the cam gear.*

The cam timing can also be changed by using *offset crank keys*. Also, some timing chain sets include crankshaft sprockets with *multiple keyways*. By selecting the appropriate slot in the crank sprocket, the cam phasing can be advanced or retarded from 4° to 8°. In all honesty, multiple keyway sprockets are not a particularly good or convenient way to alter cam timing. Before you can get to the sprocket, you must remove the degree wheel, which means you have to go through the entire drill of finding TDC again. Also, these sprockets do not always put the cam phasing right where you want it, so you may still need offset bushings to fine tune the cam timing.

DEGREEING ASYMMETRICAL CAMS

There is one category of camshafts that cannot be degreed using the intake centerline method described earlier. These cams are called *asymmetrical* profiles. A conventional camshaft lobe has the same shape on both sides. This causes the valve to open and close at the same rate. With an asymmetrical lobe, the two sides of the lobe are not mirror images of each other. Cam designers have learned that they can increase both the engine operating range and the torque output by using different opening and closing *rates*. These asymmetrical profiles were formerly found only on exotic roller racing cams, but now the same technology is starting to appear on high-performance flat-tappet cams. While asymmetric cam lobes offer the promise of improved performance, they also demand a different degreeing technique.

Since the opening and closing sides of an asymmetrical cam lobe differ, you cannot accurately determine the lobe centerline with a dial indicator. To degree an asymmetrical cam, you must go by the cam grinder's "fifty-thousandths" numbers. Instead of using the intake centerline for a reference point, you use the points at which the tappet is 0.050-inch off the base circle. A typical set of "50-numbers" for a performance cam might tell you that the intake tappet reaches 0.050-inch lift on the opening ramp at 32° before TDC, and returns to 0.050-inch lift at 58° after BDC on the closing side.

To check cam timing using these 50-numbers, you set up the dial indicator on the edge of the lifter just as

The dowel pin hole in the camshaft gear must be drilled out to fit the offset bushings.

If the cam phasing must be moved more than two or three degrees, elongate the bolt holes in the cam gear with a rat-tail file.

Some high-performance timing chain crank gears use multiple keyways to alter camshaft phasing. This gear provides three choices in cam timing: "straight up," four degrees advanced, and four degrees retarded.

you would when using the intake centerline method. Slowly rotate the crank in the direction of normal rotation, stopping as soon as the lifter rises 0.050-inch. Note the reading on the degree wheel, then continue to turn the crank until the lifter returns to 0.050-inch lift on the closing ramp. Take a second reading on the degree wheel, and compare these numbers with the specs on the camshaft card. If necessary, the cam can then be advanced or retarded with offset bushings.

CAM GRAPHING

The numbers on a timing card don't always tell the whole story about a camshaft. Even if you know the key characteristics of a cam design—valve lift, opening and closing points, and lobe centers—there are other factors to consider. How fast do the valves open and close? How long are the valves at their maximum lift? Two cams with similar lift and duration numbers may have wildly different profiles, depending on the answers to these questions. There are also times when the camshaft specs are a mystery. Finding the figures for a discontinued factory high-performance cam can be a real struggle. The only way to learn what is really happening in the valvetrain is to graph the cam lobes.

The perfect time to graph a cam is

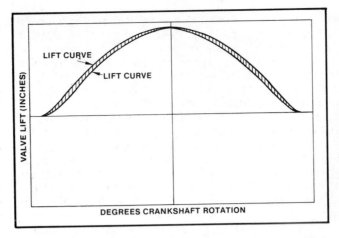

while you are degreeing it. To graph the cam, you simply record the tappet lift at regular intervals—every 5° of crank rotation, for example. Graphing the entire opening and closing cycles of both the intake and exhaust valves requires two complete crankshaft revolutions, or 720° of rotation. You can make this chore easier by first preparing a chart on a long piece of notebook paper, starting at the top with TDC and numbering to 720 by five's. Thankfully, each valve is closed for at least one of these two crank revolutions, so you will need to record only about 70 dial indicator readings for each valve (depending on the camshaft duration) to get a good picture of the cam profile.

The charts you produce from this

exercise are a valuable tool for making cam comparisons. You can actually plot the camshaft lift curve on a piece of graph paper from this data, or simply use the tappet lift numbers to compare valve opening rates between different cams. Remember to compensate for differences in the lobe centerlines when you are making side-by-side comparisons of various cam profiles from these charts. A cam with an advanced intake centerline will open the valves sooner than the same grind with a slightly retarded centerline—and it will also close the valves sooner. What you should concentrate on in these comparisons is the *shape* of the valve lift curve, since this is what determines the flow of air through the engine.

Graphing the lift curve tells you what the valves are really doing. The cams represented by these two curves have the same lift and duration figures, but one is a much "fatter" profile that opens and closes the valves quickly.

CAMSHAFT GLOSSARY

Asymmetric Lobe: A camshaft lobe that has a different lift curve on its opening and closing sides.
Centerline: The point of maximum lift on a cam lobe. It is measured by recording the number of degrees the crankshaft turns past TDC until the tappet reaches its maximum lift. The centerline of the number-one intake lobe is commonly used as a reference point to degree a camshaft.
Coil Bind: The point at which the individual coils of a spring stack solid, preventing the spring from compressing further. Coil bind can cause rapid lobe wear and valvetrain breakage.
Dual Pattern: A camshaft that has different profiles for the intake and exhaust lobes. An example of a dual-pattern cam is Chevy part number 389629, which has 296° duration/0.390-inch valve lift on the intakes, and 310° duration/0.410-inch valve lift on the exhausts.
Duration: The length of time that a valve is opened, measured in degrees of crankshaft rotation. Since there is

little airflow through a valve at very low lift, duration is usually measured from the point when the tappet is 0.050-inch off the base circle on the opening side to when it is 0.050-inch off the base circle on the closing side. *Advertised duration* usually includes the lobe clearance ramps, when the valve is not actually off the seat and flowing any air. For example, the advertised duration of Chevy part number 3863151 is 320°; measuring the duration at 0.050-inch tappet lift produces the more realistic figure of 221°.
Lift: The distance a valve moves off the seat. *Theoretical* lift is calculated by multiplying the camshaft lobe lift by the rockerarm ratio. *Net* lift is the true valve lift measured at the valve. Net lift is always less than the theoretical lift because it takes into account valve lash (on mechanical and roller-lifter cams), pushrod deflection, tolerances in the rockerarm ratio, resistance of the valvespring, and other factors that reduce the actual lift at the valve head. A cam with 0.300-inch lobe lift and I.5:I

ratio rocker arms would have a theoretical lift of 0.450-inch. The net lift, however, might be only 0.400-inch because of lash and deflection in the valvetrain.
Lobe Center: The angle measured in camshaft degrees between the point of maximum lift on the intake lobe and the point of maximum lift on the companion exhaust lobe. Lobe center is fixed when the camshaft is ground, and can only be changed by regrinding the lobes. Lobe centerlines, in contrast, can be adjusted by advancing or retarding the cam timing.
Overlap: The period of time when the intake and exhaust valves are open simultaneously. This occurs near the end of the exhaust stroke and the beginning of the intake stroke.
Single Pattern: A camshaft that has the identical profile on both the intake and exhaust lobes. Chevy part number 3863151, for example, is a single pattern cam: it has 221° of duration and 0.447-inch valve lift on both the intake and exhaust valves.

CHAPTER 8
COMPRESSION RATIO

COMPUTING COMPRESSION RATIOS

The *compression ratio* has a tremendous impact on the performance characteristics of an engine. A street engine must be able to live with the dismal octane rating of current low-lead or no-lead gasolines. On the other hand, a gas-burning race motor needs a compression ratio that extracts the maximum power from high-octane racing fuel without inviting destructive detonation. An engine that runs on alcohol runs little risk of encountering detonation, but it needs the highest possible compression ratio to make up for lower heat value in alcohol fuels. Thus, whether you are blueprinting an engine for the boulevard or for the Daytona 500, calculating the compression ratio is a vital step.

The actual arithmetic required to compute compression ratio is relatively easy. The real work is coming up with the numbers to plug into the compression equation. Compression ratio is defined as the ratio between the volume above the piston at bottom-dead center and the volume above it at top-dead center. Since combustion chambers, piston domes, and valve notches are very irregular shapes, the only way to determine their exact volume is by measuring how much liquid they hold or displace. Once these preliminary measurements have been made, you will be able to compute the compression ratio in just a few minutes

on a pocket calculator.

COMBUSTION CHAMBER VOLUME

Measuring the combustion chamber volume is popularly called "cc'ing the chambers." This refers to the fact that chamber volume is measured in cubic centimeters (cc). You will need a 100.00cc glass burette, a stand, and a 6 x 6-inch piece of 0.250-inch thick plexiglass for this exercise. (See the tool chapter for tips on buying burettes.) You will also need a colored liquid for the actual measurement. Solvent tinted with a few drops of machinist's dye or automatic transmission fluid works well, since these mixtures will not rust metal surfaces. If you are building an engine that must meet factory specifications for compression, then you should use the same measuring fluid that the tech inspectors use. The combustion chamber volume of NHRA Stock and Super Stock cars, for example, is usually measured with rubbing alcohol that has been dyed with food coloring. If you are running close to the edge of legality, a slight difference in chamber volume measurements may leave you with an engine that is declared illegal. This is why you should strive to use the same equipment and procedures as the tech inspectors.

You must also learn how to read a burette. The surface tension of the liquid in the burette tube causes it to form a cup that is called a *meniscus*. Take your readings at the *bottom* of the meniscus to ensure accuracy and con-

Combustion chamber volume is an important element in the compression ratio equation. Seal the edges of the chambers with a light coat of white grease. Don't forget to install a spark plug.

sistency.

The plexiglass square is used to seal the combustion chamber. Drill a 0.250-inch diameter hole near one edge of this plate, and chamfer the hole with a countersink. Insert the valves in the chamber and seal them with a light coating of white grease on the valve seats. Install a spark plug with the same heat range as the plugs you intend to use. Prop the head up on the work bench so that the deck surface is facing you. The head should be slightly high on the spark plug side of the chamber. Spread a light coat of grease around the chamber, then press the plexiglass plate on the deck surface with a slight twisting motion. The hole in the plexiglass should be at the upper edge of the combustion chamber, and the chamfer should be facing upward.

As you push the plexiglass down on the deck surface, the grease will form a seal between the plate and head. If the grease oozes into the chamber, it will affect the accuracy of your measurements; so remove the plate, clean out the grease, and try again, using less grease on the deck surface this time. On some cylinder heads, the edges of the valves may hold the plate away from the head surface. If you encounter this situation, grind a small groove in the plate where it hits the valve head. Fill this groove with grease and squeegee off the excess grease with the edge of a plastic credit card.

Once the chamber has been sealed, you are ready to measure the volume. Fill the burette with fluid, then open the valve until the meniscus is exactly at the zero mark. Check for air bubbles in the burette tube and valve. Position the tip of the burette over the hole in the plexiglass plate, open the valve, and begin filling the combustion chamber. Look for leaks in the ports, around the spark plug, and between the plate and deck surface—these will all upset the accuracy of your measurements. If the cylinder head chambers are larger than 100.00cc, you must close the burette valve when the meniscus reaches the 100.00cc mark, then refill and "zero" the burette again before continuing to fill the chamber.

As the measuring fluid fills the chamber, take care to prevent air pockets from forming. When the chamber is almost full, turn down the flow out of the burette so that the liquid just drips into the chamber. You may need to

move the head from side-to-side or tap on the plexiglass to dislodge any air bubbles that have collected under the sealing plate. When the fluid level just reaches the bottom of the hole in the plexiglass plate, close the burette valve. Read the volume that was required to fill the chamber, remembering to take the reading at the bottom of the meniscus. Write down this figure for later use in the compression computations.

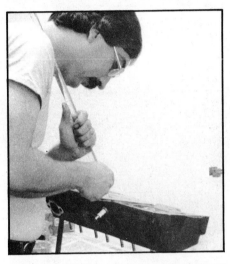

Carefully fill the chamber with colored solvent or alcohol from a burette or graduated cylinder. Check for leaks around the valves and spark plug. Tilt the head to prevent air bubbles from forming as the liquid fills the chamber.

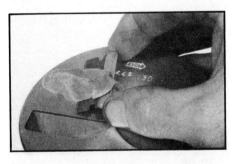

To measure the volume of the valve notches on a flat-top piston, fill one relief with clay.

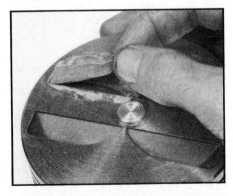

Carefully remove the clay mold and drop it a half-filled burette. The change in the fluid level equals the volume of the valve relief.

putations.

If you are building a legal engine for class racing, you must check the volume of all the remaining combustion chambers to make sure there are no chambers that will push the compression ratio over the allowable limit! Even if the engine will never be examined by a tech inspector, it is a good idea to check the volume of several other chambers. Always check at least a pair of chambers in each cylinder head to prevent basing your compression ratio calculations on wrong numbers.

Congratulations! You have just cc'd your first cylinder head.

VALVE RELIEF VOLUME

The volume of the valve notches in the piston, like the size of the combustion chambers, will have an effect on the compression ratio. If the piston tops are perfectly flat—without valve reliefs and without a dome—then the volume of the cylinder can be easily computed from the bore and stroke dimensions. If, however, the piston top is notched, dished, or domed, the volume of these features must be measured before the compression ratio can be accurately determined.

This section is concerned with the simplest and most common type of piston: a flat-top with one or more valve reliefs. (If the engine is equipped with domed or dished pistons, you will have to use the technique described in the following section.) You will need a chunk of modeling clay and a burette to measure the volume of the valve notches.

First soften the clay by squeezing it with your fingers until it becomes pliable. Fill one of the valve reliefs with the soft clay, taking care to push the clay into the corners of the notch. Then skim the clay with a metal rule to level it with the piston top. The next step is to carefully remove the clay from the notch without compressing or squeezing it. A sharp pen knife or small screwdriver is helpful when coaxing the clay out of the valve notch.

To measure the volume of this clay impression of the valve notch, fill a burette tube or graduated cylinder to a convenient point on the scale—50.00cc, for example. Then drop the clay into the liquid and note how far the liquid level in the burette rises. If the fluid rises to the 52.00cc mark, the volume of the valve notch is 2.00cc.

Most production pistons have a number of identical valve notches on the tops. If a single valve relief in a four-notch Chevrolet flat-top piston, for ex-

Press a plexiglass plate firmly against the grease. The grease should form a continuous seal without oozing into the chamber. Make sure the filling hole in the plate is at the highest point in the chamber. If the edges of the valves hit the plate, grind small clearance notches in the plexiglass and fill them with grease.

ample, has a volume of 2.00cc, then the *total* valve relief volume would be 8.00cc. If the piston has notches of unequal size—typically, there may be a large intake relief and a smaller exhaust relief—then each notch must be measured separately and the volumes added to come up with a total valve relief capacity.

DOME VOLUME

Some piston manufacturers provide dome volume figures, but they are not to be trusted. Usually these published dome volumes do not take into account the volume of the valve reliefs. A dome that is advertised as being 18.00cc may actually displace only 10.00cc after the volume of the valve notches is considered. Engine builders who compute compression ratios based on piston manufacturers' optimistic dome volumes would be quite disheartened to learn how little compression their engines really have. Of course, if you are using made-to-order pistons, or if you have modified the piston tops by radiusing the dome edges or deepening the valve reliefs, you must measure the dome volume for yourself. This is how it's done.

The dome volume is measured with the piston in the cylinder bore. After installing the crankshaft and cleaning the cylinderwalls, insert a piston/rod assembly in the cylinder and tighten the rod cap. The piston must have the compression rings in place to seal the cylinder. Rotate the crank to bring the piston to bottom-dead center, then coat the cylinderwall with a thick ring of white grease approximately 1.50 inches below the deck surface. Now carefully turn the crank and bring the piston toward TDC. Stop the piston exactly 1.00 inch below the deck, checking the position with a dial indicator or depth micrometer. Make sure that the piston is square in the cylinder bore by measuring the depth at several places around the circumference. Carefully wipe off the grease on the cylinderwall and piston top, taking care not to disturb the grease seal between the ring lands and the cylinder bore.

Now measure the volume of the space above the piston top, following the same procedure you used when cc'ing the combustion chambers. Seal a plexiglass plate to the deck surface of the block with a thin layer of grease, and tilt the engine slightly to allow air in the cylinder to escape through the hole in the plexiglass. Depending on the size of the cylinder, you may have to refill the burette two or three times

To determine piston dome volume, install the piston in the cylinder and coat the cylinderwall with grease approximately 1.500 inches from the top of the bore.

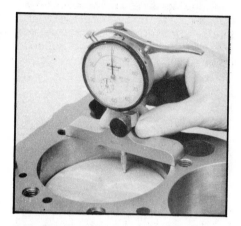

Bring the piston toward top-dead center by slowly turning the crankshaft. Stop when the piston is exactly 1.000 inches below the deck. Carefully remove any grease on the piston top and cylinderwall without moving the piston.

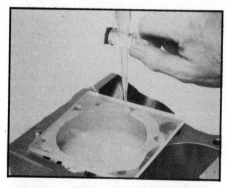

Seal the top of the cylinder with a plexiglass plate and grease. Fill the volume above the piston with fluid from a burette; you may need to refill the burette several times. Make sure there are no air pockets, and check the bottom of the cylinder for leaks. Then compute the piston dome volume as outlined in the text.

before the space above the piston is filled. Check the underside of the piston for leaks, since solvent may dissolve the seal around the piston before you are finished taking your measurements. Record the total volume of liquid needed to fill the cylinder. When

you are finished, remove the plexiglass plate and pour the fluid into a solvent pan (by rotating the engine stand).

To compute the dome volume of the piston, you must first calculate the volume of a cylinder with the same diameter as the engine cylinder and with a height of exactly 1.00 inch. Use the following formula to figure this volume:

$$\text{Volume of 1-inch tall cylinder (cc's)} = \left(\frac{d}{2}\right)^2 \times 51.48$$
where d = cylinder diameter in inches

This calculation tells you the volume of liquid that would have been required to fill the space above the piston if it had a perfectly flat top, without valve reliefs or a dome. To find the *true dome volume*, subtract the actual amount of fluid you needed to fill the cylinder from the theoretical cylinder volume you have just computed. The difference is the true dome volume.

The following example—using "real world" numbers—illustrates how this works. Say that you had an engine with 4.00-inch cylinder bores. You installed your finished piston in the number-one cylinder, brought it up to 1.00 inch below the deck surface, and sealed the gap between the piston and the cylinderwall. You filled the volume above the cylinder and found that it contained exactly 198.00cc. So far so good.

To calculate the volume of a 1.00-inch tall cylinder with the same diameter as the cylinder bores—4.00 inches—substitute the bore diameter in the equation above and calculate the answer:

$$\left(\frac{d}{2}\right)^2 \times 51.48 = \left(\frac{4.00}{2}\right)^2 \times 51.48 = 205.92cc$$

Now you know that if you had filled the space above a flat top piston with liquid, it would have held exactly 205.92cc. Your piston, however, held only 198cc. The difference between these numbers is the dome volume. In this example, the dome volume equals 205.92cc, minus 198.00cc, which equals 7.92cc. Record this number on your compression ratio worksheet, because you'll need it later. And it's a lot of work to recalculate the dome volume if you misplace the number.

DECK HEIGHT & GASKET VOLUME

The last unknowns in the compression ratio equation are the *piston deck height* and the *head gasket volume*. The empty space above the piston represented by these numbers has to be considered when calculating the compression ratio. Although rod stretch and bearing clearances can reduce the effective clearance between the piston and cylinder head to almost zero when an engine is running at high rpm, this does not occur on the compression stroke. During the compression cycle, the piston and rod are loaded by the gases being squeezed into the combustion chamber, so the rod is compressed, not stretched. To have an accurate image of the actual compression ratio, the space above the piston created by the deck height and head gasket must be considered.

The mechanics of measuring piston deck height and head gasket thickness are discussed in the chapter on engine blocks. Before the compression ratio can be calculated, the cylinder volume included in the deck height and gasket thickness must be determined. To compute the volume in the deck-height clearance use the following formula:

$$\text{Deck height volume in cc's} = \left(\frac{d}{2}\right)^2 \times 51.48 \times h$$

where d = cylinder diameter in inches
where h = deck height in inches

This assumes that the engine has a *negative deck height*. This means that the quench area of the piston lies below the deck surface when the piston is at TDC. If the engine has a zero deck deck—the piston is exactly even with the deck surface—the deck height volume does not have to be considered, since the head gasket provides all of the piston-to-head clearance. If the piston has a *positive deck height*—the quench area is above the deck at TDC—the deck height volume will have to be *subtracted* from the gasket volume.

Returning to our earlier engine example, imagine that the pistons in a motor with 4.00-inch cylinder bores all have a negative deck height of 0.015-inch (when the pistons are at TDC the quench flats of the pistons are 0.015-inch below the block deck surface). The volume this represents is computed as follows:

$$\left(\frac{d}{2}\right)^2 \times 51.48 \times h = \left(\frac{4.00}{2}\right)^2 \times 51.48 \times 0.015 = 3.09 \text{cc}$$

If these same pistons were 0.015-inch above the deck at TDC—a positive deck height—the volume would remain unchanged, but it would be *subtracted* from the head gasket volume we are about to calculate.

Head gaskets are rarely the same size as the cylinder bores they seal. If the cylinders are 4.00 inches in diameter, the holes in the head gaskets are likely to be 4.060 inches diameter or even larger. Also, the holes in the head gasket are seldom perfectly round; they may have small notches or reliefs that follow the contours of the combustion chambers. When calculating the volume of the head gasket, you should use the *true diameter* of these holes, not the bore size. If the holes are markedly eccentric, you will have to *estimate* the volume they add to the head gasket space. The following formula is used to calculate the head gasket volume:

$$\text{Head gasket volume in cc's} = \left(\frac{d}{2}\right)^2 \times 51.48 \times t$$

where d = gasket hole diameter in inches
where t = compressed gasket thickness

Plugging in some representative numbers, the calculation looks like this for a 0.020-inch thick head gasket with 4.060-inch diameter cylinder openings:

$$\left(\frac{d}{2}\right)^2 \times 51.48 \times t = \left(\frac{4.060}{2}\right)^2 \times 51.48 \times 0.020 = 4.24 \text{cc}$$

With these preliminaries completed, you are finally ready to calculate the actual compression ratio. Recall that at the beginning of this chapter the compression ratio was defined as the ratio between the volume above the piston at BDC and the volume above the piston at TDC. If you keep this concept in mind, it will be easy to understand how this calculation works.

The only difference between the top and bottom half of the formula is the *swept volume*, or the actual displacement of the cylinder. The swept volume is determined solely by the cylinder diameter and the crankshaft stroke. As long as these two dimensions are unchanged, the swept volume remains constant. Changing any of the other factors—combustion chamber volume, head gasket thickness, dome volume, etc.—changes the compression ratio. This is why you can increase or decrease the compression by swapping cylinder heads, using a thinner head gasket, or installing pistons with larger domes. All of these modifications change the volume above the piston at TDC.

To calculate compression ratio, substitute the figures for your particular engine into the following equation:

$$CR = \frac{C - P + G + D + V}{C - P + G + D}$$

where: C = combustion chamber volume (cc's)
P = piston dome volume (cc's)
G = head gasket volume (cc's)
D = deck height volume (cc's)
V = cylinder swept volume (cc's)

Notes: 1. Add P if valve relief volume is greater than dome volume.
2. Subtract D if piston has positive deck height (quench is above surface).
3. To compute V (cylinder swept volume in cc's) use formula:

$$\left(\frac{b}{2}\right)^2 \times s \times 51.48 \quad \text{where:} \quad b = \text{cylinder bore diameter in inches}$$
$$s = \text{crankshaft stroke in inches}$$

The example below illustrates how this formula works using typical numbers for a 302ci Chevy motor.

$$CR = \frac{C - P + G + D + V}{C - P + G + D} \quad \text{where:} \quad \begin{array}{l} C = 64\text{cc} \\ P = 7.92 \\ G = 4.24 \\ D = 3.09 \\ V = 621.88 \end{array}$$

$$CR = \frac{64 - 7.92 + 4.24 + 3.09 + 621.88}{64 - 7.92 + 4.24 + 3.09}$$

$$CR = \frac{685.29}{63.41} \qquad CR = 10.8$$

Thus, the actual compression ratio for this particular engine works out to 10.8:1.

Understanding the factors that contribute to the compression ratio will make you a better engine builder. Some of the elements—deck clearance and head gasket volume, for example—are virtually "locked in" by the engine design. If the engine is already built to the limit, you cannot decrease the deck height or gasket thickness without the risk of the pistons hitting the cylinder heads. A relatively small change in dome volume, in contrast, can have a dramatic effect on the final compression ratio figure. Just a 2.00 or 3.00cc increase in dome volume can boost compression by half a point in some engines. This works both ways, though: if you have to deepen the valve notches in the piston to increase the piston-to-valve clearance, you may see the compression ratio take a nose dive.

As a final note on compression ratios, you should be aware that it is easier to obtain high compression ratios from a large displacement engines than from a small displacement motor. The bore and stroke of a big engine gives an engine builder *more swept volume to pack into the combustion chamber*. The smallblock Chevrolet, which has been offered with a variety of bore and stroke combinations, provides an excellent example of this relationship. The same cylinder heads, gasket and deck height that produce a 9.0:1 compression ratio on a 283ci block (3.00-inch stroke) would squeeze over 14.0:1 compression out of a 400ci motor (3.750-inch stroke)! While this much compression might be terrific in an alcohol-burning race motor, it would be an absolute disaster in a street machine. This effectively highlights, once again, why the few minutes required to measure and calculate the actual compression ratio is a vital part of every blueprinting job.

111

CHAPTER 9 BALANCING

BALANCING

Every driver has felt the effects of an out-of-balance tire. The entire car shakes and shimmies, and the steering wheel almost vibrates out of your hands. Now just imagine what takes place inside an unbalanced engine. Instead of turning at a leisurely 600rpm like a tire, the crank may be spinning at over 6000rpm. At these engine speeds, the pistons, rods, and crankshaft all become incredibly heavy; a piston whose weight is measured in ounces can exert thousands of pounds of force when it changes direction at TDC. A minor imbalance on a crankshaft counterweight is magnified many times by the centrifugal force of the spinning assembly. A single ounce of metal (28 grams) has a dynamic weight of over 700 pounds when it's placed on a rapidly turning crankshaft counterweight. This is why *balancing* is a vital part of engine blueprinting.

Balancing a tire is a breeze compared to balancing an engine. A tire rotates in one plane; an engine has a crankshaft that is turning, pistons that are moving up and down, and connecting rods that are doing a little of both. This helter-skelter motion produces some very strange vibrations. The number and arrangement of the cylinders also has a tremendous impact on engine balance. A conventional V-8 engine with cylinder banks spread 90° is a beautiful solution to many balancing problems. Yet if you lop off two cylinders to make a 90° V-6—as several automakers have recently done—you have an engine that is a disaster from the standpoint of balancing. To keep such an engine from shaking itself apart, the engineers have to devise all sorts of ingenious solutions, including offset crankpins, super-soft engine mounts, and special balancing techniques.

There are some engine designs that can never be perfectly balanced, no matter how much time, money, and equipment you devote to the project. This is why some automobile and motorcycle manufacturers use complex *counterbalancing shafts* on inline fours when smoothness is an important consideration. Rearrange those four cylinders into a Vee with the proper angle between the cylinder

There are no low-buck alternatives when it is time to balance an engine. The equipment is expensive, and it takes a skilled machinist to do the job right.

banks, however, and the reciprocating assembly can be balanced much more easily. You don't have to understand the detailed physics behind these effects to appreciate that some motors will always have a reputation as "shakers," while others, with a different number or configuration of cylinders, can be silky smooth.

ROTATING & RECIPROCATING WEIGHT

For balancing purposes, the parts of the crankshaft assembly are divided into two categories: *rotating weight* and *reciprocating weight*. The crankshaft spins, so it is obviously part of the rotating mass. So are the components that spin with it, like the rod bearings. The pistons, rings, and wrist pins, on the other hand, move up and down, so they are part of the reciprocating weight. The connecting rods are a mixed case: the small end reciprocates, while the big end rotates. When an engine is balanced, all the components that which are part of the reciprocating weight are matched so that none of the piston/rod assemblies is heavier than the others. In a well-balanced engine, the weight of one piston is always offset by the weight of another piston moving in the opposite direction.

Before balancing the rotating components, a machinist must first compute the *bob weight*. The bob weight is the mass on a single rod journal. It takes into account the weight of the piston, pin, piston locks, rings, the reciprocating and rotating parts of the rod, and the rod bearings. When calculating the bob weight for a conventional V-8 engine, the formula used by most machinists calls for adding 50% of the total reciprocating weight to the bob weight. Other engines can require a different percentage, however. The formula used to compute the bob weight for a 90° V-6 Chevrolet, for example, calls for adding only 46% of the reciprocating mass.

The ringer in all bob weight calculations is the weight of the oil on the components. If you dip a piston and rod assembly into a can of oil and then weigh them, the oil will add between two and ten grams to the total weight. How much oil actually clings to the rods and pistons inside a running engine—and how much it affects rotating and reciprocating weight—is a difficult question. Some engine builders feel that the oil mist in the crankcase clings together to form a rope-like cloud that twists around the spinning crank and rotates with the assembly, which will,

Before the crankshaft is balanced, the bobweight must be computed. The formula used to calculate the bobweight varies according to the engine design. The estimated weight of the oil on pistons and rods and the percentage of overbalance (if any) must also be included in the calculations.

When the crankshaft counterweights are not heavy enough to balance the engine assembly, additional weights are added to the flywheel (or convertor flexplate) and harmonic balancer. This flexplate and damper are from an externally balanced 400ci Chevrolet small-block.

of course, affect the balance. Experienced engine balancers usually include an arbitrary amount of weight in the bob weight calculation to represent the oil film on the moving parts.

High-rpm racing engines are sometimes *overbalanced*. When an engine is overbalanced, the percentage of the reciprocating weight that makes up the bob weight is increased from the customary 50% to about 51% or 52%. Although there may be some theoretical advantages to overbalancing, the benefits are difficult to discern. Advocates of overbalancing point out that bearing life is increased, while disbelievers maintain that the practice makes no difference in either power or

reliability. Overbalancing is one of those engine building techniques that falls into the gray category labeled "Probably Doesn't Hurt." For a street-performance engine, using the traditional bob weight formula will provide perfectly satisfactory results.

INTERNAL AND EXTERNAL BALANCING

Engines that have extremely long strokes or heavy reciprocating weights are often *externally balanced*. External balancing is required when the crankshaft counterweights do not have enough mass to offset the bob weight. Examples of externally balanced engines include the 400ci smallblock and 454ci big-block Chevrolet V-8s. Balancing is a problem with these engines because the outside diameter of the counterweights is limited by the physical dimensions of the engine block or by interference problems with the pistons and cam.

An engine is externally balanced by adding weight to one side of the harmonic balancer and flywheel (or converter flexplate). An internally balanced engine, in contrast, has enough counterweight mass on the crankshaft to offset the reciprocating weight without any additional external weight. Many engines have extra wings or counterweights on the crankshaft flywheel flange—327 and 350ci Chevys, for example—but these are not usually considered external balancing devices.

Since an externally balanced engine depends on weights attached to the balancer and flywheel, these components must always be installed in the same position relative to the crank counterweights. If a harmonic damper or flywheel is changed, the assembly must be rebalanced. With an internally balanced engine, you can swap flywheels and harmonic balancers without causing problems. As long as the new balancer or flywheel is itself balanced, the balance of the crankshaft assembly is unaffected. Some engine builders also feel that an externally balanced crankshaft is more likely to twist and flex because of the eccentric balance weights located at the extreme ends of the crank. For these reasons, many externally balanced engines are converted to internal balancing when they are destined for high-performance use.

An externally balanced engine can be converted to internal balancing by reducing the reciprocating weight or increasing the counterweight mass. The lightweight pistons and connecting rods used in racing engines cut the reciprocating weight, which in turn reduces the need for extremely heavy crankshaft counterweights. The counterweight mass can be increased either by adding more counterweights or by installing slugs of *heavy metal* or *Mallory metal* in the existing crank weights. Heavy metal is made of exotic materials, like tungsten or depleted uranium, and is much denser (and therefore heavier) than the steel or cast iron it replaces in the crankshaft counterweights.

Heavy metal plugs are pressed into holes (in the counterweights) that are bored parallel to the crankshaft axis. If the holes are drilled perpendicular to

the crank axis, the centrifugal force of the spinning crank could cause them to fly out of the counterweights. The holes are drilled and then reamed to size to provide the correct interference fit for the heavy metal.

BALANCING TECHNIQUES

Accurate measuring equipment is essential to engine balancing. All weights are measured in grams (rather than the more familiar ounces) using a very precise scale called a *Shadowgraph*. The first step in balancing an engine is to weigh all of the components. Weight differences between pins,

locks, and rings are usually negligible, but there can be wide variations among piston and rod weights. The usual procedure is to find the lightest piston and rod, and then equalize the weights by removing material from the heavier components.

Piston weights are relatively easy to equalize. Stock pistons generally have balance pads under the pin bosses. Milling a slight amount of aluminum off these pads will bring the piston weights into line. Finding places to safely remove material from a lightweight racing piston can be more difficult, however. It is important not to weaken the piston by cutting

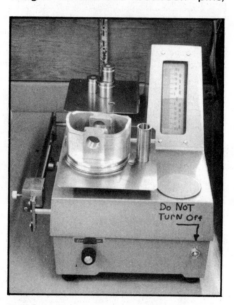

A precision scale weighs each rotating and reciprocating component in the engine. Piston weights are matched to the lightest piston.

Pin bosses are carefully machined to equalize weights without effecting the reliability of the pistons.

The big end of connecting rod is weighed by suspending the rod on a low-friction fixture. This portion of the rod is considered part of the rotating weight of the engine, since it turns with the crankshaft.

Factory connecting rods generally have balancing pads on both ends. The pad material can be ground away, as necessary, to equalize rod weights. Connecting rods designed specifically for racing are usually packaged as balanced sets by the manufacturer.

The reciprocating end (small end) of the connecting rod is weighed after turning around the scale fixture. Note the polished beam on this Chevy rod prepared for Super Stock drag-racing competition.

Bobweight cannisters are filled with lead shot—to simulate the weight of the pistons and rods—while the crankshaft is spun in the balancing machine.

aluminum at a critical point. The metal thickness under the pin needs to be at least 0.125-inch to keep the pin from pulling out of the bosses. If the thickness of the pin bosses have already been trimmed to the minimum during the lightening process, then shallow cuts on the side of the bosses may be enough to equalize the piston weights. The underside of the deck and the inside of the skirts can also be machined, providing the metal cross-sections are not dangerously thin.

Balancing the rods is more complex. Because a rod represents both rotating and reciprocating weight, each end of the rod must be weighed separately. A fixture is used to suspend the rod by the rod bearing and piston pin holes on the scale. The big ends of the rod set are balanced first. The rod with the lightest big end is determined by weighing each rod on the scale fixture, then the balancing pads on the heavier rods are ground to equalize the weights. After all of the big end weights match, the rods are turned around and the small ends weighed. Again, the heavy rods are ground until they match the lightest rod.

When all of the piston and rod weights have been equalized, the bob weight is computed according to the formula required by the particular engine design. Since it is impractical to spin a crankshaft on the balancing machine with the rods and pistons attached, their weight is duplicated by filling small bob weight cannisters with shot and clamping them to the rod journals.

The crankshaft balancer is part lathe, part drill press, and part light show. The crankshaft is supported on the end journals by roller bearings and spun with a motor-driven belt. As an out-of-balance crank vibrates, it triggers a strobe light that "freezes" the crank motion with a flash of light and indicates where metal needs to be removed or added to the crank counterweights. Balancing holes are drilled in the thick counterweights at the ends of the crank; minor adjustments are made by drilling smaller diameter holes in the inner counterweights.

Occasionally weight must be added to a crank to bring it into balance. This is done with plugs of heavy metal, as described in the preceding section on rebalancing externally balanced crankshafts. The position of the metal is as important as its mass. Existing balance holes can be filled with welding material or plugged with heavy metal. If plugs are inserted in holes that have already been drilled in the counterweights, they should be welded around the entire circumference to prevent them from getting loose inside the engine. A slug of heavy metal that is jettisoned from a rapidly

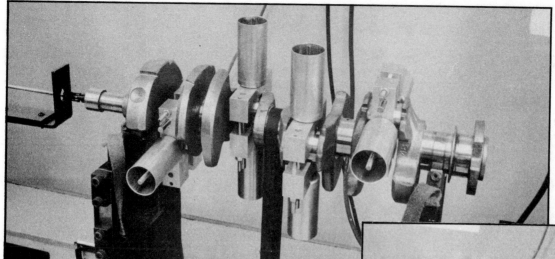

Bobweights are clamped to each of the rod journals before the crankshaft is balanced. A motor-driven belt spins the crank while sensitive pickups on the front and rear main journals detect vibrations that indicate the crank is not properly balanced.

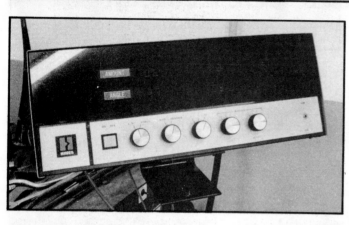

This state-of-the-art electronic balancer pinpoints the location of the imbalance and indicates how much metal must be removed to achieve proper balance. Less sophisticated machines require a time-consuming trail-and-error technique.

In most cases, the bobweight for a high-performance engine is lighter than a stock engine, so material must be removed from the counterweights. Here Kip Martin lightens the rear counterweight of a Chevy cranks with a precisely located hole. Stroker cranks or heavy pistons may require adding mass to the counterweights.

spinning crankshaft will go through the crankcase like an armor-piercing bullet.

If the engine is externally balanced, you must supply the machinist with the harmonic balancer and flywheel (or flexplate) that you intend to use. When the engine is assembled later, the flywheel must be installed in the same position on the crank as when it was balanced. Usually there is a dowel pin or keyway that registers the flywheel; if not, your machinist will mark the crank and flywheel so they can be reassembled correctly. Even if the engine is internally balanced, it is still good practice to have the harmonic damper, flywheel, and clutch balanced. These components should be balanced separately so that individual items can be replaced without disturbing the balance of the entire assembly. If the clutch and flywheel are balanced together, you cannot change the pressure plate or flywheel weight without rebalancing them as a unit.

Balancing is the last step in blueprinting before final engine assembly. Before delivering the pistons, rods, and crankshaft to the balancing service, you must be certain that they are absolutely, positively "finished." If you discover later that there is insuffi-

Slugs of heavy metal can be used to internally balance an externally balanced crank. The metal inserted in the counterweight is denser than the steel or iron it replaces. Installing the heavy metal parallel to the crankshaft axis prevents it from flying out at high rpm.

The first step in adding weight to a crank is to drill the counterweight.

cient piston-to-valve clearance, or that the domes hit the cylinder heads, or that the connecting rod bolts collide with the cam lobes, then you will have wasted the money you spent on balancing. Balancing an engine requires expensive, sophisticated equipment; there are no "low-buck" alternatives.

When you pick up your freshly balanced parts from the machinist, you will receive a card that lists the weights of the individual components as well as the total bob weight. Keep this card with your engine building records. If it is later necessary to replace a piston or rod, your machinist can duplicate the weights of the original pieces and save the cost of rebalancing the entire assembly. Also, you should spend some time detailing the parts when you bring them home after balancing. Lightly deburr all sharp edges on the pistons, rods, and crank counterweights where they have been machined. Inspect the crank journals for pits or welding splatter on the journals, and check that the big and small ends of the connecting rods have not become dangerously thin. When you are satisfied that everything is in order, you can start making preparations for final assembly of the engine.

After drilling, the counterweight hole is reamed to the finished diameter.

A bar of heavy metal is turned in a lathe to produce the correct interference fit in the counterweight.

The heavy-metal slug is cut to size and then driven or pressed into the hole in the counterweight.

ENGINE ASSEMBLY TIPS

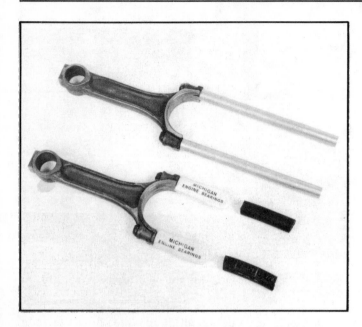

Rod bolt protectors eliminate the possibility of nicking or gouging the crankshaft when installing the pistons. Many bearing sets include a pair of plastic rod bolt "booties," or you can improvise by slipping short lengths of rubber hose over the bolts. Threaded pieces of aluminum tubing are more elegant, and can help guide the rod onto its journal.

When torquing down the connecting rod bolts, insert two feeler gauge strips between the adjacent rods. This aligns the rod caps and forks, and ensures that each pair of rods will retain the same side clearance dimension which was measured during engine preassembly.

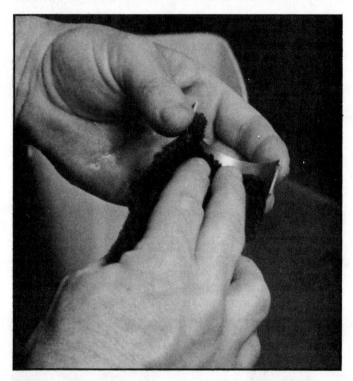

Modern engine bearings are overplated with extremely thin coatings of various metals. The top protective layer is generally a soft lead which improves the insert's "embedability," or tolerance to small metal particles. In high output engines, this top coating has a tendency to smear across the bearing face, which is why many engine builders remove it by polishing the bearing with fine Scotchbrite—despite the fact that bearing manufacturers frown on this practice. Removing this lead layer has a neglible effect on bearing clearance.

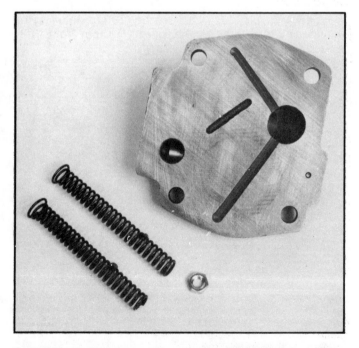

If oil is the lifeblood of an engine, then the oil pump must be its heart. In Chevrolet V-8s (and many other engines), oil pressure is regulated by the stiffness of the bypass relief spring. The difference between standard production and high-performance pumps is often just the resistance of this bypass spring. To increase oil pressure, you can install a stiffer spring, or shim the existing spring with small nuts or washers. If you choose to add shims, make certain that the valve does not block the bypass passage when the spring is fully compressed.

The oil pump can effect the accuracy of the smallblock Chevrolet ignition timing at high rpm because of a condition known as "pump chatter." Smallblock oil pump gears have only seven teeth, which causes the pump shaft to load and unload as the gears rotate. This in turn effects the distributor shaft, which drives the oil pump. This pump has been modified by milling pressure balance grooves in the pump body and cover to curtail chatter and to prevent cavitation which can aerate the oil.

The oil pump pickup for a wet sump lubrication system should be adjusted so that it is 1/4- to 3/8-inch from the bottom of the pan. This clearance can be checked by placing a ball of clay over the pickup, installing the pan, and then measuring the thickness of the compressed clay after the pan is removed. Stock-type tubular pickups can be adjusted by turning the pickup in the pump body; then fix the pickup in place by brazing or epoxying the tube to the pump. (If you braze the pickup in place, be sure to remove the bypass spring first so the tension will not be affected by the heat of the welding torch.) Aftermarket oil pump pickups can be adjusted by inserting spacers between the pump and the rear main cap.

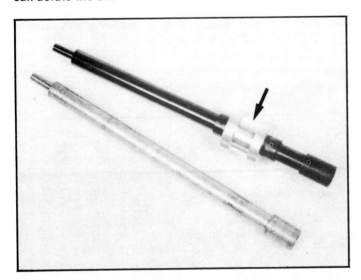

One of the most important steps in final assembly is to pre-oil the engine before initially firing it. Proper pre-oiling ensures that the oil pump is primed, the filter is full, and all the passages are filled with lubricant. These pre-oiling tools engage the Chevrolet oil pump shaft through the distributor hole. The professional model from B&B Performance has a machined collar (arrow) which seals the passenger side oil gallery of a smallblock V8, just as the distributor housing does when it is installed in the block. This directs oil to the lifters and rockers on the right side of the engine during pre-oiling. Use a 3/8-inch or larger electric drill to turn the oil pump for at least a minute after the oil gauge indicates that the engine has oil pressure. Turn the crank by hand several times during pre-oiling to expose all of the oil holes in crankshaft journals.

Rapid lobe wear with flat tappet cams is usually caused by improper break-in procedure. When final assembling an engine equipped with flat or mushroom lifters, coat the lobes and tappet bottoms with moly lube (molybdenum disulfide). It is also good practice to add a pint of oil additive such as GM Engine Oil Supplement to the lubricant when breaking in a new cam. When the motor first fires, immediately bring the engine speed to 2500 rpm for at least 20 minutes. Then drain the oil and replace the filter element.

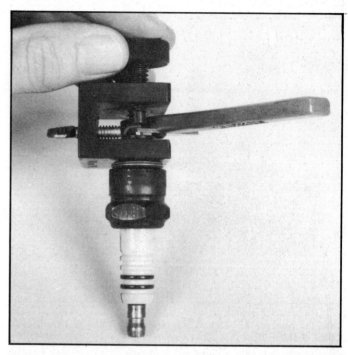

A few moments devoted to preparing the spark plugs can pay performance dividends. Many engine builders prefer side-gapped plugs because they are less susceptible to fouling and because they expose the spark directly to the charge in the combustion chamber. A conventional plug can be side-gapped by trimming the ground electrode with wire cutters or an abrasive wheel so that it extends just to the edge of the center electrode.

Modern high-energy ignition systems can tolerate much wider plug gaps than conventional coil ignitions. Wide plug gaps can show an improvement in performance, since making the spark jump a wide gap increases the chances of encountering a combustible mix of fuel and oxygen molecules. Plug gapping tools like this one are available to simplify the chore of opening up the gaps to 0.060-inch or larger. Remember, though, that wide plug gaps increase electrical resistance. The spark plug wires and ignition system must be in top condition to prevent misfires.

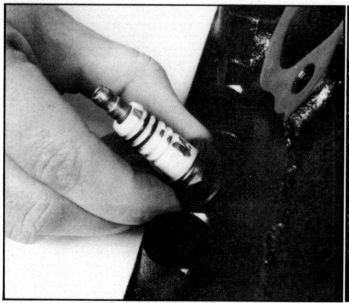

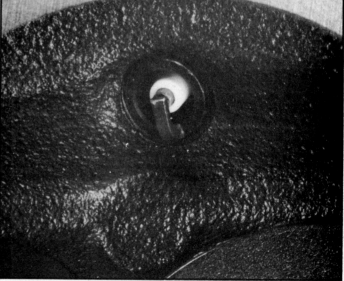

Engines equipped with high-dome pistons often require the spark plugs to be "indexed" to prevent interference between the dome and ground electrodes. When the plug is properly indexed, the electrode is near the top of the chamber (as shown). To index a set of plugs after the heads have been installed, mark a line on each ceramic insulator in line with the ground strap. You will probably have to try several plugs in

each cylinder until you find one that has the electrode in the right position after it has been tightened. Once you have selected a complete set, number each plug so it can be reinstalled in the corresponding cylinder. If some of your plugs are unusable in any of the cylinders, you can adjust the electrode position by inserting special spark plug washers of various thicknesses between the plugs and cylinder head.

If you are replacing a silent timing chain with a high-performance roller chain, make sure there is adequate clearance between the chain and block. Double-roller chains are considerably wider than Morse-type chains, and may rub on the oil gallery boss or timing chain cover.

Soft plugs used to seal oil galleries will stay in place if you stake them with a chisel as shown. Although many engine builders like the security of screw-in pipe plugs, standard expansion plugs are usually troublefree if installed properly.

To minimize the chances of a rear main seal weeping oil, rotate the seal slightly so the parting line is not aligned with the parting line between the main cap and block. Then apply a thin coat of gasket sealer between the main cap and block to head off oil leaks.

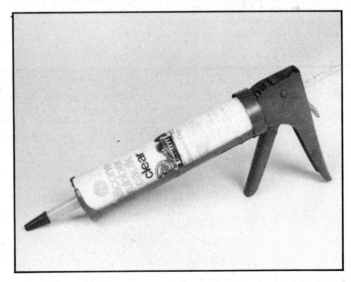

Tubes of silastic rubber are indispensible when assembling an engine. The factories have eliminated half the gaskets in new motors by substituting formed-in-place silastic gaskets. An engine builder could go bankrupt buying tiny tubes of silastic, but there's an economical alternative: Bring home a big tube of silastic and a caulking gun. The caulking gun lets you squeeze out a uniform bead just where you need it.

A fully degreed harmonic balancer is an expensive luxury if all you need is a mark to set the ignition timing. You can provide a reliable reference point for setting total ignition advance by marking the damper at 40 degrees (or whatever figure is appropriate for your particular engine). Bolt the degree wheel to the balancer and find TDC using the same procedure used when degreeing the cam. Then rotate the degree wheel to 40 degrees before TDC and mark the balancer in line with the timing tab. Paint the area around this new timing mark with contrasting paint to improve visibility.

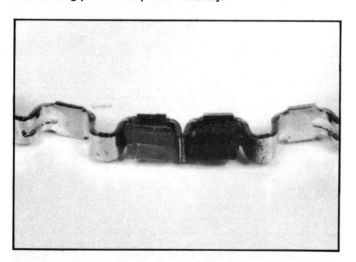

Take care to prevent the ends of the oil ring expander from overlapping. If the ends overlap, the ring will not have the proper tension and oil control will suffer. This Speed Pro oil ring expander has plastic blocks which prevent it from being installed improperly.

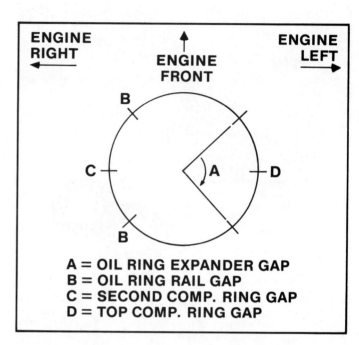

A = OIL RING EXPANDER GAP
B = OIL RING RAIL GAP
C = SECOND COMP. RING GAP
D = TOP COMP. RING GAP

When installing piston rings, pay attention to the position of the end gaps. Note that the gaps for the top and second compression rings are placed 180-degrees apart to minimize blowby. Don't be surprised, though, if the gaps have moved when you disassemble the engine later; rings will normally rotate unless they are restricted or pinned in place.

Most high-speed racing engines do not need an ignition advance curve, but variable spark timing is a necessity for a performance street engine. The distributor centrifugal advance is usually governed by a combination of springs and weights. Performance distributor kits include an assortment of springs which allow an engine builder to tailor the spark timing to specific requirements. A distributor machine simplifies this procedure, but a running engine can be used as a distributor test bench. Note the spark advance at 500 rpm intervals and record the total advance available with each combination of springs and weights.

The distributor gear can be a source of unexpected trouble. Stock gears are compatible with the iron cam cores used for most flat tappet grinds, but they will wear quickly when used with a steel roller camshaft. Aftermarket aluminum/bronze gears should be used with steel cam cores. And while you're replacing the distributor gear, you might as well shim the shaft to provide the recommended 0.005-inch end play.

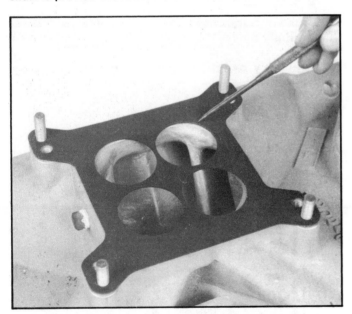

Even a shiny new aluminum intake manifold may require minor preparation before it is ready for installation. Make sure there are no sharp edges at the top of the plenum to interfere with the carburetor throttle blades or to disturb the air and fuel entering the manifold. Place a gasket or carburetor base plate on the plenum and note any obstructions. You can either radius the plenum entry with a die grinder, or drill out the holes in the carburetor base and reposition the carb over the plenum opening. You may also need to enlarge the manifold bolt holes to allow you to shift the intake manifold slightly so the runners align with the head ports. Use a small flashlight to check the manifold/port alignment. If you cannot see down the runners, a length of welding rod with a small hook on the end will let you feel any sharp edges where the manifold meets the cylinder head.

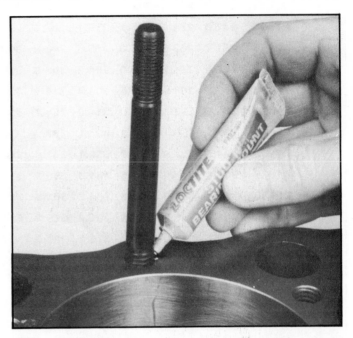

Cylinder head studs are generally recommended for supercharged and endurance racing engines. When first installing studs, coat the coarse threads with red Loctite and screw the studs into the block by hand. Then install the head and torque the stud nuts before the thread compound has hardened. This will align the studs with the holes in the cylinder head, making it easier to remove and reinstall the head for servicing.

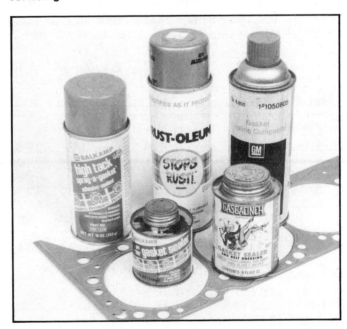

Selecting the correct sealer is essential to preventing problems with blown or leaking head gaskets. Different gasket materials require different sealers. Steel shim gaskets generally perform well with sticky adhesives such as GM gasket compound or NAPA Hi-Tack sealer. Silver aluminum paint is an inexpensive alternative that can be found nearly anywhere. Most composition and all Teflon-coated head gaskets should be installed dry (without sealer). If the head bolts enter the water jacket, be sure to seal the threads with brush-on sealer.

CUBIC INCH CONVERSION CHART

BORE DIAMETER	2.750	2.875	3.000	3.125	3.250	3.375	3.500	3.625	3.750	3.875	4.000	4.125	4.250
3.7500	243.0	254.0	265.1	276.1	287.2	298.2	309.3	320.3	331.3	342.4	353.4	364.5	375.5
3.8125	251.1	262.6	274.0	285.4	296.8	308.2	319.6	331.1	342.5	353.9	365.3	376.7	388.1
3.8750	259.5	271.2	283.0	294.8	306.6	318.4	330.2	342.0	353.8	365.6	377.4	389.2	401.0
3.9375	267.9	280.1	292.2	304.4	316.6	328.8	340.9	353.1	365.3	377.5	389.7	401.8	414.0
4.0000	276.5	289.0	301.6	314.2	326.7	339.3	351.9	364.4	377.0	389.6	402.1	414.7	427.3
4.0625	285.2	298.1	311.1	324.1	337.0	350.0	362.9	375.9	388.9	401.8	414.8	427.8	440.7
4.1250	294.0	307.4	320.7	334.1	347.5	360.8	374.2	387.6	400.9	414.3	427.6	441.0	454.4
4.1875	303.0	316.8	330.5	344.3	358.1	371.8	385.6	399.4	413.2	426.9	440.7	454.5	468.3
4.2500	312.1	326.3	340.5	354.7	368.8	383.0	397.2	411.4	425.6	439.8	454.0	468.1	482.3
4.3125	321.3	336.0	350.6	365.2	379.8	394.4	409.0	423.6	438.2	452.8	467.4	482.0	496.6
4.3750	330.7	345.8	360.8	375.8	390.9	405.9	420.9	436.0	451.0	466.0	481.1	496.1	511.1
4.4375	340.2	355.7	371.2	386.6	402.1	417.6	433.0	448.5	464.0	479.4	494.9	510.4	525.8
4.5000	349.9	365.8	381.7	397.6	413.5	429.4	445.3	461.2	477.1	493.0	508.9	524.8	540.7
4.5625	359.7	376.0	392.4	408.7	425.1	441.4	457.8	474.1	490.5	506.8	523.2	539.5	555.9
4.6250	369.6	386.4	403.2	420.0	436.8	453.6	470.4	487.2	504.0	520.8	537.6	554.4	571.2
4.6875	379.7	396.9	414.2	431.4	448.7	465.9	483.2	500.5	517.7	535.0	552.2	569.5	586.7
4.7500	389.9	407.6	425.3	443.0	460.7	478.5	496.2	513.9	531.6	549.3	567.1	584.8	602.5

Equation: Cubic Inches = 0.7854 x Number of Cylinders x Stroke x bore x bore.
   To convert cubic inches to cubic centimeters (CC) multiply by 16.39.
   For example: 283 cubic inches = 4638CC = 4.638 liter.
   To convert cubic centimeters (CC) to cubic inches multiply by 0.061.
   For example: 3000CC = 3000 x 0.061 = 183 cubic inches.

DECIMAL & MILLIMETER EQUIVALENTS

INCH	INCH	MM	INCH	INCH	MM	INCH	INCH	MM
1/64	.015625	0.397	23/64	.359375	9.128	11/16	.6875	17.462
1/32	.03125	0.794	3/8	.375	9.525	45/64	.703125	17.859
3/64	.046875	1.191	25/64	.390625	9.922	23/32	.71875	18.265
1/16	.0625	1.587	13/32	.40625	10.319	47/64	.734375	18.653
5/64	.078125	1.984	27/64	.421875	10.716	3/4	.75	19.050
3/32	.09375	2.381	7/16	.4375	11.113	49/64	.765625	19.447
7/64	.109375	2.778	29/64	.453125	11.509	25/32	.78125	19.884
1/8	.125	3.175	15/32	.46875	11.906	51/64	.796875	20.240
9/64	.140625	3.572	31/64	.484375	12.303	13/16	.8125	20.637
5/32	.15625	3.969	1/2	.5	12.700	53/64	.828125	21.034
11/64	.171875	4.366	33/64	.515625	13.097	27/32	.84375	21.431
3/16	.1875	4.762	17/32	.53125	13.494	55/64	.859375	21.828
13/64	.203125	5.159	35/64	.546875	13.890	7/8	.875	22.225
7/32	.21875	5.556	9/16	.5625	14.287	57/64	.890625	22.622
15/64	.234375	5.953	37/64	.578125	14.684	29/32	.90625	23.019
1/4	.25	6.350	19/32	.59375	15.081	59/64	.921875	23.415
17/64	.265625	6.747	39/64	.609375	15.478	15/16	.9375	23.812
9/32	.28125	7.144	5/8	.625	15.875	61/64	.953125	24.209
19/64	.296875	7.541	41/64	.640625	16.272	31/32	.96875	24.606
5/16	.3125	7.937	21/32	.65625	16.669	63/64	.984375	25.003
21/64	.328125	8.334	43/64	.671875	17.065	1	1	25.400
11/32	.34375	8.731						

ENGINE BLUEPRINTING RECORD

The following forms can be photocopied to organize your engine blueprinting project and to provide a permanent record of your engine's dimensions.

DATE: _____ ENGINE: _____

BORE: _____ STROKE: _____ DISPLACEMENT: _____

PISTON-TO-WALL CLEARANCE:

CYLINDER NO.	1	2	3	4	5	6	7	8
BORE DIAMETER								
PISTON DIAMETER								
CLEARANCE								

PISTON-TO-HEAD CLEARANCE:

CYLINDER NO.	1	2	3	4	5	6	7	8
HEAD GASKET THICKNESS								
PISTON DECK HEIGHT								

TOTAL CLEARANCE _____ _____ _____ _____ _____ _____ _____ _____

PISTON DOME VOLUME

VALVE RELIEF DEPTH								
INTAKE:								
EXHAUST:								

MAIN BEARING CLEARANCE:

JOURNAL NO.	1	2	3	4	5
BEARING ID					
JOURNAL OD					
CLEARANCE					

FASTENER TORQUE   INNER: _____ OUTER: _____

ROD BEARING CLEARANCE:

JOURNAL NO.	1	2	3	4	5	6	7	8
BEARING ID								
JOURNAL OD								
CLEARANCE								
CRANKSHAFT STROKE								

THRUST CLEARANCE _____

PISTON RINGS:

CYLINDER NO.	1	2	3	4	5	6	7	8
END GAP TOP	___	___	___	___	___	___	___	___
SECOND	___	___	___	___	___	___	___	___
OIL	___	___	___	___	___	___	___	___

SIDE CLEARANCE

	1	2	3	4	5	6	7	8
TOP	___	___	___	___	___	___	___	___
SECOND	___	___	___	___	___	___	___	___
OIL	___	___	___	___	___	___	___	___

CONNECTING RODS

ROD NO.	1	2	3	4	5	6	7	8
WRIST PIN OD	___	___	___	___	___	___	___	___
SMALL END ID	___	___	___	___	___	___	___	___
CLEARANCE:	___	___	___	___	___	___	___	___

FASTENER TORQUE: _____

ROD NOS:	1 + 2	3 + 4	5 + 6	7 + 8
SIDE CLEARANCE	___	___	___	___

VALVESPRINGS

CYLINDER NO.	1		2		3		4		5		6		7		8	
VALVE	I	E	I	E	I	E	I	E	I	E	I	E	I	E	I	E
INSTALLED HEIGHT																
SHIM																
SEAT PRESSURE																
OPEN PRESSURE																
COIL BIND																
PISTON-TO-VALVE CLEARANCE:																

CAMSHAFT

GRIND NUMBER: _____ DURATION @ 0.050'': _____ LOBE CENTER: _____

INSTALLED @ INTAKE CENTERLINE _____ LOBE LIFT: _____

ROCKERARM RATIO: _____ THEORETICAL LIFT: _____ ACTUAL LIFT: _____

VALVE LASH INTAKE: _____ EXHAUST: _____ HEAD FASTENER TORQUE: _____

DRILL SIZES

LETTER OR WIRE GAUGE	DRILL DIAMETER INCH		
Z	0.413	27	0.1440
Y	0.404	28	0.1405
X	0.397	29	0.1360
W	0.386	30	0.1285
V	0.377	31	0.1200
U	0.368	32	0.1160
T	0.358	33	0.1130
S	0.348	34	0.1110
R	0.339	35	0.1100
Q	0.332	36	0.1065
P	0.323	37	0.1040
O	0.316	38	0.1015
N	0.302	39	0.0995
M	0.295	40	0.0980
L	0.290	41	0.0960
K	0.281	42	0.0935
J	0.277	43	0.0890
I	0.272	44	0.0860
H	0.266	45	0.0820
G	0.261	46	0.0810
F	0.257	47	0.0785
E	0.250	48	0.0760
D	0.246	49	0.0730
C	0.242	50	0.0700
B	0.238	51	0.0670
A	0.234	52	0.0635
		53	0.0595
		54	0.0550
1	0.2280	55	0.0520
2	0.2210	56	0.0465
3	0.2130	57	0.0430
4	0.2090	58	0.0420
5	0.2055	59	0.0410
6	0.2040	60	0.0400
7	0.2010	61	0.0390
8	0.1990	62	0.0380
9	0.1960	63	0.0370
10	0.1935	64	0.0360
11	0.1910	65	0.0350
12	0.1890	66	0.0330
13	0.1850	67	0.0320
14	0.1820	68	0.0310
15	0.1800	69	0.0292
16	0.1770	70	0.0280
17	0.1730	71	0.0260
18	0.1695	72	0.0250
19	0.1660	73	0.0240
20	0.1610	74	0.0225
21	0.1590	75	0.0210
22	0.1570	76	0.0200
23	0.1540	77	0.0180
24	0.1520	78	0.0160
25	0.1495	79	0.0145
26	0.1470	80	0.0135

SOURCES AND ACKNOWLEDGEMENTS:

The author expresses his gratitiude to the following individuals and organizations for enduring constant interruptions to their schedules and for patiently answering his countless questions. This publication would not have been possible without their kind cooperation and extensive technical knowledge.

BILL HENDREN
Hendrens's Auto Machine
1570 Soquel Dr.
Santa Cruz, CA

LARRY HOLLUMS
Hollums Racing Engines
37111 Post St.
Fremont, CA 94536

DAVID REHER
BUDDY MORRISON
Reher-Morrison Racing Engines
1120 Enterprise Pl.
Arlington, TX 76017

SCOOTER BROTHERS
Racing Head Service
2795 Hangar Rd.
Memphis, TN 38118

ALLAN PATTERSON
KIP MARTIN
GARY PEARMAN
DARREL WIKLE
Patterson/Martin Machine
425 Walnut
Augusta, KS 67010

BOBBY ROWE
Chrome-A-Shaft
280 Tillman
Memphis, TN 38112

SOURCES:

The following companies offer many of the specialized tools and equipment required for engine blueprinting. Most have catalogs available; contact the firms directly for ordering information.

B&B PERFORMANCE SALES
23190 Del Lago Dr.
Laguna Hills, CA 92653
714-586-0561
(specialty tools)

B-H-J PRODUCTS
6756 Central Ave.
Newark, CA 94560
415-797-6780
(machining fixtures and specialty tools)

CAM DYNAMICS
460 Walker St., Bldg. A-18
Holly Hill, FL 32017
904-258-8845
(Tune-A-Cam kit)

CHICAGO LATEX PRODUCTS
1030 Morse Ave.
Schaumberg, IL 60193
312-893-2880
(latex for port molds)

MANLEY PERFORMANCE
13 Race St.
Bloomfield, NJ 07003
201-743-6577
(specialty tools)

MOROSO PERFORMANCE
Carter Drive
Guilford, CT 06437
203-453-6571
(specialty tools)

PRECISION MEASUREMENT SUPPLY
P.O. Box 28097
San Antonio, TX 78228
512-681-2405
(precision tools)

YOTHER PERFORMANCE PRODUCTS
16848 Alisal Court
San Lorenzo, CA 94580
415-481-1671
(specialty tools)

There's A <u>How-To-Do-It Book</u> For You In Each Performance Series Below

ENGINE
5 Books

- Ford Performance
- Chevy Performance
- Mopar Performance
- V-6 Performance
- Engine Blueprinting

The S-A Design <u>Engine Series</u> has no equal in providing high-quality, high-performance information. Each book contains easy-to-read tech along with hundreds of photos, charts, and graphs. Our <u>Engine Series</u> gives you the information you'll need to build a reliable, high-horsepower engine for street, track, drag racing, or off-road use.

CARBURETION
2 Books

- Holley Carburetors
- Carter Carburetors

Cut through the black magic of selecting, tuning, modifying, and rebuilding Holley and Carter carburetors. The <u>Carburetion Series</u> has helped tens of thousands of enthusiasts get the most from their induction system. From selecting jets for more economy to modifying metering circuits for racing, you can count on our <u>Carburetion Series</u>: no magic here — just tested, accurate info.

SUPER INDUCTION
3 Books

- Nitrous-Oxide Injection
- Street Supercharging
- Superpower

If you're interested in real ground-pounding horsepower, the <u>Super-Induction Series</u> is what you're looking for. Everything from the subtleties of hidden nitrous-oxide injection, to outrageous belt-driven supercharging is explained in easy-to-read text. We show you how to avoid the pitfalls, select the system, bolt on the hardware, and get the most for your money.

EXPERT
2 Books

- Smokey Yunick's Power Secrets
- The Chevrolet Racing Engine

Ever wondered how top experts find more horsepower per cubic inch than many knowledgeable people thought was possible? The <u>Expert Series</u> gives you an inside look at the "secrets" of two of the country's most successful engine builders: Bill "Grumpy" Jenkins and Smokey Yunick. These two unique books reveal techniques and insights that you can use to build reliable stock or Pro-Stock horsepower into your engine.

* Available in 1988

BOLT-ON
5 Books

- Guide To Bolt-On Street Power
- Performance With Economy
- How To Build Horsepower*
- Hot Rodder's Handbook*
- Building The Smallblock Chevy*

The S-A Design <u>Bolt-On Series</u> will help you select everything from mufflers to manifolds, gear ratios to gear drives, and tires to tachometers. All written for easy reading, these books are the nuts and bolts of hot rodding, and they will become the most valuable references in your performance library. This series will help anyone understand the complex world of performance technology.

SUPERSTREET/ SUSPENSION
2 Books

- Building A SuperStreet Mopar
- Drag Racing Chassis & Suspension*

If you'd like to build a car that corners as fast as it accelerates, the <u>SuperStreet/Suspension Series</u> has it. If you just need guidelines for component selection, or if you're looking for in-depth information about suspension function and design, this series has the answers you want. Includes everything from selecting brake fluids to details about center-of-gravity, roll couple, plus engine building tips; all written in understandable terms. Find out how to make your car handle like a Porsche and run like a Musclecar. Look into the books in this series.

PAINTING BODYWORK
2 Books

- Custom Painting
- Basic Painting & Bodywork*

Reading the S-A Design <u>Painting and Bodywork Series</u>, can help you produce silk-smooth, factory-matched repaints or eye-popping custom paint tricks in your own driveway. Many enthusiasts believe that top-quality painting and bodywork can only be done by experts, and while it's true that experts have the know-how, the books in this series can show you the right way to start, help you while you practice, and have you doing "expert" work in short order.

ALTERNATE FUELS
1 Book

- Propane Conversions

Gasoline produces horsepower, but it also produces smog, increases ring and cylinder-bore wear, contaminates engine oil, promotes erratic running when cold, can "vapor lock" when hot, and more. The <u>Alternate Fuels Series</u> book Propane Conversions provides a fascinating look at the use of propane for street performance. Learn how a straightforward conversion to LPG or propane can nearly double engine life, increase performance, reduce emissions (to virtually nothing), and improve driveability!

We encourage individuals to purchase books from a local retailer. S-A Design Books are sold internationally in speed shops, book stores, and automotive parts outlets. However, if you cannot find our books locally, you may order direct from S-A Design by pre-paying $12.95 plus $2.00 (postage and handling) per copy (California residents add 78¢ tax each). Mail to S-A Design Order Desk, 515 West Lambert, Bldg. E, Brea, CA 92621-3991, or call 714-529-7999.

Join Our Book Users Group — It's FREE!

Join the S-A Design Book Users Group now! Just some of the benefits are:

- Free newsletter keeps you in contact with our authors and readers
- Special discounts on books
- Technical updates
- Info on latest publications
- Join BUG and stay in touch

YES! I would like to activate my membership in the S-A Design Book Users Group now!

Name _____

Address _____

City _____

State _____ Zip _____